BADGES AND INCIDENTS

Michael J. Kaufman undertakes an interdisciplinary investigation of American education law and pedagogy. He weaves together the invaluable insights of law, education, history, political science, economics, psychology, and neuroscience to illuminate the ways in which the design of the American educational system does not reflect how human beings live and learn.

Kaufman examines the principles of the nation's Founders. He demonstrates how a distorted presentation of the Founders' views curtailed the development of a truly democratic educational system. He also exposes the influence of this distortion on several critical Supreme Court decisions. These decisions, Kaufman concludes, have largely failed to facilitate the educational system the Founders envisioned. In addition, he places contemporary challenges in context and endorses social constructivist pedagogy as the best path forward.

This study will prove invaluable to advocates for equity in education, helping them navigate a contentious political climate with an eye toward future reform efforts.

Michael J. Kaufman serves as Dean of the School of Law, Loyola University Chicago. He has published more than thirty books and countless articles in the areas of his expertise, including education law, policy, and pedagogy.

CAMBRIDGE STUDIES ON CIVIL RIGHTS AND CIVIL LIBERTIES

This series is a platform for original scholarship on US civil rights and civil liberties. It produces books on the normative, historical, judicial, political, and sociological contexts for understanding contemporary legislative, jurisprudential, and presidential dilemmas. The aim is to provide experts, teachers, policymakers, students, social activists, and educated citizens with in-depth analyses of theories, existing and past conditions, and constructive ideas for legal advancements.

General Editor Alexander Tsesis, Loyola University, Chicago

Badges and Incidents

A TRANSDISCIPLINARY HISTORY OF THE RIGHT TO EDUCATION IN AMERICA

MICHAEL J. KAUFMAN

Loyola University Chicago School of Law

CAMBRIDGE
UNIVERSITY PRESS

University Printing House, Cambridge CB2 8BS, United Kingdom

One Liberty Plaza, 20th Floor, New York, NY 10006, USA

477 Williamstown Road, Port Melbourne, VIC 3207, Australia

314-321, 3rd Floor, Plot 3, Splendor Forum, Jasola District Centre, New Delhi - 110025, India

103 Penang Road, #05-06/07, Visioncrest Commercial, Singapore 238467

Cambridge University Press is part of the University of Cambridge.

It furthers the University's mission by disseminating knowledge in the pursuit of education, learning and research at the highest international levels of excellence.

www.cambridge.org
Information on this title: www.cambridge.org/9781316649930
DOI: 10.1017/9781108226981

© Michael J. Kaufman 2020

This publication is in copyright. Subject to statutory exception and to the provisions of relevant collective licensing agreements, no reproduction of any part may take place without the written permission of Cambridge University Press.

First published 2020
First paperback edition 2022

A catalogue record for this publication is available from the British Library

ISBN 978-1-316-51043-8 Hardback
ISBN 978-1-316-64993-0 Paperback

Cambridge University Press has no responsibility for the persistence or accuracy of URLs for external or third-party internet websites referred to in this publication, and does not guarantee that any content on such websites is, or will remain, accurate or appropriate.

Contents

Acknowledgments		*page* vi
	Introduction	1
1	The Political Philosophy of American Education	3
2	American Education from Independence to Reconstruction and the Stamp of Slavery	11
3	Older but Not Wiser: America Industrializes and Embraces the Flawed Philosophy of Behaviorism in Education	27
4	*Brown* and Resegregation	55
5	Voluntary Race-Conscious Admissions Policies in Higher Education	78
6	*San Antonio*, Inequity, and the Human Struggle	107
7	Gender Discrimination in Education	137
8	Special Education and Inclusion	159
9	Civil Rights in the Educational Environment and Student Discipline	176
10	Current Reform Initiatives and a Better Way Forward	201
Index		224

Acknowledgments

I wish to thank the foremost scholars and educators who made invaluable comments and suggestions on prior drafts of this book, particularly Alex Tsesis. I thank as well Sean Langan and Elizabeth Chase Nelson for their outstanding research and editorial assistance.

I also thank the extraordinary educators who inspired this book, including Rose Alschuler, Norman Amaker, George Anastaplo, Nina S. Appel, Mary Bell, Cathy Fishbain Brown, Svetlana Budilovsky, James P. Carey, Patricia F. Carini, Margie Carter, Harry Clor, Maureen Condon, Richard Conviser, Margie Cooper, Barbara Cross, Deb Curtis, Meredith Dodd, James Faught, Nina Faught, Amelia Gambetti, Howard Gardner, Diane Geraghty, Josie Gough, Zelda Harris, David Hawkins, Frances Hawkins, James Hayes, Alise Shafer Ivey, Brittny Lissner Johnson, Daniel Kahneman, Judy Kaminsky, Rebekah F. Kaufman, Alfie Kohn, Mary Korte, Michelle Korte, Jody Lapp, Richard Louv, Lisa Makoul, Loris Malaguzzi, Cindy McPherson, Pam Myers, Honi Papernik, Trish Parenti, Ann Pelo, Juan Perea, Neil Postman, Steve Ramirez, Alan Raphael, Carlina Rinaldi, Peter Rutkoff, William Shapiro, Ronald Sharp, Daniel Siegel, Cathy Topal, Vea Vecchi, Merrilee Waldron, Carleton Washburne, Anita Weinberg, Carolyn Wing, and Lynn White.

For their wisdom and guidance regarding education law and policy, I am indebted to the directors and attorneys of the United States Department of Education, Office for Civil Rights, especially Kenneth A. Mines and John Fry; elected school board members and public servants, Rebecca Baim, Joan Herczeg, Debbie Hymen, Michael Lipsitz, Jerrold Marks, and Terri Olian; school district administrators, Gregory M. Kurr and Michael Lubelfeld; and school lawyers, Nancy Krent, Mike Loizzi, Bob Kohn, Heather Brickman, John A. Relias, and James C. Franczek, Jr.

Thanks also to the caring and dedicated colleagues I have encountered from early childhood education to law and graduate school: the Ravinia Nursery School staff, including Marilyn Straus, Rosalie Edelstein, Midge Hechtman, Ginger Scott, Ginger Uhlmann, and Roberta Wexler; the "teachers' teachers" at National-Louis

University and Baker Demonstration School in Evanston, Illinois, especially Paula Jorde Bloom, Marge Leon, Kathleen McKenna, Cynthia Mee, Alan Rossman, and Jane Stenson; the students, faculty, and administrators of Erikson Institute, particularly Stephanie Bynum and Rhonda Gillis; the wonderful teachers, board members, and families of Winnetka Public School Nursery; and the visionary education experts of Family Network and the Community Family Center – particularly Barbara Haley, William S. Kaufman, Ruth Stern, Herbert S. Wander, and Rosalie Weinfeld.

For their invaluable research, editorial assistance, and feedback on early drafts of the book, I am also grateful to an outstanding group of Loyola University of Chicago law students and Graduate Fellows, including Ashli Giles-Perkins, Kelsey Smith, Adam Betzen, Traci Copple, Katherine A. Buchanan, Leah G. Feldhendler, Sarah B. Ferguson, Megan L. Ferkel, Sarah Giauque, Amy S. Hammerman, Anne M. Graber, Elizabeth H. Greer, Anuradha Gupta, Gretchen M. Harris, Meghan Helder, Alison L. Helin, Erin Hickey, Caroline Hosman, Joanne Krol, Nicole Williams Koviak, Alisha J. Massie, Beth Miller-Rosenberg, Shannon Reeves-Rich, Beatriz Rendon, Laura R. Rojas, Sarah Smith, Helaine N. Tiglias, Nicole Torrado, Christina L. Wascher, Pam Witmer, and John Wunderlich.

Finally, for their incredible inspiration and support, I would like to express my profound gratitude to Bryan Stevenson, Nathaniel R. Jones, James Faught, Jerome Overbeck, S.J., Wendi Geffen, Ryan Daniels, Jo Ann Rooney, Margaret Callahan, James Prehn, S.J., Janet Sisler, Miranda Johnson, Maureen Hager, Jo Beth D'agostino, Joanna Pappas, David Prasse, John Pelissero, Susan Stabile, Maura Mast, Jean Dole, Katie Rohrer, and the compassionate community-servants on the Family Action Network Board.

Introduction

The Thirteenth Amendment to the Constitution was ratified on December 6, 1865. The first section of the Amendment declares: "Neither slavery nor involuntary servitude, except as a punishment for crime whereof the party shall have been duly convicted, shall exist within the United States, or any place subject to their jurisdiction." The Amendment is unique within the structure of the United States Constitution. It does not merely prohibit governmental action. Rather, the Amendment prohibits purely private, interpersonal conduct. It bars every person from holding slaves or from engaging in any other form of involuntary servitude (except as punishment for a crime).

The immediate impact of the Thirteenth Amendment was to end slavery in the southern United States and to bar a wider range of labor arrangements that constituted involuntary servitude. In addition, the second section of the Thirteenth Amendment grants to Congress the "power to enforce" the Amendment's prohibitions by passing "appropriate legislation." The Supreme Court has long held that this second section allows Congress to pass laws to eradicate not just slavery and involuntary servitude, but also the lingering "badges and incidents" of slavery. Congress and the Supreme Court, however, have never fully recognized that the ongoing lack of educational opportunities afforded to African Americans is attributable to those badges and incidents.

To the contrary, this book will show how American law has legitimated and perpetuated dramatic disparities in educational opportunities based upon race, sex, gender identity, sexual orientation, socio-economic status, native language, and disability. Those disparities have been sustained and justified not only by legal and political structures, but also by long-disproved theories of human development and educational psychology.

This book will challenge the history of educational disparities in America and analyze the civil right to an education from an interdisciplinary perspective. The book brings together the persuasive authority of judicial precedent and legal analysis; the wisdom, coherence, and depth of political and educational philosophy; the foresight of the Founders of the American regime; the observations, experiences, and profound understandings of educators; the prudence of policy-makers; the data sets and statistical regression analyses of economists; and the experiments and empirical evidence of cognitive psychologists and neuroscientists.

Throughout each of its chapters, the book raises and resolves the following question: What would the legal structures governing American education look like if they were based upon a proper understanding of the ways in which human beings actually learn?

The book will show that the American educational system sustains its inequities in part by projecting a misleading view of human learning and development. I will trace the evolution of the American educational system to the principles of behaviorist educational psychology which presume that human beings learn through operant conditioning. This presumption then leads to an educational system based on individual and systemic rewards and punishments, which ultimately serves to justify an inequitably funded and segregated regime. The book demonstrates how the checkered history of the right to education in America has been legitimated by this flawed presumption.

As this book will show, pathbreaking new research from the disciplines of neuroscience and educational psychology have belied the flawed behaviorist foundations that have long undergirded the legal structures supporting the American educational regime. The book will demonstrate that human beings actually learn by constructing knowledge together through meaningful relationships. I will carefully analyze that research, which reveals that all learning is constructed socially through meaningful relationships.

This book will also show that if the American educational system were founded on the correct understanding that all knowledge is socially constructed through meaningful relationships, it would recognize a civil right to adequate and equitable educational resources; it would fulfill the Founders' vision of a regime in which knowledge is diffused through important associations; it would develop diverse, inclusive, and equitable pedagogies and practices; it would extirpate the badges and incidents of discrimination; and it would teach all students the habits of mind that prepare them to be innovative leaders in a participatory democracy.

1

The Political Philosophy of American Education

This first chapter will chronicle the history of educational thought that informed the nation's Founders. Specifically, the leaders who participated in the Constitutional Convention of 1787 accepted from classical political philosophers, including Plato and Aristotle, the view that education must be a public concern because it has the power to shape character and support the regime. The Founders also accepted from modern political philosophers like Locke, Montesquieu, and Rousseau the view that secular education is vital to moral freedom and self-government. They considered public, common, and secular education indispensable to the survival and growth of the new democratic nation.

This chapter will also carefully articulate the Founders' pedagogy. Although they were familiar with an educational system dominated by private and parochial schools, the Founders also understood that knowledge is constructed through meaningful social relationships and associations. The success of their democratic experiment depended in large part on the extent to which the citizens could avail themselves of the opportunity to learn in this manner. From the start, the Founders perceived that the general diffusion of knowledge to the citizenry through a common educational system would prove vital to the survival of the American democracy. Although the Founders justified certain "nondemocratic" aspects of their constitutional structure by suggesting that it was necessary to counter the natural tendency of human beings to pursue their individual self-interest, they took a far more egalitarian view of education.

This chapter shows that the Founders' conception of American educational policy supports the development of programs designed to encourage students to construct knowledge through meaningful relationships and associations. Indeed, many of the views espoused by the philosophers held in esteem by the Founders bear a remarkable resemblance to the contemporary social constructivist approach to education discussed throughout the book. They envisioned young learners growing and developing by building associations between disparate ideas while cultivating meaningful relationships with their fellow citizens. At the same time, the regime was built on a foundation of slavery, which continues to support racial subjugation in education.

CLASSICAL PHILOSOPHIES OF EDUCATION: EDUCATION MUST BE A PUBLIC CONCERN BECAUSE IT HAS THE POWER TO SHAPE CHARACTER AND SUPPORT THE POLITICAL REGIME

Plato's *Republic* is arguably the greatest text articulating the philosophy of education.[1] The regime envisioned in the *Republic* is built upon critical assumptions about the educational process.[2] First, the goal of education is to create relatively stagnant and stratified role players for the good of the state; it is a purely public concern. Second, education is extremely powerful; it is capable of altering a person's natural instincts – including the instinct of love of one's own – and of shaping character.[3]

In Book VIII of the *Politics*, Aristotle expressly shares Plato's assumption that "education should be regulated by law and should be an affair of the state."[4] Aristotle declares that the "citizen should be molded to suit the form of government under which he lives." Each type of government has a "peculiar" character, and its educational system should strive to replicate the character required in its citizens to preserve its peculiar form.[5] Since the whole regime has one end, "it is manifest that education should be one and the same for all, and that it should be public, and not private."[6]

In the *Politics*, Aristotle also concludes that the type of "education of citizens" in a regime must depend on the political structure of that regime. Education in a democracy, for example, must teach all citizens the political skills necessary to participate in both ruling the regime and in being ruled by popular choice.[7] Democratic education must be specifically designed to develop in children the capacity to govern others by appreciating their needs and also the capacity for self-governance. As classical educational theorists, Aristotle and Plato share a belief in the supreme importance of public education for the health of the regime.

ENLIGHTENMENT EDUCATIONAL PHILOSOPHY: PUBLIC EDUCATION IS VITAL TO FREEDOM AND SELF-GOVERNMENT

In *Some Thoughts Concerning Education* (1693), John Locke emphasizes the significance of rationality and reason in the education of each child. Most people,

---

[1] Steven M. Cahn, *Classic and Contemporary Readings in the Philosophy of Education* (New York: Oxford University Press, 1997).
[2] See Plato, *Republic*, reprinted in Cahn, *Classic and Contemporary Readings*, 39–109.
[3] The question about whether educators can, and should, shape character arises in the contemporary debates about the merits of character education in public school. In Plato's *Protagoras* dialogue, Socrates appears to concur in Protagoras's argument that virtue can indeed be taught, agreeing after his arguments that "human care can make men good." See Plato, *Protagoras*, reprinted in Cahn, *Classic and Contemporary Readings*, 35–39.
[4] See Aristotle, *Politics*, Book VIII, reprinted in Cahn, *Classic and Contemporary Readings*, 137.
[5] Ibid.
[6] See Aristotle, *Nicomachean Ethics*, reprinted in Cahn, *Classic and Contemporary Readings*, 111–118.
[7] See Aristotle, *Politics*, Book VIII, 134.

Locke writes, are "good or evil, useful or not, by their education."[8] Like the ancients, therefore, Locke understands the power of education. Yet education is designed to teach the child to comprehend reason so that there is no need for external, political, or religious forms of discipline.[9] Locke believes that reason, if rightly understood and taught, can be the instrument of political freedom and self-governance.

In his seminal 1748 work, *The Spirit of the Laws*, Montesquieu concurs with Locke on the importance of public education for democracies.[10] In a democratic society that values freedom and self-government, public education is critical to social cohesion. Only public education can inspire the civic virtues requisite to democratic government, including the "love of the laws" and a preference for community, social, and public life over private life.

Rousseau, as well, shares Locke's emphasis on individual educational development, declaring that the "supreme good is not authority, but freedom."[11] In the *Emile* (alternately titled *On Education*), he expressly couples the development of a free people with a proper education: "This is my fundamental maxim. Apply it to childhood and all the rules of education follow."[12] Rousseau associates freedom with mankind's natural childhood state and authority with mankind's unnatural social condition. The rules of education, if they are to serve the supreme good of freedom, must be aligned with a child's natural condition.[13]

Rousseau understood that children are by nature competent and curious. Educators must understand the "distinctive genius" of each child, and allow the child "full liberty" to grow.[14] Hence, Rousseau creates the foundation for contemporary arguments against a standardized curriculum and in favor of child-centered education. He suggests that any educational process that neglects to "differentiate" – to take into account the unique developmental needs of each child – will fail.

In their calls for an education that promotes freedom and self-government, Locke, Montesquieu, and Rousseau share a fundamental distrust of direct instruction, dogma, or unquestioned presumptions as educational tools. Locke's belief in the power of reason suggests the subordination of preconceived notions to individual examination and rational thought. Slavish adherence to dogma is inimical to self-governance and self-determination. Thus, an education for self-government must develop in children the capacity to construct knowledge by questioning accepted beliefs.

---

[8] See Locke, *Some Thoughts Concerning Education*, reprinted in part in Cahn, *Classic and Contemporary Readings*, 145.
[9] Ibid. at 147 ("Every man must some time or other be trusted to himself").
[10] Montesquieu, Charles de, *The Spirit of the Laws*, translated by Thomas Nugent. Digireads.com, 2010. Book. 49–51.
[11] See Rousseau, *Emile, Book II*, reprinted in Cahn, *Classic and Contemporary Readings*, 167.
[12] Ibid.
[13] Ibid. at 170 ("Let the childhood ripen in children").
[14] Ibid. at 171.

In Montesquieu's thought, public education also is necessary to replace private religious zeal with a uniform, national allegiance to law and country. Rousseau, as well, believes that a proper education is the antidote to politically imposed moral doctrines. If allowed to develop their own interests free from such artificial constraints, children will naturally seek to form or construct socially useful alliances and boundaries, and they will naturally avoid socially destructive behavior.

PRIVATE EDUCATION IN COLONIAL AMERICA

The history of American education usually begins with the story of the importation of the English educational system to colonial America.[15] Contrary to common understanding, the educational tradition brought by the European settlers who colonized America was not based on a singular New England mode of educational hierarchy and religious conformity.

Rather, education in the colonial period was diffuse, localized, haphazard, and heterogeneous. There were significant differences between the educational practices in the northern, southern, and middle colonies as well as significant differences within each individual colony.[16] Nonetheless, it is fair to say that American colonists attempted for the most part to recreate the heavily religious educational institutions with which they were most familiar from their European experience.[17]

In 1647, for instance, the Massachusetts General Court enacted the "Old Deluder Satan Act." The Act declared that because Satan was keeping people in the colony from understanding scripture, every town with at least 50 families must provide for

---

[15] See, e.g., Kern Alexander & M. David Alexander, *American Public School Law* (Belmont, CA: West/Thomson Learning, 2001), 21–23. Well before the colonists brought to America their notions of schools, however, Native Americans had developed their own approach to education, an approach that was purposefully discarded by the settling Europeans. For two excellent and thorough discussions of the history of Native American education, see Wayne Urban & Jennings Wagoner, *American Education: A History* (McGraw Hill: 2000), ch. 1; Margaret Szasz, *Indian Education in the American Colonies, 1607–1783* (Lincoln: University of Nebraska Press, 1988). Despite variations among Native American tribes, precolonial education had common objectives. The primary goal of education was the development of skills essential to survival. Education in these skills was closely joined with spiritual education. The European missions first attempted to replace Native American spiritual teachings with Catholicism. The elimination of Native American culture and educational practices continued in earnest throughout the late 1800s and early 1900s in the form of boarding school programs designed to "rid" Native American children of their culture through "assimilation." See Joel Spring, *Deculturalization and the Struggle for Equality: A Brief History of Education of Dominated Cultures in the United States* (New York: McGraw-Hill Higher Education, 2000); Alan Peshkin, *Places of Memory: Whiteman's Schools and Native American Communities* (New York: Routledge, 1997); David Adams, *Education for Extinction: American Indians and the Boarding School Experience, 1875–1928* (University Press of Kansas, 1995); Bernard W. Sheehan, *Seeds of Extinction: Jeffersonian Philanthropy and the American Indian* (Chapel Hill: The University of North Carolina Press, 1973).

[16] Urban & Wagoner, *American Education: A History*, 15.

[17] Kenneth A. Lockridge, *Literacy in Colonial New England: An Enquiry into the Social Context of Literacy in the Early Modern West* (New York: W.W. Norton, 1974).

instruction in reading and writing. If a town had 100 or more families, it also had to provide grammar schools that would prepare boys for higher education at Harvard. The law threatened the town with a fine if it did not comply. While expressed in terms that may sound unusual to the modern ear, the Act reflected a conceptual link between more widespread education and an improved society. Although the Massachusetts General Court's impulse was more explicitly religious than the view of their Enlightenment counterparts, the two disparate groups both saw the need for a more systemic approach to education. The significance of this unlikely commonality was not lost on the Founders.

Despite this somewhat modest initial movement toward community-based education, those families with educated adults continued to rely primarily on the home as the institution of learning. Children who did not have the advantage of a learned adult in the home were sent to other homes occupied by adults who offered to teach groups of children together. These early private schools were run by men and women who typically instructed their own children and, for a fee, instructed the neighborhood children as well.

These private schools soon developed a shared curriculum with a strong religious flavor. Children were taught to read by first memorizing the Bible. As was true in England, the lessons were often presented on hornbooks – pieces of parchment placed on a wooden paddle, covered with a strip of clear horn to protect them from being smudged.

The lesson typically included a prayer, biblical passage, religious maxim, or psalm. The hornbooks were coupled with primers, such that religion and literacy were literally tied together. For example, the *New England Primer* contained the letters of the alphabet arranged so that each letter began a verse from the Bible. A series of illustrated rhymes taught children both the alphabet and the doctrine of original sin. The primary goal of these lessons was to teach children to read, but the lessons employed religious doctrine as the setting for language.

A variety of church-affiliated or church-sponsored schools sprang up together with the officially established religious institutions. The many religious sects in America all maintained parochial schools. Moreover, splinters that developed in the numerous Protestant denominations led to competing schools even within the same religion. The various sects soon competed vigorously for the scarce public resources devoted to education.

THE FOUNDERS' EDUCATIONAL PHILOSOPHY: DEMOCRATIC EDUCATION MUST DEVELOP MEANINGFUL RELATIONSHIPS BETWEEN INDIVIDUALS AND THE COMMUNITY

After Independence and before the Constitution was drafted, the nation's Founders were well aware that the nation was not yet a union. The Founders grew to believe that one of the most effective ways to achieve common values was to create a shared system of education. As Urban and Wagoner have observed, "[e]ducation, then, emerged as an essential consideration in the minds of those who faced the momentous task of establishing the new nation."[18] The political structure of the new regime became dependent on the educational structure of the regime, and therefore the "architects of the American nation clearly and deliberately fused educational theory with political theory."[19]

Benjamin Franklin, for example, argued consistently for the education of each individual in practical skills, useful in the world.[20] For Franklin, learned treatises and other established texts were important, but only insofar as they generated ideas that could be put into practice. Ultimately, Franklin wrote *Poor Richard's Almanack* between 1732 and 1757 for the purpose of "conveying instruction among the common people, who bought scarce any other books."[21] To express Franklin's approach in more contemporary terms, he sought to present knowledge in a broadly accessible manner. Any literate citizen could connect new ideas by building associations between the ideas in Franklin's texts and the everyday concepts the reader already understood. In addition, they could take the next step by cultivating meaningful relationships with the other readers of the extremely popular book. Together they could explore the text in further detail and gain new, shared insights.

In order to create collections of books that could be used by more than a wealthy few, Franklin and his colleagues created the first colonial library by donating their most precious books to a common collection called the "Library Company of Philadelphia." The collection contained classic works such as *Plutarch's Lives*, as well as history books and maps.

In his *Proposals Relating to the Education of Youth in Pennsylvania* (1749), Franklin designed the "Philadelphia Academy," whose mission was to create not a cadre of select scholars, but a generation of common men able to perform practical skills and community service.[22] Although Franklin's success in implementing his ideas was limited, he generated a vital discourse regarding the type of education that would serve the new nation and its people.

Thomas Jefferson attempted to advance the ideal of public education in his "Bill for the More General Diffusion of Knowledge," which he placed before the Virginia legislature in 1779.[23] Rooted in his philosophy that public education was necessary to support the new republic and its democratic government,

---

[18] Urban & Wagoner, *American Education: A History*, 70.
[19] Ibid.
[20] See Leonard W. Larabee et al., *The Autobiography of Benjamin Franklin* (New Haven, Connecticut: Yale University Press, 1964); John Hardin Best, *Benjamin Franklin on Education* (Teachers College Press, 1962); Leonard W. Larabee and Whitfield J. Bell, *The Papers of Benjamin Franklin* (New Haven, CN: Yale University Press, 1959).
[21] See *Poor Richard's Almanack*, in Larabee & Bell, *The Papers of Benjamin Franklin*.
[22] See *Proposals*, in Best, *Benjamin Franklin on Education*.
[23] Thomas Jefferson, *Bill for the More General Diffusion of Knowledge*, *The Educational Work of Thomas Jefferson* (New York: Russell & Russell, 1964), 199–204; see also Thomas Jefferson, *Writings* (Library of America: 1984); John Adams, *The Adams-Jefferson Letters* (New York: Simon & Schuster, 1971).

Jefferson proposed a system of free elementary-level education administered by separate counties or divisions. Each of these so-called little republics would provide children with basic literacy skills and with knowledge of history. Jefferson's system would allow the young pupils to make new associations across the different subjects presented. It would also encourage them to build meaningful relationships with their classmates. Over a century before the emergence of social constructivism in education, the basic ingredients of this approach presented themselves in Jefferson's proposal.

Jefferson's vision was that American children would have the education necessary to prepare them to participate as citizens in a democracy. He believed that the benefits of education should not be reserved solely for the established aristocracy or for any religious group.[24] The government had a compelling interest in providing sufficient resources to insure all young Americans gained the skills needed for democratic citizenship.

In fact, Jefferson believed that a public education was vital to the preservation of liberty. He wrote that a publicly supported educational system would raise the morals of children to the "high ground of moral respectability necessary to their own safety, and to orderly government."[25] The "most certain and the most legitimate end of government," according to Jefferson, was the provision of a free, public education to its citizens.[26]

Jefferson's system of public education is not hostile to private education; rather, it simply understands private education to be inadequate to accomplish the political objective of educating all citizens for participation in their own government. To the extent that private education depletes resources from the public educational system, which is indispensable for the survival of democracy, private education is inimical to the ultimate realization of the democratic ideal.

---

[24] See *Act Establishing Religious Freedom* (1779), in Adrienne Koch & William Pedren, *The Life and Selected Writings of Thomas Jefferson* (Modern Library, 1998), 289–291.

[25] Urban & Wagoner, *American Education: A History*, 73–74 (citing Thomas Jefferson to John Adams, Oct. 28, 1813).

[26] Ibid. As Urban & Wagoner put it: "equal educational opportunity was to allow the identification and proper education of those capable of leadership and worthy of public trust. Jefferson placed himself in opposition to those of his own social background, many of whom constituted the 'artificial aristocracy.' Content with private education for their own children, they were willing to leave the education of others to random local initiative, church benevolence, or perhaps to the well-meaning charity of a concerned citizen-benefactor. To Jefferson, however, the education required for participation and leadership in the new American social order was far too important to be left to chance, parental whim, or restricted to a traditional elite." Ibid. at 74. One of the tragic ironies of Jefferson's efforts to spread the benefits of education among American citizens, of course, is that his system completely excluded all Native Americans, all African Americans and virtually all women. See *Notes on the State of Virginia* (1781), in Koch & Pedren, *The Life and Selected Writings of Thomas Jefferson*, 243–244; E. M. Halliday, *Understanding Thomas Jefferson* (HarperCollins Publishers, 2001), 234 (describing Jefferson's exclusion of African Americans and Native Americans as an "obvious travesty").

CONCLUSION

As they sought to build a sustainable and durable democratic society, the Founders drew on a wealth of philosophical traditions. From the classical era, they applied the principles of Plato and Aristotle. From the Enlightenment, they imbibed the theories of Locke, Montesquieu, and Rousseau. They synthesized these strands of thought, and added the original contributions of thinkers like Benjamin Franklin and Thomas Jefferson to create a new approach to education. The Founders came to realize that educating the citizenry stood among the foremost duties of a democratic government. Indeed, they would have viewed it as a fundamental responsibility. The Founders prized learning through the development of meaningful associations and relationships – between different ideas and different people. In short, they anticipated by over a century the main themes of the social constructivist approach to education.

2

American Education from Independence to Reconstruction and the Stamp of Slavery

The structure governing American education is supported by the Founders' educational philosophy, which in turn is based upon the Founders' view of human nature and human development. That view is nuanced. Although the Founders justified their constitutional structure with their fear that human beings have a natural desire to pursue their self-interest, they also created a regime dependent upon the human capacity to construct knowledge through meaningful relationships.

The Founders rationalized their constitutional structure by arguing that it reflects aspects of human nature. There is evidence that the Founders feared that human beings would be overcome by their natural desire to serve their own self-interest, necessitating a constitutional order designed to check that desire. That perception of human nature can be, and has been, employed to justify a pedagogy based on behaviorism. Yet, as demonstrated in this chapter, the Founders actually held a nuanced view of human nature that led them to construct a regime premised on the principal that humans learn by constructing knowledge through meaningful relationships.

In addition to examining the contours of the Founders' conception of human nature and human development, this chapter will explore the major trends in the American educational system from the ratification of the Constitution through Reconstruction. It will present the successes of the common school movement, the heroic efforts undertaken by slaves and freedmen to secure an education in the face of daunting barriers, and the attempts to implement Reconstruction-era civil rights legislation. The chapter will conclude with an examination of Supreme Court jurisprudence from the Reconstruction era, and a discussion of the lingering implications of those consequential decisions.

THE FOUNDERS' NUANCED UNDERSTANDING OF HUMAN NATURE AND HUMAN DEVELOPMENT

The Federalist Papers are a collection of eighty-five essays written by James Madison, Alexander Hamilton, and John Jay. Originally published as a series of newspaper columns signed by "Publius" between 1787 and 1788, they provide the fundamental justification for the United States Constitution. They also contain important evidence of the Founders' understanding of human nature and development.

In Federalist 51, James Madison writes: "What is government itself, but the greatest of all reflections on human nature?"[1] The Founders presumed that human nature was flawed. Men are not angels; they are driven by passions that are difficult for them to overcome. In Federalist 55, Madison explicitly declares: "In all numerous assemblies, of whatever characters composed, passion never fails to wrest the scepter from reason."[2] Alexander Hamilton in Federalist 6 similarly presumes the "depravity in mankind" asking, "Has it not ... invariably been found that momentary passions, and immediate interests, have a more active and imperious control over human conduct than general or remote considerations of policy, utility or justice?"[3] These passions can lead individuals to pursue their own interests at the expense of others.

As Madison declares, "If men were angels, no government would be necessary."[4] Government is necessary to "control" the governed because men are generally incapable of self-control.[5] In fact, the Founders expressed the view that "sown in the nature of men" is a "propensity" to "fall into mutual animosities."[6]

Madison also argues that a regime's "parchment barriers" are not adequate by themselves to guard against the "encroaching spirit of power."[7] Rather, the only way for civil society to control the natural passions of mankind is to diffuse them. The passions of one person or group can be diffused only when they interact with the passions of another person or group. As Madison writes, "Ambition shall be made to counteract ambition."[8]

Madison further expounded on this theme at the Virginia Constitutional Convention. Speaking before his fellow delegates on June 20, 1788, he noted: "That union is the first object for the security of our political happiness, in the hands of gracious Providence, is well understood and universally admitted through all the United States."[9] To the Founders, "union" embodied both the solidarity between states and the cohesion of the body of citizens. Contrasting the American project to non-democratic forms of government, he continued: "The causes of half the wars that have thinned the ranks of mankind, and depopulated nations, are caprice, folly, and ambition ... where the passions of one, or of a few individuals,

---

[1] James Madison, *The Federalist Papers*, no. 51 (New York: New American Library, 1961), 322.
[2] Madison, *The Federalist Papers*, no. 55, 340.
[3] Alexander Hamilton, *The Federalist Papers*, no. 6, 51–53.
[4] Madison, *The Federalist Papers*, no. 51, 322.
[5] Ibid.
[6] Madison, *The Federalist Papers*, no. 10, 78.
[7] Madison, *The Federalist Papers*, no. 48, 308.
[8] Ibid. at 309.
[9] James Madison, "Federal Experiments in History," in *The Constitution of the United States of America and Selected Writings of the Founding Fathers* (Barnes & Noble, 2012), 711.

direct the fate of the rest of the community."[10] In Madison's view, a viable government not only needed diffuse sources of power but also required leaders who grasped that their individual well-being was inextricable from that of their fellow citizens. Madison's words highlight the Founders' realization that for human beings in general – and democratic citizens in particular – the ability to learn through building meaningful relationships is vital. Indeed, the Founders viewed it as a prerequisite to the success of the American experiment.

In light of the apparent propensities of human nature, therefore, the Founders devised a constitutional structure and regime that seems to be based on "animosities." The separation of legislative, executive, and judicial powers, for instance, is designed to diffuse, not to elevate, the passionate pursuit by each branch of government of its own power, ambition, and self-interest. Similarly, the Founders attempted to diffuse, not elevate, the passions by retaining the sovereignty of the states and placing that sovereignty in tension with that of the limited national government.[11]

In addition, the Founders intended the judicial branch to play a critical role in diffusing the passions of mankind. In Federalist 78, Alexander Hamilton argues that the limits on governmental power could be "preserved in practice no other way than through the medium of the courts of justice." The courts must guard the Constitution and the rights of individuals against the natural "ill humours" of mankind pursuing its own powerful self-interests.[12]

The regime that the Founders constructed is therefore predicated on their view that humans are driven by their natural instinct to survive, and are overcome by their own emotions and desires. Indeed, the Founders cautioned that in the absence of meaningful social relationships, individuals would pursue their own self-preservation and self-interest.

THE GROWTH OF THE FOUNDERS' MODEL OF PUBLIC EDUCATION FOR CHILDREN THROUGH COMMON SCHOOLS

Benjamin Rush, who had signed the Declaration of Independence and served as Surgeon General of the revolutionary army, was instrumental in advancing a free and uniform system of public education.[13]

In particular, Rush argued that a general tax should be used to finance a system of American public education, asserting that such a system would in the long run lessen taxes for all. In arguments that foreshadow contemporary debates about

---

[10] Ibid.
[11] Madison, *The Federalist Papers*, no. 39, 241.
[12] Madison, *The Federalist Papers*, no. 51, 343.
[13] See Benjamin Rush, *A Plan for the Establishment of Public Schools and the Diffusion of Knowledge in Pennsylvania; to Which are Added, Thoughts Upon the Mode of Education, Proper in a Republic* (Philadelphia PUBLISHER if available?, 1786). See also Urban & Wagoner, *American Education: A History*, 79–85.

public education, Rush even claimed that all taxpayers benefit from public education because criminal activity and the expenses of the criminal justice system would be reduced in a nation of educated, law-abiding citizens. Moreover, a national system of education for all children would bring diverse people together through a shared patriotic love of country that would allow them to internalize prudential restraints on their own freedom. This system, Rush argued, would offer a vital, tangible reinforcement to the parchment barriers invoked by Madison.

The Founders' idea of a uniform, free, public, and publicly funded educational system was further realized in the "common school" movement of the early 1800s. Horace Mann, a Massachusetts legislator and Secretary of the Massachusetts Board of Education, was a leading advocate for common schools. Mann believed that the public, common school could bring diverse peoples and cultures into a common bond. Although Mann's own values were aligned with Protestant beliefs, he advocated broad, unifying principles of morality. Division in religion and class could be overcome by a common education in a shared civic morality.

Like Rush, Mann argued that publicly financed education for the masses was good for society as a whole. In particular, he convinced wealthy property owners that proper education would give to the working class a respect for the property and wealth of others that would help to preserve the existing power structure.[14]

He argued that property landowners had a special obligation to fund public education in proportion to their ownership. Yet Mann also believed that property was a national asset entrusted to individual owners for their use in ways that served the common good. Hence, the state had the right to tax personal property for public uses such as the education of all children in an integrated, state-controlled system of common or "normal" schools.[15]

In 1852, Massachusetts became the first state to enact a compulsory attendance law, thereby exercising the type of power Mann argued states should employ in regulating the education of children.[16] By 1918, every state had passed some form of compulsory school attendance statute.[17] As public school attendance significantly increased in the late 1800s and early 1900s, the illiteracy rate among Americans significantly declined.[18]

---

[14] See Urban & Wagoner, *American Education: A History*, 102–103.
[15] Ibid. at 108–109. Urban and Wagoner also trace the rise of women in the teaching profession to Mann's "common" or "normal" school movement.
[16] Ibid. at 173.
[17] Ibid. at 172.
[18] Ibid. at 174 (attendance increased at the turn of the century from 49 percent to 64 percent, while illiteracy declined from 20 percent to 13 percent). In *Brown v. Board of Education*, 347 U.S. 483 at n.4 (1954), the Supreme Court traces the development of public schools and compulsory school attendance laws, both of which grew dramatically after the adoption of the Fourteenth Amendment in 1868.

THE BADGES AND INCIDENTS OF SLAVERY

For all the noble sentiments espoused by the Founders in the Declaration of Independence, Constitution, and Bill of Rights, a glaring hypocrisy characterized the nation's treatment of African Americans. The theories of government adopted by the Founders – not to mention the educational philosophies they endorsed – should have resulted in the prompt emancipation of the millions of enslaved African Americans. This failure to practice their principles would have profound effects on every facet of national life. America's "original sin" cast, and continues to cast, a long shadow over the nation's educational system. Time and time again, this nation has failed to extirpate the badges and incidents of this horrible injustice.

In *Self-Taught, African American Education in Slavery and Freedom*,[19] Heather Andrea Williams demonstrates that most white southern slaveholders were opposed to the education of their slaves because they feared an educated slave population would threaten their authority. Williams documents a series of statutes that criminalized any person who taught slaves or supported their efforts to teach themselves. For example, in 1830, North Carolina passed a statute that declared that "any free person, who shall hereafter teach, or attempt to teach, any slave within this State to read or write, the use of figures excepted, or shall give or sell to such slave or slaves any books or pamphlets, shall be liable to indictment in any court of record in this state."[20]

Slaves who attempted to educate themselves suffered physical and psychological consequences. Nonetheless, even under the strict limitations of slavery, slaves still developed strategies in order to learn reading and writing. Williams describes slaves who received their instruction in "pit schools," which were "pit[s] in the ground way out in the woods away from the master's surveillance."[21] She also writes about slaves who "hid spelling books under their hats to be ready whenever they could entreat or bribe a literate person to teach them."[22] During the Civil War, some black soldiers studied during their lunch breaks. She found that "during the transition from slavery to freedom, many African Americans simultaneously attempted to satisfy material needs with intellectual longings."[23]

Upon emancipation, white southerners' fear of an educated black population did not dissipate; they used violence and arson to prevent attempts to educate the freed slaves. Yet, in spite of the danger and meager resources, many freed slaves constructed and operated their own schools. Williams details how students would ask for longer class days and shorter vacations in order to maximize their instructional time. They would walk miles from their homes to the nearest school, some "barefoot,

---

[19] (Chapel Hill: University of North Carolina Press, 2005).
[20] Ibid. at 206.
[21] Ibid. at 20.
[22] Ibid.
[23] Ibid. at 30.

wearing torn, ragged clothing."²⁴ These independent African American schools, Williams argues, served as "the central point of an educational sphere."²⁵

"With so much invested in the empowering potential of education," Williams discovered that "freedpeople identified teaching as a critical job for building self-sufficient communities and called both men and women into service."²⁶ S. W. Magill, an American Missionary Association employee who sought complete control over Savannah's black educational institutions, was outraged that the freed slaves had established the Savannah Educational Association. In response he "complained that black people expected him to work with them rather than hand over authority."²⁷ Placing black teachers and administrators in black schools was part of the freed slaves' larger campaign for self-determination.

Williams posits that the newly emancipated African American communities' success in establishing their own educational institutions impacted and "transformed" education in the American South.²⁸ State legislatures eventually established educational facilities for large numbers of poor whites who would otherwise not have had any formal education. Williams points out that the idea of a literate and free African American population both threatened and inspired white southerners to seek educational opportunity for their own communities.

A recent study published by the Institute of Labor Economics attempts to quantify the ongoing effects of slavery. In "The Evolution of the Racial Gap in Education and the Legacy of Slavery," Graziella Bertocchi and Arcangelo Dimico conclude:

> The initial gap still exerts a significantly positive impact on the subsequent degree of inequality, which means that initial conditions as of 1940 have shaped educational attainment in a persistent fashion. Moreover, this initial inequality can be linked to the legacy of slavery, which confirms the conjecture that current racial educational inequality has indeed deep roots in the history of the country.²⁹

They continue: "Using the 1860 slave share as an instrument, we establish that indeed the initial gap negatively affects growth. In other words, in 1940 the degree of racial educational inequality is still determined by the 1860 slave share. It is through this channel that slavery hampers economic development."³⁰ In conclusion: "The legacy of slavery still looms over American society."³¹

Their research shows that the current degree of racial inequality in education is affected by slavery through its effect on the level of the gap at the eve of World War

---

[24] Ibid. at 142.
[25] Ibid.
[26] Ibid. at 111.
[27] Ibid. at 88.
[28] Ibid. at 6.
[29] Graziella Bertocchi & Arcangelo Dimico, "The Evolution of the Racial Gap in Education and the Legacy of Slavery," IZA DP No. 6192 (December 2011).
[30] Ibid.
[31] Ibid.

II. This influence is identified by Graziella Bertocchi and Arcangelo Dimico through a two-step strategy that allows them to obtain consistent estimates of the persistence of racial educational inequality throughout the 1940–2000 period.[32]

Over the same period, Bertocchi and Dimico also find that income growth is negatively affected by the initial educational disparities between blacks and whites, which uncovers a negative influence of slavery on development that runs through the accumulation of human capital.[33] The badges and incidents of slavery remain.

THE RE-FOUNDING, THE ORIGIN OF CIVIL RIGHTS, AND THE SETBACKS OF RECONSTRUCTION

The end of the Civil War brought Amendments to the United States Constitution that promised a re-founding of the republic. They marked a sustained effort by Congress to remove the badges and incidents of slavery from African Americans. Ratified on December 6, 1865, the Thirteenth Amendment abolished slavery in the United States: "Neither slavery nor involuntary servitude, except as a punishment for crime whereof the party shall have been duly convicted, shall exist within the United States, or any place subject to their jurisdiction."[34]

Shortly after the end of the Civil War, Congress passed the Civil Rights Act of 1866, which provided:

> All persons born in the United States ... are hereby declared to be citizens of the United States; and such citizens, of every race and color, without regard to any previous condition of slavery or involuntary servitude, except as a punishment for crime whereof the party shall have been duly convicted, shall have the same right, in every State and Territory in the United States, to make and enforce contracts, to sue, be parties, and give evidence, to inherit, purchase, lease, sell, hold, and convey real and personal property, and to full and equal benefit of all laws and proceedings for the security of person and property, as is enjoyed by white citizens.[35]

The Fourteenth Amendment was ratified on July 9, 1868, and granted citizenship to "all persons born or naturalized in the United States," which included persons formerly enslaved. The Amendment also forbids states from making or enforcing "any law which shall abridge the privileges or immunities of citizens of the United States; nor shall any state deprive any person of life, liberty, or property, without due process of law; nor deny to any person within its jurisdiction the equal protection of the laws." Section 5 of the Fourteenth Amendment declares: "The Congress shall have power to enforce, by appropriate legislation, the provisions of this article."[36]

---

[32] Ibid.
[33] Ibid.
[34] U.S. Const. amend XIII.
[35] Ch. 31, 14 Stat. 27 (reenacted by Enforcement Act of 1870, ch. 114, § 18, 16 Stat. 140, 144 (codified as amended at 42 U.S.C. §§ 1981–1982 (2012).
[36] U.S. Const. amend XIV, §5.

The Constitution's Fifteenth Amendment, ratified in 1870, provides: "The right of citizens of the United States to vote shall not be denied or abridged by the United States or by any State on account of race, color, or previous condition of servitude." Section 2 of the Fifteenth Amendment gives to Congress the power to enforce the Amendment "by appropriate legislation."[37]

Historian Eric Foner of Columbia University offers valuable insight into the prevailing views of the lawmakers who ratified the Fourteenth Amendment. He notes:

> If there's one thing you can say about the Thirty-ninth Congress, it was not thinking about school segregation when it passed the Fourteenth Amendment. There's no question about that. They set up a segregated school system in Washington, D. C. right at the same time. Most black leaders were not thinking about it. The issue of segregation versus integration was not an issue at that time. . . . The issue at the time was *access* to education, and whether African Americans should *have* education. Under slavery it was illegal to educate a slave. In presidential reconstruction, some of the southern states began making provision for public education but only for whites. So in a sense, the Thirty-ninth Congress said no, blacks have to get education too. It is illegal to set up a school system just for whites. That was the issue: exclusion from education, not integration or segregation.[38] (Emphasis in original)

Congress, striving to act pursuant to its authority under these Amendments, passed the Civil Rights Act of 1875. That legislation was initially designed to prevent states and private enterprises from discriminating on the basis of race in public schools, the selection of juries, and public accommodations – including inns, forms of public transportation, and places of public amusement, such as theaters and concerts.[39] Although the public accommodations provision extended to enterprises operated by private individuals, such enterprises were taken to be open to members of the public generally, so the line between state and private action did not seem significant.[40] By the time the Act was passed by Congress in early 1875, the public schools provision had been dropped.[41]

That statute in pertinent part provided:

> SEC. 1. That all persons within the jurisdiction of the United States shall be entitled to the full and equal enjoyment of the accommodations, advantages, facilities, and privileges of inns, public conveyances on land or water, theaters, and other places of public amusement, subject only to the conditions and limitations established by law and applicable alike to citizens of every race and color, regardless of any previous condition of servitude.

---

[37] U.S. CONST. amend XV, §2.
[38] Eric Foner, "The Original Intent of the Fourteenth Amendment: A Conversation with Eric Foner," 6 NEV. L.J. 425 (2006).
[39] G. Edward White, "The Origins of Civil Rights in America," 64:3 CASE WEST. RES. L. REV. 755 (2014).
[40] Id.
[41] Id.

SEC. 2. That any person who shall violate the foregoing section by denying to any citizen, except for reasons by law applicable to citizens of every race and color, and regardless of any previous condition of servitude, the full enjoyment of any of the accommodations, advantages, facilities, or privileges in said section enumerated, or by aiding or inciting such denial, shall for every such offence, forfeit and pay the sum of five hundred dollars to the person aggrieved thereby, to be recovered in an action of debt, with full costs, and shall also, for every such offence, be deemed guilty of a misdemeanor, and, upon conviction thereof, shall be fined not less than five hundred nor more than one thousand dollars, or shall be imprisoned not less than thirty days nor more than one year.[42]

THE CIVIL RIGHTS CASES AND THE FALSE DISTINCTION BETWEEN STATE ACTION AND PRIVATE CHOICE

In the *Civil Rights Cases*,[43] the Supreme Court declared unconstitutional the Civil Rights Act of 1875. The Court, in an eight to one majority opinion written by Justice Bradley, reasoned that the post-Civil War Reconstruction Amendments do not empower Congress to enact legislation protecting African Americans from the actions of private individuals. The Fourteenth Amendment can be enforced by legislation that prohibits state action, not interpersonal conduct:

> It is proper to state that civil rights, such as are guaranteed by the Constitution against State aggression, cannot be impaired by the wrongful acts of individuals, unsupported by State authority in the shape of laws, customs, or judicial or executive proceedings. The wrongful act of an individual, unsupported by any such authority, is simply a private wrong, or a crime of that individual; ... An individual cannot deprive a man of his right to vote, to hold property, to buy and sell, to sue in the courts, or to be a witness or a juror; he may, by force or fraud, interfere with the enjoyment of the right in a particular case; he may commit an assault against the person, or commit murder, or use ruffian violence at the polls, or slander the good name of a fellow citizen; but, unless protected in these wrongful acts by some shield of State law or State authority, he cannot destroy or injure the right; he will only render himself amenable to satisfaction or punishment, and amenable therefor to the laws of the State where the wrongful acts are committed. Hence, in all those cases where the Constitution seeks to protect the rights of the citizen against discriminative and unjust laws of the State by prohibiting such laws, it is not individual offences, but abrogation and denial of rights, which it denounces and for which it clothes the Congress with power to provide a remedy. ...
>
> [The Fourteenth Amendment] does not invest Congress with power to legislate upon subjects which are within the domain of state legislation; but to provide modes of relief against state legislation, or state action, of the kind referred to. It

---

[42] Ch. 31, 14 Stat. 27 (reenacted by Enforcement Act of 1870, ch. 114, § 18, 16 Stat. 140, 144 (codified as amended at 42 U.S.C. §§ 1981–1982 (2012)).
[43] 109 U.S. 3 (1883)

does not authorize Congress to create a code of municipal law for the regulation of private rights; but to provide modes of redress against the operation of state laws, and the action of state officers, executive or judicial, when these are subversive of the fundamental rights specified in the amendment. Positive rights and privileges are undoubtedly secured by the Fourteenth Amendment; but they are secured by way of prohibition against state laws and state proceedings affecting those rights and privileges, and by power given to Congress to legislate for the purpose of carrying such prohibition into effect; and such legislation must necessarily be predicated upon such supposed state laws or state proceedings, and be directed to the correction of their operation and effect.[44]

The Court also concludes that the Thirteenth Amendment did not authorize Congress to pass the Civil Rights Act because the statute did not target the "badges" of slavery:

It would be running the slavery argument into the ground to make it apply to every act of discrimination which a person may see fit to make as to guests he will entertain, or as to the people he will take into his coach or cab or car; or admit to his concert or theater, or deal with in other matters of intercourse or business. Innkeepers and public carriers, by the laws of all the states, so far as we are aware, are bound, to the extent of their facilities, to furnish proper accommodation to all unobjectionable persons who in good faith apply for them. . . ..

When a man has emerged from slavery, and by the aid of beneficent legislation has shaken off the inseparable concomitants of that state, there must be some stage in the progress of his elevation when he takes the rank of a mere citizen, and ceases to be the special favorite of the laws, and when his rights as a citizen, or a man, are to be protected in the ordinary modes by which other men's rights are protected. There were thousands of free colored people in this country before the abolition of slavery, enjoying all the essential rights of life, liberty, and property the same as white citizens; yet no one, at that time, thought that it was any invasion of their personal status as freemen because they were not admitted to all the privileges enjoyed by white citizens, or because they were subjected to discriminations in the enjoyment of accommodations in inns, public conveyances, and places of amusement. Mere discriminations on account of race or color were not regarded as badges of slavery. . . ..

Congress has a right to enact all necessary and proper laws for the obliteration and prevention of slavery with all its badges and incidents, is the minor proposition also true, that the denial to any person of admission to the accommodations and privileges of an inn, a public conveyance, or a theatre does subject that person to any form of servitude, or tend to fasten upon him any badge of slavery? If it does not, then power to pass the law is not found in the Thirteenth Amendment.[45]

Justice Bradley's opinion was informed by his view that, "surely it is no deprivation of civil right to give each race the right to choose their own company." Bradley

[44] 109 U.S. 3, 18, 11–12 (1883).
[45] Id. at 24–25, 21.

believed that the right to choose one's own company was a "social" right rather than a civil right. In his *Civil Rights Cases* opinion, he writes, "Congress did not assume ... to adjust ... the social rights of men and races in the community; but only to declare and vindicate those fundamental rights which appertain to the essence of citizenship."[46]

In his dissent, Justice Harlan argues that Congress had the power to enact the Civil Rights Act to protect African Americans from racial discrimination. He contends that the rights protected by the statute were not merely "social" rights; they were legal rights:

> What I affirm is that no state, nor the officers of any state, nor any corporation or individual wielding power under state authority for the public benefit or the public convenience, can, consistently either with the freedom established by the fundamental law, or with that equality of civil rights which now belongs to every citizen, discriminate against freemen or citizens, in their civil rights, because of their race, or because they once labored under disabilities imposed upon them as a race. The rights which Congress, by the act of 1875, endeavored to secure and protect are legal, not social, rights.[47]

Justice Harlan concludes:

> If the constitutional amendments be enforced, according to the intent with which, as I conceive, they were adopted, there cannot be, in this republic, any class of human beings in practical subjection to another class, with power in the latter to dole out to the former just such privileges as they may choose to grant. The supreme law of the land has decreed that no authority shall be exercised in this country upon the basis of discrimination, in respect of civil rights, against freemen and citizens because of their race, color, or previous condition of servitude.[48]

Harlan writes, "that government has nothing to do with social, as distinguished from technically legal, rights of individuals. . . . I agree that if one citizen chooses not to hold social intercourse with another, he is not and cannot be made amenable to the law for his conduct in that regard; for even upon grounds of race."[49] Harlan concedes, "no legal right of a citizen is violated by the refusal of others to maintain social relations with him."[50]

The Civil Rights Cases call into question the distinction between natural rights and social rights. According to the majority, the Constitution only empowers Congress to enforce natural rights against their encroachment by the government. Those rights are given to the individual. Justice Harlan's dissent, however, argues that social rights as between citizens of the United States also require legal

---

[46] White, "The Origins of Civil Rights in America."
[47] 109 U.S. 3, 59 (1883).
[48] *Id.* at 62.
[49] *Id.* at 59.
[50] *Id.*

protection. These social rights are legal rights that require protection from encroachment by other members of society. By rejecting the existence of protectable social rights, the majority returns to a construct of individual rights that the Founders discounted. It takes an atomized view of human nature and democratic citizenship that bears little resemblance to the concepts of union and community articulated by James Madison, Alexander Hamilton, Horace Mann, and many others. If social rights are not legal rights worthy of protection, one wonders how the cultivation of meaningful social relationships envisioned by the Founders could occur.

Moreover, by emphasizing the distinction between legal rights and social rights, the Court glosses over a compelling argument that would, in various formulations, appear in later battles over race and education: the concept of fundamental or natural rights. The Court repeatedly notes the importance and validity of civil rights. Given that these rights attempt to effectuate the principle of equality under the law, and given that inequality premised on a citizen's race attacks that citizen's dignity, would it not be reasonable to view civil rights as natural or fundamental rights?

Rather than engage directly with this argument, the Court deferred to the prevailing view that most civil rights were creatures of state law. Whether the sources of those rights were natural law, antebellum common law, the Civil Rights Act of 1866, or judicial efforts to identify "fundamental rights" associated with citizenship, the consensus view was articulated by Bradley in the *Civil Rights Cases*: namely, the civil rights of individuals were, on the whole, to be enforced by state rather than federal courts, unless it could be shown that states had willfully or negligently failed to protect those rights.

THE LEGACY OF RECONSTRUCTION AND ITS LINGERING CONSEQUENCES

Historian Eric Foner argues:

> A historical narrative of Reconstruction repudiated by historians continues to exert an outsized *influence on Supreme Court jurisprudence*, and that judicial unwillingness to overturn flawed Reconstruction-era precedents hinders the cause of equality before the law even today. It suggests that the overdue judicial repudiation of precedents resting, in part, on a faulty interpretation of Reconstruction's history would have a salutary effect on the Supreme Court's Thirteenth and Fourteenth Amendment jurisprudence. (Emphasis added)
>
> Racial inequality in education, it showed, stemmed from a wide array of interlocking and reinforcing causes – school location decisions by public officials, highway construction patterns, the policies of real estate companies, private employment practices, urban renewal projects, disciplinary decisions by individual teachers, and on and on. Some were primarily public, some private – but to disentangle them is virtually impossible. Judicial precedents and current decisions that take as a given a hard and fast distinction between private and state

discrimination reinforce an understanding of the history of race and racism in the United States that is fundamentally misleading but deeply embedded in current jurisprudence.[51]

In "Reconstruction Revisited," Foner writes,

[T]he establishment of schools for blacks by federal authorities and northern missionary associations and the creation of state-supported common school systems in the South were once hailed as the finest legacy of Reconstruction. Now a series of studies indicted northern teachers for seeking to stabilize the plantation order and inculcate "middle class" northern values like thrift, self-discipline, temperance, and respect for authority. ... Like northern common schools, black education in the South was increasingly seen as a form of cultural imperialism, an effort to create a disciplined and docile labor force.[52]

Yet, according to Foner,

"Reconstruction [also] gave birth to the modern black community, whose roots lay deep in slavery, but whose structure reflected the consequences of emancipation."[53] Nonetheless, he acknowledges that "Reconstruction's promise certainly exceeded its accomplishments."[54] Its accomplishments failed to meet its promise in large part because discrimination's roots continued to be nourished by government-sponsored social institutions. The historical consensus paints Reconstruction as, at best, a very limited success. Yet, the work of scholars like Foner demonstrates that the unduly optimistic view of Reconstruction taken by the judiciary has had serious implications for crucial precedents. In the context of education law, this phenomenon manifests itself through a widespread inability to appreciate the institutionalized nature of the obstacles faced by many minorities.

In *The Color of Law: A Forgotten History of How Our Government Segregated America*, Richard Rothstein documents in painstaking detail why the distinction between state action and private choices in the area of racial segregation is a false dichotomy.[55] Thus, he shows how the faulty reasoning buttressing the majority opinion in *Civil Rights Cases* opened the door to insidious forms of discrimination. Rothstein demonstrates how the government purposefully and systematically created or maintained racially segregated schools and neighborhoods. In particular, the government manipulated school placement and school construction to produce racially segregated schools and racially segregated attendance zones. In northern states where racially segregated schools were not explicitly mandated by state law,

---

[51] In *Symposium: The Thirteenth Amendment: Meaning, Enforcement, and Contemporary Implications: Panel II: Reconstruction Revisited: The Supreme Court and the History of Reconstruction – and Vice-Versa*, 112 COLUM. L. REV. 1585.
[52] Eric Foner, "Reconstruction Revisited." *Reviews in American History* 10, no.4 (1982), 86.
[53] Ibid. at 88.
[54] Ibid. at 95.
[55] Richard Rothstein, *The Color of Law: A Forgotten History of How Our Government Segregated America* (New York: Liveright Publishing Corporation, 2017).

the government nonetheless took calculated steps to steer families into racially segregated schools and attendance areas.[56] As Rothstein concludes, government mandates for school construction and school site programs were the "key" to preserving racially segregated schools long after they were declared unconstitutional in *Brown*.[57] Residential segregation was in fact created by state action, not by private choices.[58] Accordingly, the premise that racially segregated schools are not the product of state action, but of independent private choices, is based on a profoundly flawed conception of American history. Schools are more segregated now than they were before *Brown* because the state deliberately created racially segregated attendance zones.[59]

Similarly, Glenn E. Bracey II traces the evolution of critical race theory scholarship describing the "state as a constellation 'of *institutions*, the *policies* they carry out, the *conditions and rules* which support and justify them, and the *social relations* in which they are imbedded.'"[60] According to critical theorists, "[t]he state is inherently racial because every state action has racial consequences and because the state itself is structured to accomplish racial goals. In other words, the state both shapes and is shaped by racial conflict."[61]

Specifically, according to these thinkers, the State embodies the following tenets:

1. Every aspect of the state is racialized, meaning it shapes and is shaped by racism.
2. The state is white institutional space and, thus, inherently white racist. The state cannot be considered racially neutral.
3. The state is a tool, not a social actor unto itself. Whites have instrumental control of the state.
4. With respect to racial justice, the state only changes in accordance with the principles of interest-convergence.
5. Boundaries, both theoretical and empirical, between state and non-state (i.e., public and private) actors are fluid and contingent.
6. Each of these elements is permanent.[62]

Bracey continues:

Because racism is a fundamental part of American society, every aspect of the state is inescapably racialized. This racialization is due to the dialectic relationship between race and state, in which racial conflict structures the state and vice versa. Whites designed the state to be white institutional space, rendering it inherently racist and permanently under whites' instrumental control. Consequently, they can

---

[56] Ibid. at 132–137.
[57] Ibid. at 137.
[58] Ibid. at 179.
[59] Ibid. at 179, 215.
[60] Glenn E. Bracey II, "Toward a Critical Race Theory of State," *Critical Sociology* 2015, 41(3) 555.
[61] Ibid.
[62] Ibid. at 563–564.

insure that the state operates in their collective racial interests, effecting racial change only when and to the extent that it advances some other white concern. Whites' instrumental control also blurs the conceptual and practical division between state and non-state action, as whites' private actions are implicitly backed by state force. Indeed, the state is a vital instrument of racism because, through it, whites: define, unify, and organize themselves; arbitrate intra-racial disputes; mobilize and legitimize force; coerce people of color; and relieve their emotional costs by laundering racial oppression through a formal, "impersonal" apparatus. Ultimately, because whiteness is tacitly institutionalized at its core and because its utility for white racism is so great, the characteristics of state defined in the tenets of (critical race theory) of State are permanent.[63]

This research belies the notion that there is a meaningful practical difference between state action and private choices. As we have seen, this dubious distinction was used by the Supreme Court in the Civil Rights Cases to justify limiting the reach of the Civil Rights Act and the power of the Thirteenth and Fourteenth Amendments. The distinction also is used by the Court throughout its history to justify the maintenance or exacerbation of racial discrimination, segregation, and inequity in education.

In its pathbreaking work, which is summarized in *"Segregation in America,"* the Equal Justice Initiative has demonstrated that the current conditions of racial segregation and subjugation in education can be traced directly from slavery, to post-reconstruction lynching and racial terrorism, to Jim Crow, to segregation, and to mass incarceration. As the Equal Justice Initiative shows, the Supreme Court, with rare exception, has disregarded the evidence of this lineage, and instead has been complicit in the maintenance of strategies of racial subordination in education.

CONCLUSION

From the earliest deliberations of the 1787 Constitutional Convention in Philadelphia, the Founders realized they were constructing a democratic government unlike any the world had yet seen. The institutions and structures specified in the Constitution require a citizenry capable of collaborating and compromising in order to address the pressing questions of the day. Thomas Jefferson, James Madison, and Benjamin Rush understood this principle intuitively. Their writings and speeches reveal an abiding commitment to the shared construction of knowledge – both in the context of solving the nation's daily problems through effective government and in the more general sense of the pursuit of knowledge for its own sake. Reformers like Horace Mann carried the Founders' torch and laid the foundations for the comprehensive system of public education that continues today.

The Constitution that these Founders ratified, however, also endorsed an injustice. America's "original sin" of slavery could not coexist with the ideals described in

[63] Ibid.

the rest of the document; one strain of thought would eventually have to defeat the other. Although the new nation tolerated slavery for nearly a century, Reconstruction offered the United States a chance to atone for the wrongs it inflicted on African Americans. Yet, Reconstruction proved to be a missed opportunity. While the period is often remembered as one of important improvements in racial justice, recent scholarship has painted a more accurate picture of dashed hopes and unfulfilled promises. In particular, critical theorists have demonstrated that the judiciary's failure to comprehend the realities of Reconstruction has continued to have an adverse effect on the pursuit of justice in this country.

In the next chapter, we will explore the period lasting from the end of Reconstruction through World War II. Commonly known as the Gilded Age and Progressive Era, it featured an increased involvement of government in everyday life – particularly in education. We will examine how this increased involvement combined with broader societal trends like industrialization to alter the American approach to education.

3

Older but Not Wiser: America Industrializes and Embraces the Flawed Philosophy of Behaviorism in Education

In the decades following the Civil War and Reconstruction, the United States experienced a period of tremendous growth. During the seventy years between the end of Reconstruction and the end of World War II, the nation became a highly industrial, urbanized, and diverse society. The America of 1945 bore little resemblance to the America of 1875. During these seven decades, the modern United States came into being.

The massive, often unwieldy, expansion of manufacturing and the teeming, overcrowded cities that appeared as a consequence of this development sparked a desire to impose order on an increasingly dynamic and chaotic society. This impulse permeated all aspects of American life during this period, and was especially pronounced in the increased prominence of federal and state government. Attempting to bring some semblance of organization, government at all levels expanded its regulatory reach. For the first time, the American educational system became the object of clearly defined government standards and regulations – as demonstrated by a number of seminal Supreme Court decisions.

Developments in the economy also cast a shadow over educational practices in the United States. The factory model and its corresponding emphasis on mass production, routinization, and standardization permeated American pedagogy. Coupled with the principles of so-called scientific management, this emphasis gave rise to a behaviorist model of education. This development not only deviated significantly from the worldview of the Founders, but also had lasting consequences that reverberate in the present day.

This chapter will begin by exploring the avenues for government influence on education at the federal and state level. It will also – through an investigation of controlling Supreme Court jurisprudence – discuss the limits of that influence. Next, this chapter will expose the pervasive and ongoing impact of behaviorist theory on the American educational system. It will then offer compelling critiques of this antiquated approach from sources as varied as neuroscientists and child psychologists – and from thinkers like Thomas Jefferson and Albert Einstein. Finally, the chapter will conclude by juxtaposing the Founders' view of human nature with the deficient caricature offered by behaviorist theories. It will demonstrate that attempts to justify a behaviorist approach by pointing to the Founders' supposed vision for society must fall short in light of historical evidence.

THE RELATIONSHIP BETWEEN FEDERAL AND STATE CONTROL OVER EDUCATION

Although parents and guardians have a constitutional liberty interest in directing the upbringing of their children, the state has tremendous power to establish public schools, and to require that all children be educated according to its standard curriculum – even in private school or a homeschool environment. The state also has the authority to determine the age at which formal education must begin and thus has the power to regulate early childhood education.

As this chapter indicates, however, the state's power over education is influenced by federal legislation passed primarily under the Constitution's Spending Clause and is limited by the language of applicable amendments – notably the First Amendment and Fourteenth Amendment. The right of the government to mandate education for children must be balanced against these fundamental guarantees.

The Constitution does not grant to the federal government any direct power to regulate education. It does not even contain the word "education." In the absence of an express delegation to the federal government of constitutional power to regulate schools, therefore, that power is reserved to the states.

The Tenth Amendment to the Constitution reserves to the states all powers that are not expressly delegated to the federal government. That reservation of non-delegated powers to the states insures that the state and local governments generally retain sovereignty over affairs such as the education of their own citizens. As such, education law in America is primarily a matter of state and local concern. So long as they do not run afoul of constitutional or federal statutory prohibitions, state and local governments have virtually unlimited discretion to regulate the education of children.

LOCAL CONTROL OF EDUCATION

The states have virtually unlimited discretion to regulate education. A state has the power to pass legislation mandating attendance at school, punishing the failure of children at specific ages to attend school without legitimate justification, and imposing reasonable regulations on basic education, including: (1) required and elective curriculum, (2) instructional practices, (3) facilities, (4) attendance zones, (5) transportation, (6) security, (7) teacher qualifications, (8) policies and procedures, and (9) assessments. The states' power to mandate education and to regulate instructional practices extends to all private schools, and even to homeschooling.

The states' interests in compelling schooling and promulgating reasonable school regulations include: standardizing children; preparing citizens for political life; preparing citizens to be self-sufficient; instilling a love of country; facilitating the diffusion of knowledge; preventing children from prematurely entering the workforce; shaping character; developing critical thinking skills; developing intellectual autonomy; preparing students to interact in a culturally, ethnically, religiously, and racially diverse community; and developing habits of mental and physical wellness.

In exerting their control over education, the states typically delegate their power to local educational agencies or school boards. School boards set policies that incorporate legal requirements for the school district. Boards also establish specific rules governing district administration, personnel, community relations, student rights, dispute resolution, curriculum, and instructional practices.

The school board also is empowered to establish a school district's mission, belief statement, strategic objectives, and annual goals. School boards typically are composed of elected, volunteer public servants. The locally elected public officials, in turn, often delegate their managerial authority to an educational professional such as a chief administrator or superintendent.

The theme of "local control" is a recurring one throughout education law. In his dissent in *Board of Education of the Westside Community Schools v. Mergens*,[1] Justice Stevens explored the "pedagogical, political, and ethical" arguments supporting local control of education:

> As a matter of pedagogy, delicate decisions about immersing young students in ideological cross-currents ought to be made by educators familiar with the experience and needs of the particular children affected, and with the culture of the community in which they are likely to live as adults. ... As a matter of politics, public schools are often dependent for financial support upon local communities. The schools may be better able to retain local favor if they are free to shape their policies in response to local preferences.[2] As a matter of ethics, it is sensible to respect the desire of parents to guide the education of their children without surrendering control to distant politicians.[3]

FEDERAL CONGRESSIONAL POWER TO INFLUENCE EDUCATION

Although state and local governments have significant direct control over education, the United States Constitution invests Congress with the power to influence educational practices by regulating interstate commerce and its authority under the Spending Clause.

---

[1] 496 U.S. 226 (1990).
[2] See *San Antonio Independent School Dist. v. Rodriguez*, 411 U.S. 1 (1973), 49–53.
[3] See *Meyer v. Nebraska*, 262 U.S. 390 (1923), 399–403.

The Commerce Clause gives Congress the power to regulate the channels of interstate commerce, persons or instrumentalities of interstate commerce, and activities that substantially affect interstate commerce. Congress's power to regulate education under the Commerce Clause, however, is limited. For example, the Supreme Court has held that Congress has no power to pass a statute criminalizing gun possession in a "school zone" because such possession alone does not "substantially affect" interstate commerce.[4]

The federal government, therefore, regulates education primarily through the Spending Clause. Under the Spending Clause, Congress may attach conditions to the states' receipt of federal funds, so long as: (1) the expenditures are used by the states for the general welfare, as opposed to a purely local concern; (2) the conditions imposed by Congress on funding are clear and unambiguous; (3) the conditions imposed by Congress on funding are reasonably related to the purpose of the expenditures; and (4) the conditions imposed by Congress do not violate any independent constitutional prohibition. In addition, the Supreme Court also has made clear that the conditions Congress attaches to its funding must not be coercive. In other words, the conditions of the grant must afford the states a genuine choice of whether to forego the funding stream.[5]

Acting pursuant to its "spending" power, Congress has passed an array of federal statutes that regulate school affairs, including the employment of teachers;[6] the treatment of female students;[7] the education of children with learning disabilities;[8] the privacy rights of teachers and students;[9] the rights of teachers to take family and medical leave;[10] the access of public and private groups to educational facilities;[11] and even the qualifications of teachers, the content of curriculum, and the standards for student achievement.[12] This book will explore many of these efforts in greater detail in later chapters.

CONSTITUTIONAL LIMITS ON LOCAL CONTROL

The Constitution also places important limits on state and local control of education. For example, the Fifth and Fourteenth Amendment Due Process Clauses prohibit the state and federal governments from enacting educational programs that unilaterally deprive parents and guardians of the liberty to direct the upbringing of

---

[4] *United States v. Lopez*, 514 U.S. 549 (1995).
[5] *National Federation of Indep. Bus. v. Sebelius*, 567 U.S. 519 (2012).
[6] See, e.g., 42 U.S.C. §2000e-2 et seq. (Title VII); 29 U.S.C. §206 (Equal Pay Act).
[7] See, e.g., 20 U.S.C. §§1681–1688 (Title IX).
[8] See, e.g., the Individuals with Disabilities Education Act Amendments of 1997, 20 U.S.C. §§1400–1405.
[9] See, e.g., Family Educational Rights and Privacy Act, 20 U.S.C. §1232.
[10] See, e.g., the Family and Medical Leave Act, 29 U.S.C. §§2601, 2611, 2612.
[11] See, e.g., Equal Access Act, 20 U.S.C. §§4071–4072.
[12] See, e.g., No Child Left Behind Act (NCLB), 20 U.S.C. §6301 et seq.

their children. Moreover, the Fourteenth Amendment's Equal Protection Clause generally does not prevent the states from employing education-financing systems that produce dramatic disparities in the funds available in different school districts. However, the same Clause does preclude them from absolutely depriving children of a minimally adequate level of education. State constitutional provisions may also proscribe inadequate and inequitable education funding systems.

THE RELATIONSHIP BETWEEN THE STATE'S POWER TO REGULATE EDUCATION AND THE CONSTITUTIONAL RIGHTS OF PARENTS AND GUARDIANS TO DIRECT THE UPBRINGING OF THEIR CHILDREN

In the seminal cases of *Meyer v. Nebraska*[13] and *Pierce v. Society of Sisters*,[14] the Supreme Court announces a constitutional right allowing "parents and guardians to direct the upbringing and education of children under their control" guaranteed by the Due Process Clause of the Fourteenth Amendment. In *Meyer*, that right precludes the state of Nebraska from criminalizing the practice of teaching in languages other than English. In *Pierce*, that right precludes Oregon from requiring all of its children to attend only public school.

In both cases, the Court emphasizes that a child in America is not "the mere creature of the state."[15] Accordingly, the state's power to "standardize" children cannot interfere with the right of parents and guardians to direct the upbringing and education of their own children. Nonetheless, even as it recognizes that the state has no power to "submerge the individual," the Supreme Court makes clear that the state has tremendous authority over the education of children.

The Supreme Court also has recognized that parents and guardians have a right to "direct the upbringing of their children" in a manner consistent with the "fundamental mode of life mandated" by their "deep religious convictions." State programs violate that right if they place a substantial burden on the free exercise of religion. In *Wisconsin v. Yoder*,[16] the parents of high school age Amish schoolchildren alleged that Wisconsin's compulsory school attendance law unduly burdened their right to raise their children in accordance with their religious beliefs. Amish cultural and religious tenets demand a near total separation from modern American society. Thus, the parents argued, forcing their children to attend high school in lieu of participating in religious instruction and communal agricultural work was directly inimical to their sincerely held religious beliefs.[17] The plaintiffs also contended that the competitive, "worldly" nature of high school education – which would take

---

[13] 262 U.S. 390 (1923).
[14] *Pierce*, 260 U.S. 535.
[15] *Id.*
[16] 406 U.S. 205 (1972).
[17] *Id.* at 211.

place at a regional school far removed from the community – presented a challenge to their religious beliefs that elementary education did not pose.[18]

The Supreme Court held that Wisconsin's compulsory school attendance law violated the constitutional rights of Amish parents to direct the upbringing of their children in a manner consistent with the fundamental mode of life mandated by their deep religious convictions.

Since *Yoder*, however, parents challenging compulsory school attendance and state regulation of the education of their children in public school, private school, and at home have rarely been able to meet the test for demonstrating a violation of their right to free exercise of religion. To satisfy the burden under *Yoder*, plaintiffs must show that: (1) their fundamental mode of life is inseparable from their deep religious convictions; (2) the state's compulsory education regime or its regulation of education sharply conflicts with, or unduly burdens, the free exercise of their religious convictions; and (3) either the state's interest is not compelling or the state's method of achieving its interest is not the least restrictive of religious exercise.

Accordingly, the state has substantial power to govern the education of its citizens. The state may establish the age at which schooling must begin; may require all children of that age to be schooled; may establish the curriculum and assessment to be administered to all of its school age children; and may even dictate the way in which education is provided and assessed for children who are homeschooled. Having examined the power vested in the state to regulate education, we will unpack the pervasive cultural influence of behaviorism. As we will see, its pedagogical and philosophical tenets are at odds both with the views of the Founders and the principles of social constructivism.

BEHAVIORISM: HISTORICAL ORIGINS, BASIC TENETS, AND CONTINUING INFLUENCE

The early twentieth century in the United States was a time of unprecedented industrial expansion. With this expansion came a corresponding emphasis on mass production. With this new emphasis came a demand for a new type of worker.

Perhaps no single work better captured the ethos of this era than Frederick Winslow Taylor's *The Principles of Scientific Management*.[19] Taylor, essentially an early prototype of what would today be called a management consultant, called for a standardized approach to all tasks – from the complex to the mundane – in pursuit of efficiency and increased production. He declared: "In the past the man has been first; in the future the system must be first."[20] Speaking of "efficiency" in almost religious terms, he maintained that, "in the case of any single individual the greatest

---

[18] *Id.*
[19] Frederick Winslow Taylor, *The Principles of Scientific Management* (New York: Harper, 1911).
[20] Ibid. at 7.

prosperity can exist only when that individual has reached his highest state of efficiency; that is, when he is turning out his largest daily output."[21]

Taylor, however, took an exceedingly dim view of the ability of human beings to reach this exalted state without the help of an enlightened cadre of managers. He argued that, absent unusual exceptions, "one type of man is needed to plan ahead and an entirely different type to execute the work."[22]

By way of illustration, Taylor relays in his *Principles of Scientific Management* an episode with a "mentally sluggish" pig iron handler.[23] The exchange between Taylor and the pig iron handler, Schmidt, demonstrates the context that fueled the rise of behaviorism in education. In an attempt to make Schmidt effectively quadruple the amount of pig iron he moves each day, Taylor offers to raise his daily wage from $1.15 to $1.85.[24] By way of motivation, Taylor asks Schmidt if he is a "high-priced man."[25] For Schmidt to raise his output to the extent required by his employer, he must submit unquestioningly to the new management methods – which differ from his established work habits.[26] As Taylor tells him, "a high-priced man has to do exactly as he's told from morning till night."[27]

The exchange between Taylor and Schmidt offers a glimpse into how behaviorist thought operates – when carried to its logical conclusion and coupled with the authoritarian approach to management often conducive to an industrialized economy. Taylor operates under the assumption that Schmidt will respond only to a mixture of threats of coercive consequences delivered in no uncertain terms with promises of a concrete, albeit paltry, reward for compliance. Under no circumstances will Schmidt be permitted to improvise or ask clarifying questions; his job is to do and obey, not think and create. There is no sense that Schmidt should or even could be trained to develop improvements to Taylor's system through his firsthand experience in the trade. Neither is there any inkling that Taylor views Schmidt as a collaborator instead of a subordinate.

Certainly, the episode with Schmidt is an extreme example. To be fair to Taylor, he expresses more charitable views toward workers like Schmidt later in his book – even suggesting that, in the unlikely event their suggestions improve the processes devised by management, workers should receive an appropriate share of the profits that arise from the improvement.[28] On balance, however, it is clear that the principles espoused by Frederick Winslow Taylor in his *Principles of Scientific Management* apply behaviorism rather than constructivism in the workplace. Given the widespread adoption of his methods in American manufacturing, it was

[21] Ibid. at 12.
[22] Ibid. at 38.
[23] Ibid. at 46.
[24] Ibid. at 45.
[25] Ibid. at 44–45.
[26] Ibid.
[27] Ibid. at 45.
[28] Ibid. at 128.

almost inevitable that a similar approach would hold sway in American education. With the emphasis on mass production and efficiency over creativity, the economy required more Schmidts than Taylors. Increasingly, American schools endeavored to fill this need – often at the expense of the students themselves.

The United States' educational system, including our legal educational system, has for generations reflected behaviorist assumptions and practices about human nature and development. The foundation of behaviorism is the belief that learning is defined as a change in observable behavior. In *Psychology as the Behaviorist Views It*,[29] John Watson built upon Pavlov's conclusions regarding conditioned responses by animals to external stimuli, showing that children could be "conditioned" to fear an object by repeatedly aligning that object with a painful experience.[30] For example, by linking a child's observation of a white rat with a harsh noise, a child could be conditioned to fear (and to avoid) all similar white objects.[31]

B. F. Skinner then extended Watson's research, finding that animals could be conditioned to perform a particular behavior (such as pushing a lever) when that behavior is repeatedly and immediately rewarded.[32] Significantly, the animals placed into a "Skinner Box" could be conditioned to perform the desired behavior regardless of their actual need for the reward itself.[33] Rats, for example, can be trained to continue to push levers in return for food even if they are not hungry, thereby becoming obese. Moreover, animals can be conditioned to compete with each other for the reward of food, even if they do not want the food or are not naturally competitive.[34]

In 1958, Skinner developed a teaching machine based upon his behaviorist approach to education. The machine presented direct instruction of information that was tested in a "carefully prescribed order."[35] Students were rewarded for correct answers and were punished for incorrect ones. As described by Skinner:

> In using the device, the student refers to a numbered item in a multiple-choice test. He presses the button corresponding to his first choice of answer. If he is right, the device moves to the next item; if he is wrong, the error is tallied and he must continue to make choices until he is right.[36]

The behaviorist assumptions about human nature and development thus can be, and have been, used to justify a regime of standardized testing.[37] Although Skinner

---

[29] John B. Watson, "Psychology as the Behaviorist Views It," 20 *Psychol. Rev.* 158 (1913).
[30] John B. Watson & Rosalie Rayner, "Conditioned Emotional Responses," 3 *J. of Experimental Psychol.* 1, 1–14 (1920), https://archive.org/stream/journalofexperimo3ameruoft/journalofexperimo3ameruoft_djvu.txt [https://perma.cc/MS5T-9XBX].
[31] Ibid.
[32] B. F. Skinner, "Teaching Machines," 128 *Science* 969, 970 (1958).
[33] Ibid.; see also B. F. Skinner, *The Behavior of Organisms: An Experimental Analysis* (1938).
[34] Skinner, *Behavior of Organisms*.
[35] Ibid. at 970.
[36] Ibid. at 969.
[37] See Phillip Harris, Bruce M. Smith, & Joan Harris, *The Myths of Standardized Tests: Why They Don't Tell You What You Think They Do* (New York: Rowman & Littlefield, 2011), 73–75.

eventually appreciated that individual behavior could not be explained merely by reactions to external stimuli, educators began to contend that children could be conditioned to demonstrate desired behavior on tests through a system of external rewards and punishments.[38] If the digestion of discrete facts is the goal of education, then tests can be devised to assess whether or not students have memorized such facts. Students who fail to demonstrate appropriate external behavior can be made to do so with negative reinforcements like poor grades and being held back in school. In this construct, the process by which the human mind functions is not particularly important. A person's thoughts, feelings, desires, emotions, intentions, and cognitive processes are less significant than observable behavior and, accordingly, less important to learning.

Behaviorist pedagogies also legitimate an authoritarian role for teachers. "The teacher who follows the behaviorist approach will rely primarily on direct instruction to transmit information to students. Direct instruction is teacher-dominated communication designed to deliver to students the facts and values deemed important by the educational institution."[39] In addition, the behaviorist approach helps to justify the development of pre-ordained and inflexible lesson plans.

As one of the nation's foremost education experts, Linda Darling-Hammond observes: "Behaviorist learning theory has had substantial influence in education, guiding the development of highly-sequenced and structured curricula, programmed instructional approaches, workbooks and other tools."[40] She notes, "The behaviorist method of operative conditioning also has been applied across schools and states. School administrators attempt to condition the behavior of teachers by rewarding and punishing them depending on the performance of their students on standardized tests."[41] As Darling-Hammond astutely points out, "Schools that fail to train their students to perform will suffer negative reinforcements such as the withdrawal of funds."[42]

The behaviorist approach appears to be a cost-effective way to provide large numbers of students with mass-produced pieces of information, the acquisition of which can be efficiently measured by standardized tests.[43] Skinner, in fact, suggested that his approach to teaching and assessment was economically efficient: "It is a labor-saving device because it can bring one programmer into contact with an indefinite number of students."[44]

---

[38] Michael J. Kaufman et al., *Learning Together: The Law, Politics, Economics, Pedagogy, and Neuroscience of Early Childhood Education* (1st ed., Lanham, MD: Rowman & Littlefield, 2015), 51. [hereinafter Kaufman et al., *Learning Together*].
[39] Ibid., note 10, at 23.
[40] Linda Darling-Hammond et al., "How People Learn: Introduction to Learning Theories" (Stanford University School of Education, 2001), 6, http://web.stanford.edu/class/ed269/hplintrochapter.pdf.
[41] Ibid.
[42] Ibid. at 11.
[43] Ibid. at 22–23.
[44] Skinner, note 11 at 971.

This understanding of human nature also can be used to erect binaries: child v. adult, reason v. passion, intellect v. emotion, and science v. art. The presumption that these animosities are natural, inevitable, and necessary even led the Supreme Court in *San Antonio Independent School District v. Rodriguez* to justify undisputed inequality in educational funding by contending that there is a "continual struggle between two forces: the desire by members of society to have educational opportunity for all children and the desire of each family to provide the best education it can afford for its own children."[45]

The presumption that individuals are naturally motivated to pursue their own self-interest, which is commonly attributed to liberal democratic principles embraced by the Founders, can be used to support an educational philosophy built on inter-personal separation and intra-personal dualities. Strangers are threats to survival. The educational success of a neighbor's child is a threat to the educational success of my child. The individual is in conflict with the community. An individual's private life is distinct from his or her public life.

These perceived binaries also are used to justify a corresponding pedagogy and system of assessments. By this view, children are naturally undisciplined, but as rational actors, their external behavior can be shaped by rewarding positive behavior and punishing negative behavior. Education shapes behavior by focusing on the intellect as separate from emotions, and then rewarding positive expressions of intellect and punishing negative expressions of passion. Positive expressions of "intelligent" behavior are assessed and rewarded through a regime of standardized tests.

Skinner's work in operant conditioning led naturally to the rewards and punishments offered by a standardized test of rote knowledge. Yet he cautioned that, while the "discipline of the birch rod" or the threat of failure may "facilitate learning," it also "breeds followers of dictators and revolutionists." Skinner celebrated the progressive educational practices advocated by John Dewey and condemned aversive learning strategies.[46] Skinner asserted only that his behaviorist approach could replace those aversive practices based on negative reinforcement of failure. Skinner knew that such aversive educational practices threatened "democratic principles" and hoped that his insights would be useful for teachers in their efforts to reach all their students.[47]

Employing aspects of the behaviorist approach fashioned by Skinner, educators began to contend that children could be conditioned to demonstrate desired behavior on tests through a system of external rewards and

---

[45] 411 U.S. 1, 49 (1973). See Chapter 6 for a more detailed examination of *Rodriguez*.

[46] See John Dewey, *Democracy and Education*, reprinted in *Classic and Contemporary Readings in the Philosophy of Education*, 288–289 (Steven M. Cahn ed., 2nd ed., 2011); John Dewey, *Experience and Education*, reprinted in *Classic and Contemporary Readings in the Philosophy of Education*, 362 (Steven M. Cahn ed., 2nd ed. 2011).

[47] See Skinner, at 977.

punishments.[48] The implementation of a system of routinized tests could be justified as an application of Skinner's model of operant conditioning, in which behavior is shaped by external stimuli.

Although behaviorists such as B. F. Skinner came to understand that both internal and external stimuli could influence observable behavior, the focus of behaviorists is upon rewards and punishments.[49] Positive external reinforcement for behavior deemed to be good combined with negative external reinforcement through punishment for behavior deemed to be bad will "teach" individuals to behave in a socially desired manner.[50] Behaviorism depends on separating the human being into distinct and often oppositional pieces. The internal, private core of the individual is virtually irrelevant to the learning process, and must be distinguished from the individual's external observable and measurable behaviors.[51]

The principle of 'operant conditioning' also suggests that teachers should deliver their external rewards and punishments immediately after the student has demonstrated the particular behavior being observed. As a consequence, teachers must present their instruction in a linear way in which one particular desired behavior is observed before the next conditioning takes place.[52] Therefore, the teacher breaks lesson plans into small, pre-packaged products, which must proceed in a fixed, linear fashion.

Only after the student has been conditioned by rewards and punishments to demonstrate one particular desired behavior can that student then proceed to be conditioned to demonstrate the next desired behavior. This method of operant conditioning requires breaking learning into small bits so that the student recognizes the precise behavior for which he or she is being rewarded or punished. The teacher therefore breaks lesson plans into small bits as well, which must proceed in a predetermined linear fashion.

While arguably efficient, this pedagogical approach has severe limitations. As Linda Darling-Hammond has observed:

> [The behaviorist approach] has proved useful for the development of some types of skills – especially those that can be learned substantially by rote through reinforcement and practice. However, evidence has accrued that tasks requiring more complex thinking and higher mental processes are not generally well-learned through behaviorist methods and require more attention to how people perceive, process, and make sense of what they are experiencing.[53]

---

[48] T. H. Leahey, "Control: A History of Behavioral Psychology," *The Journal of American History* 87(2) (2000), 686–687.
[49] Skinner, "Teaching Machines."
[50] Robert E. Slavin, *Education Psychology: Theory into Practice* (Boston: Allyn & Bacon, 2012).
[51] M. R. Lepper, D. Greene, & R. E. Nisbett, "Undermining Children's Intrinsic Interact with Extrinsic Rewards," *Journal of Personality and Social Psychology* 28 (1973).
[52] Ibid. at 22.
[53] Darling-Hammond, "How People Learn," 6.

The teacher who follows the behaviorist approach will rely primarily on direct instruction to transmit information to students. In other words, he or she will seldom deviate from lecturing – dominating all communication in the classroom. Such instruction is an efficient way to provide students with isolated pieces of information, the acquisition of which can be observed and measured by standardized tests.

The behaviorist method of operative conditioning also has been applied across schools and states. School administrators attempt to condition teacher behavior by rewarding and punishing them depending on the performance of their students on standardized tests. Under the federal regimes created by the No Child Left Behind Act and Race to the Top, states are conditioned to change school performance through a system of monetary rewards and punishments.

The behaviorist approach to education creates a mistaken perception that it is efficient. "The 'standards' movement generally accepts the idea that a single teacher can impart a single set of facts to a large number of students at the same time."[54] Consequently, this type of education appears cost-effective. However, the educational system built upon behaviorist principles is inefficient by any credible measure. After reviewing many measures of cost-effectiveness, including overall educational expenses relative to student outputs, Stephen Heyneman concluded: "The sum of this evidence would suggest that by many different measures the U.S. is less efficient than other countries and that the record of inefficiency is consistent over at least two decades."[55] Despite these insights, the history of education in America since industrialization has been characterized with an obsessive pursuit of efficiency. One classic study incisively analyzes the misguided definition of efficiency used by analysts to measure school performance and its implications on the learning environment.

In *Education and the Cult of Efficiency: A Study of the Social Forces That Have Shaped the Administration of the Public Schools*, Raymond Callahan shows how the growth of the "standards" movement in education became linked to mistaken attempts to achieve "efficiency" by assembling large numbers of students in a single classroom, conveying prepackaged information to them, and measuring their outputs as if they were factory workers.[56] Callahan explains that "[a]s the business-industrial values and procedures spread into the thinking and acting of educators, countless educational decisions were made on economic or on non-educational grounds."[57] As such, "school administrators, already under constant pressure to make education more practical in order to serve a business society better, were brought under even stronger criticism and forced to demonstrate first, last, and

---

[54] Kaufman et al., *Learning Together*, at 11.
[55] See Stephen P. Heyneman, "The International Efficiency of American Education: The Bad and the Not-so-Bad News," in *Pisa, Power, and Policy: The Emergence of Global Educational Governance* 279, 284 (Heinz-Dieter Meyer & Aaron Benavot, eds., 2013).
[56] See Raymond E. Callahan, *Education and the Cult of Efficiency: A Study of the Social Forces That Have Shaped the Administration of the Public Schools* (University of Chicago Press, 1962), 247.
[57] Ibid. at 246–247.

always that they were operating the schools efficiently."[58] The result is that: "Our schools are, in a sense, factories in which the raw products (children) are to be shaped and fashioned into products to meet the various demands of life."[59] Frederick Winslow Taylor's scientific management principles had migrated from steel mills to schoolhouses.

In 1900, the basic institutional framework of the educational system was created. Business ideals permeated the educational system, from the elementary level through universities, and by 1907 there were indications that they were being applied by the educators themselves.[60] Furthermore, the administrative makeup of the educational system was also shifting. Businessmen began to predominate school boards, which only augmented the business pressures on the system. Consequentially, schools began shifting away from the classical curriculum of literature and arts to one deemed "practical." This businesslike mindset is epitomized through a statement by a New York high school principal who stated, "[my girls] want to get in 1910 something they can use in 1911."[61]

The emerging principles of scientific management offered a solution to the perceived inefficiency in schools. One efficiency expert, Harrington Emerson, outlined how industrial factories were already successfully implementing efficient procedures. Specifically, efficient entities: (1) articulated clear and definite aims, (2) organized management structures to accomplish these aims, (3) utilized resources/equipment sufficient to achieve these aims, and (4) had "a strong executive who [was] able to carry them out."[62]

Scientific management was applied to schools through a budget analysis, and the educational value of curricula was measured in dollar value. Essentially, "decisions on what should be taught were made not on educational, but on financial grounds."[63] With this outlook, the obvious solution for education was to increase class size and the number of classes each teacher taught in order to minimize the cost per student and the number of teachers needed.[64] Educational and financial decision-making power became vested in one superintendent.[65] Only one acquainted with both those aspects of a school could insure that it was being run efficiently. From there, the nature of the superintendent position would facilitate the application of so-called scientific management across the various facets of education. As usual, efficiency and economical use of resources was emphasized. Accordingly, the superintendent increasingly functioned as a quasi-corporate manager.

[58] Ibid. at 18.
[59] Ibid. at 152 (citing Ellwood P. Cubberley, *Public School Administration* at 338).
[60] Ibid. at 6.
[61] Ibid. at 10.
[62] Ibid. at 56.
[63] Ibid. at 75.
[64] Ibid.
[65] Ibid.

The idea that teachers themselves, as the workmen, also needed certain standards and levels of efficiency, led to the belief that teachers needed to be trained so as to "[keep] up to standard qualifications for his kind of work for his entire service."[66] In these ways, scientific management appeared a natural remedy to the inefficiencies of education.

Tests, rating sheets, and other measures developed as a way to provide tangible evidence of progress and efficiency. "Educators from all over the country engaged in this activity by developing rating sheets or offering suggestions to the profession on ways and means of increasing efficiency."[67] Focus on miniscule details was emphasized. At all costs, superintendents exhorted their teachers to use their time and energy in the most "efficient" manner possible.

In 1916, the *American School Board Journal* reported on approximately 50,000 inspections of school systems. The strengths and weaknesses of the districts under inspection were laid bare. "By the end of 1918 the campaign to introduce efficiency measures into the schools had been successfully consummated."[68] By 1920, districts employed quantifiable rating systems for teachers and students alike.

Revealingly, the principal motivation for these developments was defending against public criticism of administrators.[69] Even though many educators were critical of the efficiency movement and its influence on the changes being made in their system, it was their only viable option. "This [was] an age of efficiency. In the eyes of the public no indictment of a school [could] be more severe than to say it [was] inefficient."[70]

Another effort to demonstrate efficiency improvements occurred between 1911 and 1925 through the school "plant." The factory system of full utilization of an industrial plant was applied to the schools. Attempts to replicate the physical environment of a factory in the school context only exacerbated the rush on the part of school districts to prize efficiency above all other measures of student growth.

The evolution of the superintendent from educator to business administrator had started early in the twentieth century. These changes occurred most rapidly from 1911 to 1918.[71] This evolution was stimulated by the dominance of business in American society, by the "sheer size and magnitude of the school system," and by an atmosphere of discontent from school boards.[72]

Educators criticized the composition of school boards. They sought smaller boards whose members would, ideally, "be appointed rather than elected, and be removed from partisan or municipal politics."[73] Furthermore, experts increasingly

[66] Ibid. at 89.
[67] Ibid. at 101.
[68] Ibid.
[69] Ibid. at 111.
[70] Ibid. at 112.
[71] Ibid. at 148.
[72] Ibid. at 149.
[73] Ibid.

advocated dividing administrative responsibilities – one department would perform administrative and organizational tasks while the other would focus solely on educating students.[74] Consequentially, school boards began to reduce in size and largely seated businessmen who were viewed as the most qualified to run the business side of education.[75] Because of this, administrators had to operate schools like businesses.[76]

Educators implemented these business methods, and as a result, administrators evolved from teachers to managers.[77] "The varied actions taken by administrators for this purpose are best described as educational cost accounting."[78] This included increasing time spent on records and reports, standardizing the cost of school supplies and equipment, and analyzing expenditures on employees and students.[79] Above all, they sought to standardize costs.[80] This practice was mostly focused on high schools. Given the public obsession with efficiency, this was a natural priority. However, "what was surprising was the eager way some administrators embraced and fostered the notion that educators were servants of the taxpayers and not only had to acquiesce meekly but also had to attempt to enthusiastically meet demands."[81]

As a result of this new emphasis on scientific management, administrators became familiar with "the merits and the methods involved in educational cost accounting."[82] It was quickly being implemented, and by 1918, it was well established.[83]

Actions taken by administrators to cut costs paralleled similar initiatives undertaken in factories during this era. These included increasing class sizes, classes taught by individual teachers, and the sizes of student bodies.[84] After 1910, the class size in secondary schools became a problem because there were more students and they were staying in school longer.[85] In the 1930s, formulae were developed as a means to standardize the teacher's workload. From this, the teaching load that is the norm today was created.[86]

As Callahan concludes, the "wholesale" adoption of business values as the cure-all to defects in education was a tragedy in retrospect.[87] The application of these new

[74] Ibid.
[75] Ibid. at 150.
[76] Ibid. at 151.
[77] Ibid. at 152.
[78] Ibid. at 153.
[79] Ibid.
[80] Ibid. at 158.
[81] Ibid. at 159.
[82] Ibid. at 163.
[83] Ibid. at 164.
[84] Ibid. at 232.
[85] Ibid. at 234.
[86] Ibid. at 230.
[87] Ibid. at 244.

policies proved especially disastrous. While businesses sought to deliver "the finest product at the lowest cost," educational fixes ignored the "product" (or, more precisely, the student), and only focused on "lowest cost."[88]

Thus, focus on business efficiency persisted through the 1960s at the expense of teaching and instructing students.[89] Patterns of business-inspired practices in education persisted largely due to the social consensus developing in the United States regarding education. The practices were still strong because schools were still vulnerable to public criticism and lacked funds in a nation reluctant to spend. This atmosphere relegated superintendents to a role of responding to the public with little job security, which prevented them from focusing on the curricular aspects of their schools.[90] By the 1960s, they were seen as managers first and educators a distant second.[91] Furthermore, there remained constant pressure on administrators to demonstrate their efficiency.[92]

RESEARCH REGARDING HUMAN DEVELOPMENT BELIES BEHAVIORIST THEORIES

Relying on sophisticated research techniques, including brain imaging, the world's foremost neuroscientists have discovered the existence of mirror neurons in human beings.[93] These neurons fire the same way when a person performs an activity as when a person watches someone else perform the same activity.[94] The neural connectivity between human beings is the result of human evolution;[95] it is the foundation for the natural impulse toward empathy.[96] Human beings are not hard-wired to consume or compete; rather, they are hard-wired to pursue meaningful, loving relationships, which are critical to the continued growth of their cognitive functioning.[97]

In his pathbreaking brain research, renowned child psychiatrist Dr. Bruce Perry has found dramatic evidence that we are in fact "born for love."[98] Based on his brain

---

[88] Ibid.
[89] Ibid. at 254.
[90] Ibid. at 255.
[91] Ibid. at 256.
[92] Ibid.
[93] V. S. Ramachandran, *The Tell-Tale Brain: A Neuroscientist's Quest for What Makes Us Human* (2012), 22.
[94] Ibid.
[95] Ibid. at 23.
[96] Ibid. at 261, 265 (noting the role of mirror neurons in empathy).
[97] Cf. Charles Darwin, *The Descent of Man*, at 98. ("When two tribes of primeval man, living in the same country, came into competition, if the one tribe included (other circumstances being equal) a greater number of courageous, sympathetic, and faithful members, who were always ready to warn each other of danger, to aid and defend each other, this tribe would without doubt succeed best and conquer the other.")
[98] See generally Maia Szalavitz & Bruce D. Perry, *Born for Love: Why Empathy Is Essential – and Endangered* (2010).

imaging and clinical research, Dr. Perry concludes that human beings have a distinct biological make-up and survival instinct that compels them to form meaningful relationships.[99] Dr. Perry demonstrates: "Humankind would not have endured and cannot continue without the capacity to form rewarding, nurturing, and enduring relationships. We survive because we can love."[100]

Indeed, children are born with a natural desire and capacity for "attachment," which is the ability to form and maintain emotionally significant, reliable, and enduring bonds with others.[101] Meaningful attachment relationships are based on genuine communication that supports the development of social, emotional, and cognitive functioning.[102] Early attachment experiences alter the chemicals in the brain that develop the nervous system's capacity to support emotional resilience.[103]

Loving relationships also develop the uniquely human capacity for inter-subjectivity, which is the process by which human beings understand the thoughts, feelings, and intentions of others.[104] In exercising their natural disposition toward inter-subjectivity, human beings find great joy; they realize what they have in common with others. Children who experience attachment and inter-subjectivity in early learning environments are more likely to exhibit focus, perseverance, and control over their behavior.[105] The security in feeling that any disruption in a meaningful relationship will be repaired allows a student to develop grit and resiliency in the face of life's inevitable hardships.[106]

Similarly, the natural human desire for love is vital to cognitive integration. As neuropsychiatrist Daniel Siegel has found:

> We come into the world wired to make connections with one another, and the subsequent neural shaping of our brain, the very foundation of our sense of self, is built upon these intimate exchanges between the infant and the caregiver. In the early years, this interpersonal regulation is essential for survival, but throughout our lives we continue to need such connections for a sense of vitality and wellbeing.[107]

According to Siegel, meaningful relationships develop the prefrontal cortex in the brain, thereby integrating the cognitive processes that are essential to success and well-being.[108]

Daniel Siegel's most recent book fully supports the vision that human beings are made for love. In *Mind: A Journey to the Heart of Being Human*, Siegel finds that the human mind is "an embodied and relational, self-organizing emergent process that

---

[99] Ibid. at 4, 30.
[100] Ibid. at 4.
[101] Daniel J. Siegel, *Mindsight: The New Science of Personal Transformation* (2011), 167–168.
[102] Kaufman et al., *Learning Together*, note 10, at 214.
[103] Ibid.
[104] Ibid. at 208–209, 210.
[105] Ibid. at 208–209, 215.
[106] Ibid. at 214–215.
[107] Daniel J. Siegel, *Mind: A Journey to the Heart of Being Human* (2017), note 44, at 10–11.
[108] Ibid. at 26.

regulates the flow of energy and information both within and between."¹⁰⁹ He declares that "the mind is not just within us – it is also between us."¹¹⁰ Accordingly, Siegel concludes that all human "[e]nergy and information flow happens in relationships as energy and information is shared."¹¹¹

Such relationships also can be developed between individuals and their environment. David Hawkins writes about the relationship that forms between a child, a teacher, and natural materials.¹¹² He notes that, when a teacher explores a natural material with a child, the teacher has made possible a "relation between the child and 'It'."¹¹³

The human urge to develop loving relationships is indispensable to well-being. In "A Survey Method for Characterizing Daily Experience: The Day Reconstruction Method," Nobel Prize-winning psychologist and founder of behavioral economics, Daniel Kahneman, presents his transformative research regarding the determinants of happiness and well-being. The evidence indicates that individuals experience the greatest degree of happiness from their social relationships.¹¹⁴ As Professor Kahneman's research confirms, the most significant determinant of happiness – whether measured as momentary feelings, reflective thoughts, or life satisfaction – is the quality of a person's relationships.¹¹⁵ In fact, he finds the evidence shows that "very happy people" differ from unhappy or modestly happy people in the level of their "fulsome and satisfying interpersonal lives."¹¹⁶

The research is clear: the single most important factor in fostering happiness and well-being is the quality of a person's relationships.¹¹⁷ People who have developed the ability to form and maintain meaningful relationships are "significantly happier and healthier than their peers who do not have such meaningful relationships. Moreover, those who have formed meaningful relationships are even happier and healthier than their wealthier peers who have not formed those relationships."¹¹⁸

Quality of relationships also is connected to physical well-being, health, and wellness. Meaningful relationships increase immunity to disease and infection, lower the risk of heart disease, and reduce the degree of cognitive decline through the aging

---

[109] Ibid. at 37.
[110] Ibid. at 167.
[111] Ibid. at 53.
[112] See David Hawkins, *The Informed Vision: Essays on Learning and Human Nature* (New York: Algora Publishing, 2002), 56–57.
[113] Ibid. at 59.
[114] Daniel Kahneman et al., "A Survey Method for Characterizing Daily Life Experience: The Day Reconstruction Method," 306 *Science* 1776, 1776–1780 (2004).
[115] Ibid. at 1777–78.
[116] Sherelyn R. Kaufman et al., *The Pre-K Home Companion*, 33–34 (Lanham, MD: Rowman & Littlefield, 2016) [hereinafter Kaufman et al., *The Pre-K Home Companion*] (citing Kahneman et al., "A Survey Method for Characterizing Daily Life Experience," 306 *Science* 1776, 1776–80 (2004)).
[117] Ibid. at 41.
[118] Ibid.

process. Indeed, the absence of meaningful relationships is as deleterious to health as obesity or smoking. It is not surprising, therefore, that Nobel Prize-winning economist James Heckman, in *Giving Kids a Fair Chance (A Strategy that Works)*, presents irrefutable evidence showing learning environments that develop the capacity to build meaningful relationships not only produce robust economic returns but also provide significant health advantages, including a reduction in obesity, blood pressure, and hypertension.[119] As contemporary commentators note the steep rise in "deaths of despair" and other indicators of an "epidemic of loneliness" in the United States, it is becoming all too clear that the failure to build meaningful relationships has devastating implications that reach far beyond the classroom.

In addition, the natural human desire for meaningful relationships helps produce executive function.[120] The concept of executive function has been recognized as part of recent scholarship about the importance of "grit" or "growth mindset" to learning.[121] "These popular catch phrases capture some, but not all, of the power of executive function."[122] "Executive function properly understood includes three types of capacities: working memory, cognitive flexibility, and inhibitory control."[123] Educational programs that enable students to develop meaningful, positive relationships are particularly effective in supporting the growth of executive function.[124] The relationship-building capacities of neuro-connectivity, attachment, inter-subjectivity, cognitive integration, interpersonal well-being, and executive function are uniquely human.[125] They are vital to human nature, human survival, and human evolution.

These competencies are critical to the development of the five habits of mind, which Howard Gardner argues are indispensable for future success and well-being.[126] Gardner, one of the world's most influential educational psychologists, concludes that education must be directed toward creating habits of mind that will be valuable in the future, including:

[(1)] a disciplined mind – the ability to become an expert in at least one area[;]
[(2)] a synthesizing mind – the ability to gather information from many sources, to organize the information in helpful ways and to communicate the information to others[;]

---

[119] Kaufman et al., *The Pre-K Home Companion*, note 61, at 41.
[120] *Building the Brain's "Air Traffic Control" System: How Early Experiences Shape the Development of Executive Function* 6 (Ctr. on the Developing Child at Harvard Univ., Working Paper No. 11, 2011).
[121] See generally Paul Tough, *How Children Succeed: Grit, Curiosity, and the Hidden Power of Character* (Boston: Houghton Mifflin, 2012).
[122] Kaufman et al., *The Pre-K Home Companion*, note 61, at 41.
[123] Ibid. at 42.
[124] See *Building the Brain's "Air Traffic Control" System*, note 65, at 10. See also W. Steven Barnett et al., "Educational Effects of the Tools of the Mind Curriculum: A Randomized Trial," 23 *Early Childhood Res. Q.* 299–313 (2008).
[125] John Barresi & Chris Moore, "The Neuroscience of Social Understanding," in *The Shared Mind: Perspectives on Intersubjectivity*, 39–66 (Jordan Zlatev et al. eds., Amsterdam: John Benjamins, 2008).
[126] See Howard Gardner, *Five Minds for the Future*, 5–9 (Boston: Harvard Business School Press, 2006).

[(3)] a creating mind – the ability of adults to keep alive in themselves the mind and sensibility of a young child, including an insatiable curiosity about other people and the environment, an openness to untested paths, a willingness to struggle, and a desire and capacity to learn from failure[;]

[(4)] a respectful mind – the ability to understand the perspectives and motivations of others, particularly those who appear to be different[; and]

[(5)] an ethical mind – the ability to appreciate one's social or professional role and to act in accordance with shared standards for that role.[127]

These habits of mind are developed through interpersonal relationships and in turn produce critical life-long relationship-building competencies.[128] It is these particular habits of mind – rather than just the traditionally tested abilities to consume information – that significantly increase the chance that a student will grow to experience life-long success and well-being.[129]

Moreover, recent research in neuroscience, neuropsychology, cognitive psychology, educational psychology, economics, and behavioral economics demonstrates that an authoritarian, behaviorist approach to education is counterproductive. The behaviorist approach does not provide most students with the habits of mind and heart that are necessary to life-long success and well-being. In his pathbreaking study, *The Growing Importance of Social Skills in the Labor Market*, Professor David J. Deming provides a wealth of empirical evidence which reveals the "growing demand for social skills in the U.S. labor market over the last several decades."[130] Deming demonstrates that "social skill-intensive occupations have grown by nearly ten percentage points as a share of the U.S. labor force, and that wage growth has also been particularly strong for social skill-intensive occupations."[131] He also finds that "high-paying jobs increasingly require *social skills*."[132]

According to Deming, the social skill that is the key determinant of success is "the ability to attribute mental states to others based on their behavior, or more colloquially to 'put oneself into another's shoes.'"[133] He explains:

> Reading the minds of others and reacting is an unconscious process, and skill in social settings has evolved in humans over thousands of years. Human interaction in the workplace involves team production, with workers playing off of each other's strengths and adapting flexibly to changing circumstances. Such non-routine interaction is at the heart of the human advantage over machines.[134]

[127] Kaufman et al., *The Pre-K Home Companion* at 33–34 (citing Gardner at 3, 5–9).
[128] See Gardner, at 5–9; see also Kaufman et al., *The Pre-K Home Companion* at 34–36.
[129] Kaufman et al., *The Pre-K Home Companion* at 35.
[130] David J. Deming, *The Growing Importance of Social Skills in the Labor Market* 30 (Nat'l Bureau of Econ. Research, Working Paper No. 21473, 2015), www.nber.org/papers/w21473.pdf [https://perma.cc/7R79-MNQG].
[131] Ibid.
[132] Ibid. at 3.
[133] Ibid. at 3–4.
[134] Ibid. at 30–31.

THE FOUNDERS' NUANCED VIEW OF HUMAN NATURE DOES NOT JUSTIFY BEHAVIORIST PEDAGOGIES

The behaviorist approach that has been used to rationalize educational and economic inequities cannot be fairly justified by a proper understanding of the democratic regime established by the Founders. Although the Founders justified their constitutional structure by claiming that this unique system was necessary to diffuse otherwise unbridled human passions, they also erected a regime of self-government that "presupposes" the existence of other qualities in human nature that justify a certain portion of "esteem and confidence."[135] Specifically, the Founders built legal structures into their regime that presume the natural human capacity to construct and disseminate knowledge through meaningful relationships.

The Constitution's limitation on the term of appointment of representatives to relatively short two-year increments is based on the presumption that humans are self-regulated by empathy.[136] According to the Founders, elected representatives will "anticipate the moment" when they are not in power, and will naturally put themselves in the shoes of the governed.[137] "The Founders believed that: 'There is in every heart a sensibility to marks of honor, of favor, of esteem ... which, apart from all considerations of interest, is some pledge for grateful and benevolent returns.'"[138] "There is disposition toward gratitude in human nature, by which representatives 'will be bound to fidelity and sympathy with the great mass of people.'"[139]

The structure of the American regime also presumes that the construction of knowledge requires cooperation.[140] The First Amendment's free speech and free press clauses flow from the belief that human interactions – in dialogue, in the marketplace of ideas, and in myriad forms of "expression" – are imperative to human advancement.[141] Knowledge is built and spread in the public sphere.

Indeed, the Supreme Court has recognized that the First Amendment's protections of the freedom to construct knowledge, form beliefs, and express oneself are dependent upon the freedom to develop meaningful relationships in which knowledge is shaped, belief is formed, and expression is respected:

> It is beyond debate that freedom to engage in association for the advancement of beliefs and ideas is an inseparable aspect of the "liberty" assured by the Due Process Clause of the Fourteenth Amendment, which embraces freedom of speech. Of course, it is immaterial whether the beliefs sought to be advanced by association pertain to political, economic, religious or cultural matters, and state action which

---

[135] Kaufman et al., *Learning Together*.
[136] Ibid.
[137] Ibid.
[138] Kaufman et al., *Learning Together* at 24 (quoting *The Federalist* No. 57 (James Madison)).
[139] Ibid. (quoting *The Federalist* No. 57 (James Madison)).
[140] Ibid.
[141] Ibid.

may have the effect of curtailing the freedom to associate is subject to the closest scrutiny.[142]

In Article 1, Section 8, Clause 8, the United States Constitution further reflects the Founders' appreciation of the importance of meaningful associations to the construction and dissemination of knowledge.[143] That section grants to Congress the power to promote "the [p]rogress of science and the useful arts."[144] One method by which Congress is empowered to promote such "progress" is by giving to "Authors and Inventors the exclusive right to their respective writings and discoveries."[145] The Constitution recognizes that human discovery requires the ingenuity of individual inventors.[146] Yet, the Constitution does not grant to Congress the power to give such inventors unlimited exclusive control over their inventions; rather, it provides such control only for "limited times."[147] As James Madison wrote in the Federalist Papers, the "public good fully coincides in both cases with the claims of individuals."[148]

The intellectual property protections in the Constitution can be traced to the political philosophy of John Locke. In his *Second Treatise of Civil Government*, Locke wrote that human beings have a natural right to property in their own bodies.[149] The right of individuals to their own bodies also gives them a property right to the "labors" of their bodies and the fruits of those labors.[150] A person has a natural right to own that which his labor has created.[151] Locke's understanding of a natural right to property that pre-dates civil society undoubtedly influenced the drafters of the Constitution.[152]

Yet, as the Founders understood, Locke cautioned against the excesses of the natural right to property.[153] Because the right to property is an extension of the right to self-preservation, it cannot be used to justify the appropriation of material that is not necessary for self-preservation.[154] There is no natural right to the acquisition of property that is not necessary for self-preservation.[155]

---

[142] NAACP v. *Alabama ex rel. Patterson*, 357 U.S. 449, 460–61 (1958) (citations omitted). See generally *Id.* at 461, 463; NAACP v. *Button*, 371 U.S. 415, 429–30 (1963); *Cousins v. Wigoda*, 419 U.S. 477, 487 (1975); *In re Primus*, 436 U.S. 412, 426 (1978); *Democratic Party v. Wisconsin ex rel. La Follette*, 450 U.S. 107, 121 (1981).
[143] Kaufman et al., *Learning Together* at 24 (citing U.S. Const. art. I, § 8, cl. 8).
[144] Ibid.
[145] Ibid. (quoting U.S. Const. art. I, § 8, cl. 8).
[146] Ibid.
[147] Ibid.
[148] Ibid. (quoting *The Federalist* No. 43 (James Madison)).
[149] Ibid. at 25 (citing John Locke, *Concerning the True Original Extent and End of Civil Government*, in *Two Treatises of Government* para. 27–28 (1698)).
[150] Ibid.
[151] Ibid.
[152] Ibid. at 56.
[153] Ibid. at 23; see Locke para. 25–27.
[154] Ibid. See Locke, para. 25.
[155] Ibid. at para. 30.

To the contrary, Locke believed that individuals who appropriated to themselves more property than they could efficiently use to sustain themselves, acted in a way contrary to their true natures, particularly where there is not enough left in common for others.[156] There is no natural right to appropriate that which is not useful for the improvement of knowledge, the progress of civilization, and the advancement of human happiness.

The Founders not only understood the natural limits on individual work-product, they also grasped the collaborative nature of human discovery.[157] The temporal limit on Congress's power to protect the individual creator's exclusivity was designed to insure that knowledge will enter the public domain.[158] By insuring that a discovery will enter the public domain at some point, the Founders also recognized the value of collaboration in constructing human knowledge.[159]

The Founders' understanding of the social nature of the construction of knowledge is captured by Thomas Jefferson's analysis of the nature of ideas: "If nature has made any one thing less susceptible than all others of exclusive property, it is the action of the thinking power called an idea."[160] Jefferson understood that the moment a person divulges an idea, "it forces itself into the possession of every one, and the receiver cannot dispossess himself of it."[161] Jefferson argues it is the social construction of knowledge that is natural, not the individual's property interest in any particular discovery: "That ideas should freely spread from one to another over the globe, for the moral and mutual instruction of man, and improvement of his condition, seems to have been peculiarly and benevolently designed by nature."[162]

Jefferson uses the image of a flame emanating from a candle to explain the social nature of knowledge: "He who receives an idea from me, receives instruction himself without lessening mine; as he who lights his taper at mine, receives light without darkening me."[163] An individual's ideas are like fire, they "spread from one to another"; they illuminate all without "lessening their density in any point"; and thus they are "incapable of confinement or exclusive appropriation."[164]

Jefferson's image of the candle is an apt metaphor for the tenets of social constructivism. Like Jefferson, social-constructivists appreciate that knowledge cannot be delivered or captured by any particular individual or group. Rather, knowledge is constructed when ideas are "spread from one to another" through meaningful relationships. Jefferson's conception of knowledge as a collective,

---

[156] Ibid. at para. 27, 31.
[157] Kaufman et al., *Learning Together* at 56.
[158] Tzen Wong, "Intellectual Property Through the Lens of Human Development," in *Intellectual Property and Human Development* 1, 18 (Tzen Wong & Graham Dutfield eds., Cambridge: Cambridge University Press, 2011).
[159] Ibid. at 18–19.
[160] Thomas Jefferson, *Letter to Isaac McPherson* (Aug. 13, 1813).
[161] Ibid.
[162] Ibid.
[163] Ibid.
[164] Ibid.

collaborative enterprise bears no resemblance to the approach embodied by scientific management. This dichotomy underscores the fact that, far from being the fulfillment of the principles of the Founders, the management tactics employed in mass production are a repudiation of the founding principles.

The Founders recognized that human beings have a natural instinct to collaborate with others.[165] In *Democracy in America*, Alexis de Tocqueville writes about the tendency of Americans to join associations:

> Americans of all ages, all minds constantly unite. ... As soon as several of the inhabitants of the United States have conceived of a sentiment or an idea that they want to produce in the world, they seek each other out; and when they have found each other, they unite.[166]

In a democratic regime like the United States, de Tocqueville argues, "the art of associating must be developed."[167] In fact, associations are essential to human progress: "In democratic countries, the science of associations is the mother science; the progress of all the others depends on the progress of that one."[168] Particularly to the American people, associations of all varieties are necessary because of their yearning for freedom and equality. He also notes that the "art of associating must be developed and perfected" among Americans in order to "remain civilized."[169]

The American inclination to group with neighbors into associations, both large and small, must be cultivated and celebrated. In fact, de Tocqueville argues that of all "the laws that rule human societies," the law requiring the act of associating is the most "precise" and "clear."[170] As de Tocqueville recognized, the United States regime depends upon a view of human nature that drives individuals to develop meaningful relationships through which they achieve well-being and find joy in the social construction of knowledge.

The Founders concurred wholeheartedly with de Tocqueville's views on human nature and development. Human beings are equal in their capacity to govern and to be governed. They possess the innate ability to understand another person's perspectives, feelings, and intentions. The constitutional structure of self-governance depends on the belief that individuals have a natural desire for the freedom to construct and to spread knowledge through meaningful relationships. Accordingly, the behaviorist practices that have dominated American education and rewarded consumption cannot be fairly justified by any claim that they are aligned with our founding documents or principles.

---

[165] Ibid.
[166] Alexis de Tocqueville, *Democracy in America* (H. Mansfield & D. Winthrop, eds. & trans., Chicago: University of Chicago Press, 2000), 489–492.
[167] Ibid.
[168] Ibid.
[169] Ibid.
[170] Ibid.

The Founders fully appreciated that the choices made by citizens in a democracy are not merely the product of subjective utility. The Founders relied upon the overriding human capacity for empathy as a check on the passionate pursuit of self-interest and the abuse of power. The quality of empathy enables individuals to put themselves in someone else's shoes, to understand someone else's feelings and intentions.

As we have seen, recent findings from the disparate fields of neuroscience, neuropsychology, cognitive psychology, educational psychology, economics, and behavioral economics all support the principle that human learning and development depends on building relationships. Our educational and economic systems, which reward atomistic, competitive, and consumptive behavior, and which have produced gross inequalities and environmental degradation, cannot consequently be justified as an accurate reflection of human nature.

In short, behaviorist theory views human beings as atomistic, competitive, and passive consumers of knowledge. To the contrary, these diverse fields all confirm that human beings are holistic, collaborative, and active producers of knowledge.

The current conditions of gross inequality and environmental degradation cannot be justified as a true reflection of human nature. Nor can the retention of those conditions be justified as cost-effective or as aligned with our founding documents and principles.

The behaviorist model of education has been wielded to produce a regime of consumers, who, contrary to their nature, are rewarded for the kind of unbridled consumption that leads to radical inequality and unchecked dominion over the environment. The process of rationalization begins with the education system. As John Bellamy Foster contends, "the forms of consciousness and behavior fostered by capitalist schooling are designed to reproduce existing classes and groupings, and thus are meant to reinforce and legitimize the social relations of production of capitalist society as a whole."[171] Foster demonstrates that

> [s]chools are, then, less about education than a kind of behavioral modification, preparing the vast majority of students for a life of routinization and standardization, in which most will end up employed in essentially unskilled, dead-end jobs. Indeed, most jobs in the degraded work environment of monopoly capitalist society – even those set aside for college graduates – require precious little formal education.[172]

It does not strain the imagination to see Schmidt, the pig-iron handler from Frederick Winslow Taylor's anecdote, nodding his head in agreement with Foster's critique.

Similarly, Albert Einstein recognized how our education system trains students to accept the false necessity of the unequal acquisition of resources by the most wealthy

---

[171] John Bellamy Foster, "Education and the Structural Crisis of Capital," 63 MONTHLY REV. no. 3 (July–Aug. 2011).
[172] Ibid.

and powerful: "This crippling of individuals I consider the worst evil of capitalism. Our whole educational system suffers from this evil. An exaggerated competitive attitude is inculcated into the student, who is trained to worship acquisitive success as a preparation for his future career."[173]

Roberto Mangabeira Unger also has shown how a complete understanding of the Founders' vision can support the growth of a genuine democracy in which all members of a community are encouraged to construct their knowledge through meaningful relationships and to exercise their power to perform different leadership roles. As Unger has suggested, there is nothing in human nature or in true democratic regimes that requires an adversarial relationship between the individual and the community.

To the contrary, the notion that there that must be a continual "struggle" between the educational best interests of the child and those of the community is a "false necessity."[174] That false necessity may help to legitimate a particular form of political order, but it ultimately stands in the way of the development of a genuine democracy.

Political structures justified by the belief that individuals are naturally governed by their subjective desires "undermine the conception of a shared humanity."[175] The belief that individuals should overcome their passions through reason, however, ultimately leads to an effort to negate or dissolve the individuality of the person.

The legal and political dimension of the artificial antinomy between reason and desire is the "contrast between public and private existence."[176] The "public" sphere is characterized by the necessity of being governed by common standards and laws. In the "private" sphere, by contrast, individuals are free to follow their own individual and natural desires. As a consequence, people are compelled to negate their full identities in the public realm of law and the marketplace, while they also are compelled to pursue their own desires only in isolation from the community.

The presumption that human desire is natural and negative while reason is acquired and positive makes both individual well-being and community cohesiveness difficult. The "antinomy" of reason and desire undermines the formation of a complete human being in which reason and desire act in harmony, just as it undermines the formation of a community in which individuals and others can act in harmony.

In *Law and Modern Society: Toward a Criticism of Social Theory*,[177] Unger shows how the emergence of the conception of the individual who is in opposition to society corresponds with the disintegration of community. In a community, there is

---

[173] Albert Einstein, "Why Socialism?," 1 MONTHLY REV. no. 1, 14 (May 1949).
[174] See Roberto Mangabeira Unger, *False Necessity: Anti-Necessitarian Social Theory in the Service of Radical Democracy* (Boston: Cambridge University Press, 1987).
[175] Ibid. at 57.
[176] Ibid. at 59.
[177] Roberto Mangabeira Unger, *Law and Modern Society: Toward a Criticism of Social Theory* (New York: Free Press, 1976).

a "closely held communion of reciprocal expectations, based on a shared view of right and wrong."[178] The standards of behavior are not established primarily through formal rules or positive law. Rather, there is an organic "allegiance to common moral understandings."[179]

Individual members of a community are not in opposition to the commonwealth. They have internalized the desire to remain faithful to the group's customs and they may rely comfortably on their belief that their neighbors will do the same. In the community, desire is not in opposition to reason. The individual has already internalized the group's expectations so that the individual will instinctively desire what is expected by the group. At the same time, the group's expectations are fully informed by the collective desires of its members, so that those expectations are not imposed by some external force of "reason."[180]

Unger suggests that in a genuine democracy, the artificial tension between the individual and the community would dissolve because power would be rotated and shared in meaningful associations. All members of the community would play multiple roles.

In fact, teaching children the habits of mind and heart that are required for "role playing" is essential to the development of a true democracy. Although their concerns about self-interest have been used to justify a political and educational regime based on the supposed struggle between the individual and the community, the Founders' also fully appreciated that the development of such a democracy depends on the natural capacity of children to learn to share roles, to construct meaning, and to spread knowledge through meaningful associations.

CONCLUSION

America in the Gilded Age and Progressive Era struggled to make sense of the rapid changes which it experienced during this period. An impulse to create order out of apparent chaos permeated these decades, and led in part to a national obsession with efficiency. The works of thinkers like Frederick Winslow Taylor revolutionized manufacturing and soon began changing the nature of the educational process. Standardization replaced creativity, uniform standards supplanted individualized pedagogy, and outputs overshadowed inputs. By treating knowledge as a commodity, schools began to operate like factories. Behaviorism and operant conditioning reigned supreme. While exciting advances in neuroscience and myriad other fields of inquiry have exposed these philosophies as based on erroneous assumptions, American education still relies too heavily on these nineteenth century principles.

---

[178] Ibid. at 61.
[179] Ibid. at 62.
[180] Ibid.

In the next chapter, we will begin our investigation of the Supreme Court's jurisprudence in education under the Equal Protection Clause of the Fourteenth Amendment. This section of the Constitution impacts countless facets of American life – particularly education. We will begin with perhaps the most famous application of the Equal Protection Clause in American History: *Brown v. Board of Education*.

4

Brown and Resegregation

No period in American history blends an attempt to convert the Founders' theories into action with an emphasis on the importance of education as dramatically as the Civil Rights Movement of the 1950s and 1960s. The story of the effort to desegregate the nation's schools and, in so doing, build a society inclusive of all Americans remains a pivotal episode in the history of education in America. It also offers a fascinating demonstration of the capacity of legal arguments to facilitate cultural change.

This chapter will thoroughly analyze *Brown* v. *Board of Education*, which declared legally mandated racial segregation in public schools unconstitutional. The chapter will both analyze the reasoning of the unanimous Supreme Court decision and scrutinize the gaps in the Court's opinion. In telling the story of *Brown*, it will emphasize the heroic efforts of the brave parents and students, tireless activists, and visionary attorneys who collectively ended *de jure* segregation (segregation mandated by law) in the United States. It will also investigate the foundations of this monumental decision – demonstrating how the ingenuity of constitutional lawyers slowly yet steadily laid the groundwork for desegregation and left the *Brown* Court little alternative but to rule in their favor. Finally, it will examine the progeny of *Brown* and the often-disappointing results of subsequent Supreme Court decisions dealing with race in schools. This will include an analysis of the lingering effects of *de facto* segregation (segregation not mandated by law but instead resulting from other factors including housing patterns and demographic shifts).

FROM COUNTRY ROADS TO COURTHOUSE STEPS: THE LONG WAR AGAINST *PLESSY V. FERGUSON*

The story of the decades-long struggle to declare legally segregated school systems unconstitutional is, among many other things, a story of the power of education. Systematically excluded from mainstream American society, African Americans built parallel institutions of their own. While certainly unequal when measured by access to resources and quality of facilities, they were entirely the equal of white schools in terms of dedicated teachers and emphasis on learning. In fact, the story of *Brown* cannot be told without recounting the work of an extraordinary lawyer and educator named Charles "Charlie" Houston.

Inspired to study law after witnessing multiple racially motivated courts-martial while serving in World War I, Houston turned Washington, DC's Howard School of Law into a West Point for African American lawyers. As author Juan Williams relates, "Houston made no secret of his main goal. He wanted to make the American legal system work for blacks, and to do so he was training a cadre of top-notch black lawyers."[1] Houston's students, many of whom would go on to become giants of the legal profession, were invariably turned away by segregated law schools. Rather than bow to this injustice, Houston rallied these bright young minds and trained them to beat their segregationist adversaries at their own game: constitutional law.

Keenly aware of the Supreme Court's preference for incremental holdings rather than sweeping pronouncements, Houston sought to lead the Court toward desegregation, step by step. Williams explains,

> Houston worked out his own detailed, long-range strategy. They would begin by attacking segregation in professional and graduate schools. If they could amass victory after victory, selecting the right cases to litigate and establishing precedent in a clear, ever-broadening line, they could then work their way through colleges, high schools, and finally elementary schools.[2]

With a long range plan in place, Houston could draw upon the considerable talents of his former students at Howard – many of whom he influenced not only professionally but also personally. If Houston played the role of coach while developing a game plan to defeat segregation, he found his star quarterback in Thurgood Marshall. "Marshall and Houston were a powerful combination. . . . Houston read law books with precision and an eye to the future; his skill was more than matched by Marshall's ability to read people and their motives," reports Juan Williams.[3]

In addition to Houston's legal brilliance, his pedagogical approach also deserves praise. After imparting the fundamentals of the law to his students, he brought many of them on to his team as collaborators and colleagues. While it is unclear whether he would have used the language of social constructivist educational theories, it is evident that Charlie Houston appreciated the importance of building knowledge collaboratively through meaningful relationships. This approach, actively seeking input from potential new contributors, is the antithesis of a segregated system – which, by its very nature, prevents the entire disfavored group from contributing. Rather than seeking to include as many voices as possible, segregation assumes an

---

[1] Juan Williams, *Eyes on the Prize: America's Civil Rights Years, 1954–1965* (New York: Viking, 1987), 10.
[2] Ibid. at 10–11.
[3] Ibid. at 14.

entire group of people has nothing of value to say. Charlie Houston's collaborative, visionary approach to education offered a rebuke to segregation nearly as powerful as the legal arguments he helped develop.

Even with detailed plans and dedicated personnel, the process of overturning *Plessy* and thus ending segregation in schools would prove difficult and grueling. The lawyers and advocates who sought to challenge segregation would scour the country looking for potential plaintiffs brave enough to place their names on the cover of a complaint. Danger was always present; the plaintiff in *Missouri ex rel Gaines* v. *Canada* disappeared under mysterious circumstances shortly after the Supreme Court heard the case.[4] Later, leading up to the *Brown* litigation, a minister who helped mobilize community members to fight for integrated schools had his house and church burned down and also survived an assassination attempt.[5] These by no means isolated incidents illustrate the strain under which plaintiffs, lawyers, and their supporters in the desegregation cases all labored.

The Court in *Brown* relied on both *Sweatt* v. *Painter*[6] and *McLaurin* v. *Oklahoma State Regents for Higher Education*.[7] In *Sweatt*, the Supreme Court held that the Equal Protection Clause of the Fourteenth Amendment prohibited the state of Texas from denying African American students admission to the University of Texas Law School because of their race. The Court's reasoning was based largely on the fact that the law schools available to African American students lacked "substantial equality in the educational opportunities offered."[8] The Court found that the tangible facilities and intangible qualities of the state's African American law schools were, in fact, unequal to those available at the University of Texas Law School. The Court also observed that because the African American law schools excluded "most" of the state's lawyers, judges, and officials with whom future lawyers inevitably deal, those law schools were not "substantially equal" to law schools that include such a "substantial and significant segment of society."[9]

In *McLaurin*, the Supreme Court concluded that the Equal Protection Clause also prevents states from treating students differently within the educational environment because of their race. The plaintiff enrolled as a graduate student at the University of Oklahoma, pursuing a doctorate in education. The state forced him to sit in a section of the classroom reserved for African Americans, to sit at a library table assigned to African American students, and to eat at a "special" cafeteria table assigned to African American students.[10] Although the Court assumed that these separations were "nominal" and resulted in no "disadvantage of location," it

---

[4] See James T. Patterson, *Brown v. Board of Education: A Civil Rights Milestone and Its Troubled Legacy* (New York: Oxford University Press, 2001), 39.
[5] Ibid. at XXIV-V.
[6] 339 U.S. 629 (1950).
[7] 339 U.S. 637 (1950).
[8] 339 U.S. 629, 633–634.
[9] *Id.* at 634.
[10] 339 U.S. 637, 640.

nonetheless declared: "[t]he result is that appellant is handicapped in his pursuit of an effective graduate instruction."[11]

The state's practices violated the Equal Protection Clause because, in setting McLaurin "apart from the other students," the state had imposed "restrictions" that "impair and inhibit his ability to study, to engage in discussions and exchange views with other students, and, in general, to learn his profession."[12] According to the Court, state-imposed restrictions "which prohibit the intellectual commingling of students" based on race produce "inequalities" that cannot be sustained.[13]

In both these cases, Houston, Marshall, and the rest of their team took great care to select sympathetic plaintiffs as well as particularly egregious fact patterns. They also tailored their legal arguments to operate within the confines of existing precedent rather than explicitly seeking to overturn prior cases. The attorneys in *Sweatt* and *McLaurin* did not ask the Court to overturn *Plessy*. Rather, they argued that the separate educational facilities implicated by the fact patterns could not be called "equal" in any meaningful sense and, accordingly, violated *Plessy*. To modern ears it is, of course, odd to hear *Plessy*'s odious reasoning used as a tool by advocates for civil rights. However, this maneuver illustrates the sophistication of Houston's strategy. Rather than mount a direct attack on the "separate but equal" doctrine, Houston, Marshall, and their colleagues sought to establish new precedents declaring separate facilities unequal *in light of the facts presented in a particular case*. After compiling enough of these successes and thus forcing the Court to emphasize equality in each subsequent opinion – dealing with fact patterns of increasingly broad applicability – the NAACP would argue that separate facilities were *unequal in all circumstances*. The strategy, in short, was to use the absurdities inherent in the *Plessy* doctrine to eventually overturn the precedent.

After the successes of *Sweatt* and *McLaurin*, the NAACP undertook its long-awaited attack on desegregation *per se*. By this point, "the rulings by the federal courts indicated … that the existence of segregated schools, no matter how good they were, implied inferiority – that separate could never be equal."[14] With these developments in mind, the petitioners in *Brown* made a strategic decision to attack the segregated aspects of public education rather than the tangible disparities in the quality of education between white and black students. Relying on emerging psychological research, the petitioners sought to lead the Court to the conclusion that, even in the unlikely event the facilities for African American children were similarly situated to those for white children, the deleterious effects of segregation on a child's ability to learn rendered the system inherently unequal. Historian James T. Patterson concludes: "What was intolerable, they asserted, was that the system of segregation … was legally required, and that it was enforced. Children who were

[11] *Id.* at 641.
[12] *Id.*
[13] *Id.*
[14] Williams, Eyes on the Prize, 18.

part of such an officially sanctioned system ... were made to feel inferior. And children who felt inferior would necessarily lose motivation to learn."[15]

Two weeks before the Supreme Court issued its *Brown* decision, it decided *Hernandez* v. *Texas*.[16] The Court held that the systematic exclusion of persons of Mexican descent from jury service violated the Equal Protection Clause of the Fourteenth Amendment. According to the Court, the "groups" requiring the "aid of the courts in securing equal treatment under the laws" include those who are "singled out" or subjugated by the attitudes of community members.[17]

The nearly half-century battle to overturn *Plessy* finally ended on May 17, 1954, when the Supreme Court held that the "separate but equal" doctrine violated the Equal Protection Clause of the Fourteenth Amendment. In its unanimous opinion, authored by Chief Justice Earl Warren, the Court emphasized that its decision was driven as much by the special role acquired by public education in American society as any other factor. When Congress ratified the Fourteenth Amendment, the Court noted, public education was far less systemically developed than it would eventually become. Thus, the Court reasoned, an inquiry into the exact intent of Congress would be fruitless; the Court was addressing conditions in 1954 that Congress could not have envisioned in 1868.[18]

In addition, unlike in *Sweatt*, the Supreme Court in *Brown* assumed "the physical facilities and other 'tangible' factors" in the segregated African American schools were "equal" to those of the all-white schools.[19] In contrast to its previous opinions in cases dealing with segregated educational institutions, the *Brown* Court at last addressed the inherently negative effect of segregation on the opportunity to learn. As Chief Justice Warren eloquently explained: "To separate (minority children) from others of similar age and qualifications solely because of their race generates a feeling of inferiority as to their status in the community that may affect their hearts and minds in a way unlikely ever to be undone."[20] Nestled just beneath the surface of the Court's opinion, the careful reader can find a growing sense that education depends as much on building relationships and learning to work and live together as transmitting facts and figures. The *Brown* Court did not explore this essentially social constructivist approach in any great depth.

One key passage in particular deserves close examination – both for what it says and for what it does not say.

> Today, education is perhaps the most important function of state and local governments. Compulsory school attendance laws and the great expenditures for education both demonstrate our recognition of the importance of education to our

---

[15] See *Patterson, Brown v. Board of Education*, 36.
[16] 347 U.S. 475 (1954).
[17] *Id.* at 480.
[18] 347 U.S. 490.
[19] *Id.* at 492.
[20] *Id.* at 494.

democratic society. It is required in the performance of our most basic public responsibilities, even service in the armed forces. It is the very foundation of good citizenship. Today it is a principal instrument in awakening the child to cultural values, in preparing him for later professional training, and in helping him to adjust normally to his environment. In these days, it is doubtful that any child may reasonably be expected to succeed in life if he is denied the opportunity of an education. Such an opportunity, where the state has undertaken to provide it, is a right which must be made available to all on equal terms.[21]

Here, the Court applauds public education. It enumerates the many ways in which education is indispensable to a modern, democratic society. Without it, the Court implies, the nation would cease to function properly.

However, the Court makes clear that education is a "function of state and local governments." By implication, it is also saying that education is not a responsibility of the federal government. Moreover, while the Court calls education "a right which must be made available to all on equal terms," it qualifies this pronouncement with the crucial caveat, "where the state has undertaken to provide it." The implications of this subtle phrase are profound. This language allows states to argue that, despite the clear importance of education, it is not a fundamental right protected by the United States Constitution. As later chapters will explore in detail, this caveat has the effect of undermining much of the emphasis on equality of opportunity which permeates the rest of *Brown*.

In reaching its result in *Brown*, the Supreme Court could have articulated several different arguments for the unconstitutionality of racially segregated public schools. The alternative bases available to the *Brown* Court include: (1) students who are members of a racial minority learn better when they are integrated in classrooms with children who are not members of a racial minority; (2) separate educational facilities assigned to minority children are, or inevitably become, tangibly worse than facilities assigned to non-minority children; (3) precluding members of a racial minority and members of a racial majority from congregating in the same educational environment denies to all students their First Amendment rights to freedom of association; and (4) the perpetuation of separate educational facilities, regardless of their relative quality, harms children who are members of a racial minority by stigmatizing them.[22]

The *Brown* Court has been criticized because its language does not make clear that the Constitution precludes practices of racial oppression, subordination, and injury.[23] Instead, *Brown*'s focus appears to be only (albeit importantly) on laws that

---

[21] *Id.* at 493.

[22] See, e.g., Laurence H. Tribe, *American Constitutional Law* §16–15, at 1476–1480 (2nd ed., St Paul, MN: West Academic Publishing, 1988); Herbert Wechsler, *Toward Neutral Principles of Constitutional Law* (Harv. L. Rev., 1959) 73 10.

[23] See, e.g., Derrick Bell, *Silent Covenants: Brown v. Board of Education and the Unfulfilled Hopes for Racial Reform* (New York: Oxford University Press, 2004); Sheryll Cashin, *The Failures of Integration: How Race and Class Are Undermining the American Dream* (New York: PublicAffairs, 2004).

formally separate the races. In other words, *Brown* clearly prohibits *de jure* segregation but says nothing of *de facto* segregation. Even critics of *Brown* applaud the case as a monument to racial and educational equality. Yet, they lament that its reasoning has allowed subsequent courts to frustrate the goal of genuine integration and equity.

The Court held that even if tangible factors like facilities, quality of instruction, and curriculum are indeed comparable, segregation of children in public schools solely on the basis of race deprives the "children of the minority group of equal educational opportunities."[24] The Court does not reach the issue of whether segregation adversely affects children of the majority group. Nor does the Court consider whether a diverse educational environment is valuable to all students. By focusing on the harm to African American children caused by racial segregation, *Brown* and its progeny inadvertently divided the races on the *issue* of segregation itself. This would serve only to complicate future court battles over the precise implications of the sweeping, yet often vague, language in *Brown*.

CONGRESSIONAL EFFORTS TO PROTECT CIVIL RIGHTS AND EDUCATION FOR SOME AMERICANS

As the Civil Rights Movement continually gained strength in the decade following *Brown*, Congress eventually mobilized itself to act and rendered vital assistance in the form of two landmark statutes. Congress's passage of the Civil Rights Act of 1964 and the Elementary and Secondary Education Act of 1965 promised meaningful federal involvement in protecting civil rights and insuring educational access for all Americans. This legislative effort reflected the spirit of the judicial battles waged by Charlie Houston, Thurgood Marshall, and so many others.

Civil Rights advocates won arguably their most lasting legislative victory with the passage of the Civil Rights Act of 1964. Its terms insured that the federal government would not be a party to racial or ethnic discrimination either directly or indirectly. It provided:

> No person in the United States shall, on the ground of race, color or national origin, be excluded from participation in, be denied the benefits of, or be subjected to discrimination under any program or activity receiving Federal financial assistance.[25]

The impact of this monumental legislation on American life cannot be overstated. However, in the context of our discussion of the history of education law, the close relationship between the Civil Rights Act and *Brown* is especially salient. Ushering the bill toward passage, Senator Hubert Humphrey (D-Minn.) informed his colleagues that financing schemes then in force provided federal funds to racially

---

[24] *Id.* at 394.
[25] 42 U.S.C.A. §2000d.

segregated institutions in accordance with the Court's holding in *Plessy*.[26] In light of the *Brown* decision – which discarded the "separate but equal" doctrine – this arrangement was not only fundamentally unjust but also patently illegal. Additionally, Senator Humphrey noted that the arduous process of litigation often led to delays in securing the equal protection of the laws.[27] The situation called for a robust federal intervention; Congress speaking explicitly would deprive segregationists of even the barest semblance of legal cover. In effect, the Civil Rights Act of 1964 was Congress's way of offering its assistance in the battle previously waged by advocates in the courts.

The Elementary and Secondary Education Act of 1965 (ESEA) marked the largest federal intervention in education that had occurred at that time in American history. According to the Department of Education: "The purpose of ESEA was to provide additional resources for vulnerable students. ESEA offered new grants to districts serving low-income students. ... The law also provided federal grants to state educational agencies to improve the quality of elementary and secondary education."[28] The bill reflected President Lyndon Johnson's desire to "declare a national goal of full educational opportunity."[29] ESEA's provisions and lofty aspirations echoed the impulse toward equality and delivering meaningful opportunity to all citizens that characterized the early 1960s.[30] In evaluating ESEA's legacy, Catherine A. Paul of Virginia Commonwealth University concludes that the Act, "brought education into the forefront of the national assault on poverty and represented a landmark commitment to equal access to quality education."[31] For the first time, American students enjoyed the benefit of a unified, nationwide, effort on their behalf undertaken by the federal government.

These two great legislative victories of the early 1960s continue to impact American education in a profound way. This success in Congress, however, was not entirely matched in the courts in the years following *Brown*.

FROM DESEGREGATION TO RESEGREGATION: THE PROGENY OF BROWN

In *Brown v. Board of Education* (*Brown II*),[32] the Supreme Court addressed the question of integrating districts in which a *de jure* regime of segregation had held sway prior to *Brown*:

---

[26] See www.justice.gov/crt/fcs/T6manual2.
[27] Ibid.
[28] See https://blog.ed.gov/2015/04/what-is-esea/.
[29] Ibid.
[30] See Michael J. Kaufman & Sherelyn R. Kaufman, *Education Law, Policy, and Practice* (New York: Wolters Kluwer, 2013), 363.
[31] See https://socialwelfare.library.vcu.edu/programs/education/elementary-and-secondary-education-act-of-1965/.
[32] 349 U.S. 294 (1955).

Full implementation of these constitutional principles may require solution of varied local school problems. School authorities have the primary responsibility for elucidating, assessing, and solving these problems; courts will have to consider whether the action of school authorities constitutes good faith implementation of the governing constitutional principles. ... In fashioning and effectuating the decrees, the courts will be guided by equitable principles. Traditionally, equity has been characterized by a practical flexibility in shaping its remedies and by a facility for adjusting and reconciling public and private needs. These cases call for the exercise of these traditional attributes of equity power. At stake is the personal interest of the plaintiffs in admission to public schools as soon as practicable on a nondiscriminatory basis. To effectuate this interest may call for elimination of a variety of obstacles in making the transition to school systems operated in accordance with the constitutional principles set forth in our May 17, 1954, decision. Courts of equity may properly take into account the public interest in the elimination of such obstacles in a systematic and effective manner. But it should go without saying that the vitality of these constitutional principles cannot be allowed to yield simply because of disagreement with them.

While giving weight to these public and private considerations, the courts will require that the defendants make a prompt and reasonable start toward full compliance with our May 17, 1954, ruling. Once such a start has been made, the courts may find that additional time is necessary to carry out the ruling in an effective manner. The burden rests upon the defendants to establish that such time is necessary in the public interest and is consistent with good faith compliance at the earliest practicable date. To that end, the courts may consider problems related to administration, arising from the physical condition of the school plant, the school transportation system, personnel, revision of school districts and attendance areas into compact units to achieve a system of determining admission to the public schools on a nonracial basis, and revision of local laws and regulations which may be necessary in solving the foregoing problems. They will also consider the adequacy of any plans the defendants may propose to meet these problems and to effectuate a transition to a racially nondiscriminatory school system.

During this period of transition, the courts will retain jurisdiction of these cases. ... [T]he cases are remanded to the District Courts to take such proceedings and enter such orders and decrees consistent with this opinion as are necessary and proper to admit to public schools on a racially nondiscriminatory basis with all deliberate speed the parties to these cases.[33]

Interestingly, prior drafts of the opinion reveal the Court originally wrote that desegregation must occur with "all appropriate speed," but the word "appropriate" was changed to "deliberate" in the final version of *Brown II*.[34] Indeed, there was little speed and much resistance to the federal court orders implementing *Brown II*.

---

[33] Id. at 299–301.
[34] See www.abajournal.com/magazine/article/the_court_comes_together/.

Before delving further into the progeny of *Brown*, a word of explanation regarding the Supreme Court's approach to equal protection cases is needed. While equal protection analysis could fill a full-length book by itself, a simplified summary will be adequate for our purposes here.[35] An equal protection claim arises whenever a plaintiff can show that a law treats similarly situated people differently on the basis of their membership in a protected class. While there are a number of protected classes, this book will primarily discuss race, national origin, and gender. Laws that discriminate against similarly situated people on the basis of characteristics such as these are subject to a more demanding judicial review than laws that make no such distinction.

The Court has developed three levels of review for equal protection claims: rational basis review, intermediate scrutiny, and strict scrutiny. Quite often, determining the correct level of review dictates the outcome of the case. The next three paragraphs will discuss the approach taken by the Court when the law discriminates on its face (i.e., explicitly by its very terms).

Rational basis review is employed in situations in which the government does not discriminate on the basis of a protected class. The Court has held that this level of review is appropriate for distinctions based on age. To successfully prove an equal protection claim under the rational basis test, a plaintiff must demonstrate that the law is not rationally related to any legitimate government purpose. Naturally, this is a very difficult task. Rational basis review almost always upholds the challenged law and denies the equal protection claim.

At the other end of the spectrum, the Court applies strict scrutiny to laws discriminating on the basis of race or national origin. Under strict scrutiny, the burden of proof shifts from the plaintiff to the government. In order for a law to survive strict scrutiny, the government must demonstrate that the law (1) serves a compelling government interest and (2) is narrowly tailored to pursue the articulated compelling interest. This means that the government can only discriminate on the basis of race or national origin for extremely important reasons, and must use a method that is inextricably linked to that same reason. The law or policy being challenged must pass both these prongs of the test. When strict scrutiny is applied, the majority of laws will fail at least one prong of the test.

Finally, the Court uses intermediate scrutiny for laws discriminating on the basis of gender. Under intermediate scrutiny, the burden of proof remains with the government. In order for a law to survive intermediate scrutiny, the government must prove that the classification (1) serves important governmental objectives and (2) is substantially related to those important governmental objectives. As is the case under strict scrutiny, the law must pass both prongs of this test. Effectively, this allows more deference to the government than under strict scrutiny. At the same

---

[35] For an excellent discussion of Equal Protection Clause jurisprudence, see Erwin Chemerinsky, *Constitutional Law: Principles and Policies* (New York: Wolters Kluwer, 2011), 683–811.

time, it gives plaintiffs a considerably better chance of success than under rational basis review. First adopted by the Court in the 1970s, the language used in intermediate scrutiny is more fluid and somewhat less precise than in strict scrutiny or rational basis review. For example, the Court has also on occasion formulated intermediate scrutiny as requiring the government to demonstrate an "exceedingly persuasive justification" for gender-based classifications. As a result, judges, practitioners, and commentators continue to debate the exact boundaries of intermediate scrutiny.

Laws that do not discriminate by their own terms are analyzed pursuant to the disparate impact template. Disparate impact is used to describe laws which do not explicitly discriminate yet still affect members of protected classes differently. In short, laws that are not facially discriminatory may nonetheless have the effect of discriminating based on membership in protected classes. However, for claims in which the plaintiff is challenging a law based on its alleged disparate impact, the plaintiff must demonstrate that the government formulated the facially neutral law *with the intent to discriminate*. In other words, simply showing that a neutrally worded law treats members of protected classes differently (i.e., less favorably) is not sufficient. The plaintiff must show that the drafters of the law intended to discriminate against members of protected classes and used the facially neutral language of the statute to cover their motive. To borrow a concept from criminal law, this is akin to asking the plaintiff to produce a smoking gun as evidence. Thus, disparate impact analysis favors the government and presumes its good faith absent a showing to the contrary.

With the fundamentals of equal protection jurisprudence in mind, we can unpack the progeny of *Brown*. In *Green v. County Sch. Bd. of New Kent County*,[36] the Court rejected the school board's "freedom of choice" plan, which allowed students to choose their own public school. The Board failed to show that its plan resulted in an effective transition to a unitary (fully integrated) district, and therefore the Board failed to demonstrate its compliance with its responsibility "to achieve a system of determining admission to the public schools on a nonracial basis." The Supreme Court concluded that school districts must eliminate racial discrimination in public education "root and branch."

The Court turned to *Alexander v. Holmes County Bd. of Educ.*,[37] in the wake of concerted efforts by southern states to avoid integration. In *Alexander*, the Supreme Court denounced its "all deliberate speed" standard as a "soft euphemism for delay" that allowed too much deliberation and not enough speed. The Court ordered all southern school districts to become unitary on an immediate basis.

Two years later, the Court attempted to implement general standards for desegregation plans in *Swann v. Charlotte-Mecklenburg Board of Education*.[38] The Court

[36] 391 U.S. 430 (1968),
[37] 396 U.S. 19 (1969).
[38] 402 U.S. 1 (1971).

focused on four "problem areas" in desegregation: (1) the use of racial quotas; (2) the continued existence of schools with student bodies comprised almost entirely of one race; (3) the limits of altering district lines and attendance zones; and (4) the limits on the use of intradistrict busing to achieve desegregation.[39] In outlining its approach, the Court rejected an invitation to consider the effect of broader societal discrimination. It confined itself solely to undoing the harm of a *de jure* regime of segregation in schools.[40] This decision would weigh heavily on future precedent and limit later efforts to achieve desegregation.

The Court upheld the "limited" use of quotas in desegregation plans for districts formerly operating under *de jure* segregation.[41] It approved of quotas that, broadly speaking, reflected the overall racial makeup of a given district. It did not, however, require that districts aim for student bodies that replicated the overall racial demographics of the district at each individual school.

Relatedly, the Court concluded that the continued existence of "one-race schools" did not, by itself, violate the Fourteenth Amendment.[42] So long as the student body composition did not result from past or present discriminatory action by the district, the Court saw no constitutional defect.

In addition, the Court endorsed the redrawing of attendance zones within a district to facilitate integration.[43] The Court even approved the idea that, as part of a remedial plan, the traditional attachment to the ideal of the "neighborhood school" may be overweighed by the need to build a more equitable system.

Finally, the Court approved busing schemes as part of a larger desegregation plan.[44] However, the Court noted that any busing components could be challenged on the grounds of time or distance of travel when either student health or educational quality were called into question. The Court cautioned districts to use busing as sparingly as possible when assigning younger students.

In *Columbus Bd. of Educ. v. Penick*,[45] and *Dayton Board of Education v. Brinkman*,[46] the Supreme Court found *de jure* segregation in these Ohio districts based upon evidence that Ohio public officials had knowledge of the existence of segregated schools and failed to take affirmative steps to dismantle that dual system. The Court suggested that the failure to remedy an existing dual school system was itself a constitutional violation.

In *Milliken v. Bradley*,[47] the Supreme Court made it clear that a federal court may *not* impose a multi-district, area wide remedy to a single-district *de jure* segregation

---

[39] *Id.* at 22.
[40] *Id.*
[41] *Id.* at 25.
[42] *Id.* at 26.
[43] *Id.* at 28.
[44] *Id.* at 29.
[45] 443 U.S. 449 (1979).
[46] 443 U.S. 526 (1979).
[47] 418 U.S. 717 (1974).

violation absent exceptional circumstances. Such circumstances include situations in which the other districts involved in the remedy also operated segregated school systems. Similarly, a multi-district remedy could be imposed upon a finding that the boundary lines of any affected school district were established with the purpose of fostering racial segregation in public schools. In addition, a finding that the neighboring districts committed acts which facilitated segregation within the district(s) explicitly under a desegregation order could also trigger a remedy employing the neighboring areas to integrate the district explicitly under a desegregation order. However, absent a meaningful opportunity for the included neighboring school districts to present evidence on either the propriety of a multi-district remedy or the question of the alleged constitutional violations, no multidistrict remedy may be imposed.[48]

The *Milliken* Court's reasoning was based in large part on the principle of local control:

> [N]o single tradition in public education is more deeply rooted than local control over the operation of schools; local autonomy has long been thought essential both to the maintenance of community concern and support for public schools and to quality of the educational process. Thus, in *San Antonio School District v. Rodriguez*, 411 U.S. 1, 50 (1973), we observed that local control over the educational process affords citizens an opportunity to participate in decision-making, permits the structuring of school programs to fit local needs, and encourages experimentation, innovation, and a healthy competition for educational excellence.[49]

The *Milliken* Court also addressed the issue of remedy:

> The controlling principle consistently expounded in our holdings is that the scope of the remedy is determined by the nature and extent of the constitutional violation. Before the boundaries of separate and autonomous school districts may be set aside by consolidating the separate units for remedial purposes or by imposing a cross-district remedy, it must first be shown that there has been a constitutional violation within one district that produces a significant segregative effect in another district. Specifically, it must be shown that racially discriminatory acts of the state or local school districts, or of a single school district have been a substantial cause of interdistrict segregation. Thus an interdistrict remedy might be in order where the racially discriminatory acts of one or more school districts caused racial segregation in an adjacent district, or where district lines have been deliberately drawn on the basis of race. In such circumstances an interdistrict remedy would be appropriate to eliminate the interdistrict segregation directly caused by the constitutional violation. Conversely, without an interdistrict violation and interdistrict effect, there is no constitutional wrong calling for an interdistrict remedy.[50]

[48] *Id.* at 752.
[49] *Id.* at 742.
[50] *Id.* at 745.

After *Milliken*, it became extremely difficult for urban school districts to achieve racial integration. There simply is not enough racial diversity *within* many American communities to accomplish racial integration through intradistrict school assignment plans alone. Without the participation of suburban districts, there are insufficient numbers of white students to achieve the integration of urban districts.[51]

Practically speaking, *Milliken* placed multidistrict remedies for discrimination in a segregated district off limits. None of the exceptions contemplated by the *Milliken* Court lend themselves to easy proof by a plaintiff. The Supreme Court's holding in *Milliken* sharply circumscribed future efforts to implement the constitutional guarantees announced in *Brown*. In effect, it permits even the most detailed, equitable desegregation plan to be thwarted by changing demographics and the location of school district boundary lines.

In *Freeman v. Pitts*,[52] the Court relaxed the urgency of court-mandated integration plans. The Court relied on *Board of Education of Oklahoma City Public Schools v. Dowell*,[53] in holding that the creation of a racially "unitary" school district in all its dimensions is not a *constitutional* requirement. In *Dowell*, the Supreme Court concluded that a school desegregation remedy is a "temporary" measure that should be dissolved after "local authorities have operated in compliance with it for a reasonable period of time."[54] In *Freeman*, the Court returned to the principles of equitable remedies to insure that a federal court's remedial plan is narrowly tailored to the exact constitutional violation in question. Where the constitutional violation has been redressed by a remedy, the district court may and should withdraw its jurisdiction over the monitoring and maintenance of that remedy. In other words, if resegregation subsequently occurs by virtue of private choices, the court has no equitable power to devise additional remedies to redirect those private choices. Accordingly, a federal court's remedy for a constitutional violation can be entirely frustrated by changing demographics within a district. Moreover, because a state or school district cannot take affirmative steps to desegregate its students *absent* a proven constitutional violation, a state or district generally will be unable to attempt to improve a clear condition of *de facto* segregation. The *Freeman* Court indicated that a federal court's remedial power may weaken as the condition of resegregation becomes more and more attenuated from the original constitutional violation.

In *Missouri v. Jenkins (Jenkins II)*,[55] the Supreme Court rejected the district court's order requiring the Kansas City Metropolitan School District to increase its tax rate in order to raise the funds required for implementing the district court's ambitious plans. The Supreme Court, however, indicated that such a tax increase

---

[51] *See* Chemerinsky, *Segregation and Resegregation of American Public Education*.
[52] 503 U.S. 467 (1992).
[53] 498 U.S. 237 (1991).
[54] *Id.* at 247–248.
[55] 495 U.S. 33 (1990).

could be within the federal court's remedial power if "no permissible alternative would have accomplished the required task."[56] Moreover, the Court made clear that a remedial order which does not impose its own tax increase but instead directs "a local government body to levy its own taxes is plainly a judicial act within the power of the federal court."[57]

The district court creatively employed the concept of "magnet schools" to assist in its remedial plan. The Supreme Court defines magnet schools as "public schools of voluntary enrollment designed to promote integration by drawing students away from their neighborhoods and private schools through distinctive curricula and high quality."[58] Nonetheless, the Court rejected the district court's reliance on magnet schools in *Jenkins*.[59]

EVALUATING *PICS*: LIMITING THE LEGACY OF *BROWN*

In 2007, the Supreme Court handed down its most recent ruling addressing desegregation efforts in public schools: *Parents Involved in Community Schools* v. *Seattle School Dist. No. 1* (*PICS*).[60] *PICS* remains the controlling precedent for cases involving voluntary desegregation plans at the elementary and secondary level.

The Court's opinion dealt with two separate yet factually similar disputes, one involving high schools in Seattle, Washington, and the other implicating elementary schools in Jefferson County, Kentucky – a district which includes the city of Louisville. Seattle, which had never been subject to a court order mandating desegregation, nevertheless decided to pursue the educational benefits of diversity in its high schools as part of a larger student choice plan. The district permitted its students to rank their top choices of high schools. For years in which more students chose a high school than that particular school could accommodate, the district employed a racial tiebreaker system. This system was intended to insure that the student body of each school bore some similarity to the racial composition of the city of Seattle as a whole. To achieve this, the district used two categories: "white" and "nonwhite."[61]

Meanwhile, Jefferson County used a similar approach to maintain a racial balance in its elementary schools. The Jefferson County policy applied to both student assignments and transfer requests and, like Seattle, used two categories: "black" and "other."[62] In contrast to Seattle, Jefferson County had operated under a desegregation order for decades. The order included busing arrangements that were functionally identical to the plan attacked in *PICS*. However, even after

[56] *Id.* at 51.
[57] *Id.* at 55.
[58] *Id.* at 40.
[59] *Id.* at 60.
[60] 551 U.S. 701.
[61] *Id.* at 710.
[62] *Id.*

a subsequent court order declared Jefferson County schools "unitary," Jefferson County voluntarily decided to continue some programs mandated by the court order. Quoting the District Court's dissolution of the desegregation order, Justice Breyer notes, "the Louisville School Board had 'treated the ideal of an integrated system as much more than a legal obligation – they consider it a positive, desirable policy and an essential element of any well-rounded public school education.'"[63]

Chief Justice Roberts writes the majority opinion for the Court. Five members of the Court, including Justice Kennedy, seem to join that opinion. Yet, Justice Kennedy also writes separately and clearly parts company with significant portions of the Court's opinion.

The Court first determines the level of judicial scrutiny appropriate to the constitutional challenge. Chief Justice Roberts declares that all racial classifications demand strict scrutiny, requiring the proponents of the classification to show that the classification is "narrowly tailored" to achieve a "compelling" governmental interest. The majority specifically rejects any notion that so-called "benign" racial classifications undertaken with the intent to benefit victims of discrimination should receive more lenient review.[64] The Court instead reiterates that the use of racial classifications – whatever the motive – demands strict scrutiny. It follows an objective rather than a subjective test.

Chief Justice Roberts finds two interests sufficiently compelling to justify the government taking racial considerations into account in its decision-making: (1) remedying the effects of past intentional discrimination and (2) pursuing student body diversity.[65] The majority concludes that the first of these compelling interests is inapplicable to both school districts. Seattle, the majority notes, had never practiced intentional (*de jure*) discrimination. While Jefferson County practiced past intentional discrimination, the Court concludes the district court's declaration that it had achieved unitary status placed Jefferson County on a similar footing to Seattle. In other words, Jefferson County had already remedied the effects of past intentional discrimination and thus could no longer cite such a remedy as a compelling interest.

A bloc of four justices (though, as we will see, not a majority) explicitly concludes that the second compelling interest – pursuing the educational benefits of student body diversity – is inapplicable at the elementary and secondary level.[66] According to this theory, the diversity interest recognized in *Bakke* and reaffirmed in *Grutter* "relied upon considerations unique to institutions of higher education."[67] As such, this four-justice bloc distinguishes the facts in *PICS* from *Grutter* – seemingly limiting its precedential value to the context of higher education.[68]

---

[63] *Id.* at 818.
[64] *Id.* at 742.
[65] *Id.* at 720–722.
[66] *Id.* at 722.
[67] *Id.* at 724.
[68] While *PICS* incorporates holdings announced by the Court in cases dealing with race-conscious admissions policies in higher education, *PICS* is a more direct descendant of *Brown* because it addresses the discretion available to elementary and high schools. For a detailed discussion of *Bakke*,

Chief Justice Roberts recognizes that the school districts assert other interests that might prove compelling, including reducing racial isolation, giving non-white students access to the most desirable schools, educating students in a racially integrated environment, and the educational and broader socialization benefits that flow from a racially diverse learning environment. Significantly, Chief Justice Roberts – and therefore the Court – never decides whether these interests might be compelling enough to justify narrowly tailored race-conscious student assignments.[69] However, given the skepticism which four of the five majority justices express regarding the applicability of *Grutter*, it is far from certain that the *PICS* Court would have endorsed these interests as compelling.

The Court ultimately concludes that the "racial classifications employed by the districts are not narrowly tailored to the goal of achieving the educational and social benefits asserted to flow from diversity."[70] The majority notes that the districts employed systems that seek racial balancing to mirror community demographics – an interest repeatedly rejected in prior cases.[71] This signaled an attempt not to pursue the benefits of diversity, broadly conceived, but rather diversity viewed only through the lens of race. Moreover, the majority observes that students were, in effect, reduced to members of a racial category; neither Seattle nor Jefferson County made any attempt at the individualized consideration present in *Grutter*. Finally, the majority also takes issue with the binary view of race embodied in the classification systems. Such a system would inevitably fail to capture the full spectrum of racial diversity in a district and, thus, could not be deemed narrowly tailored to achieve the benefits of the broad vision of diversity put forth in *Bakke*.

Justice Kennedy's separate opinion appears to provide a fifth vote for portions of Chief Justice Roberts's opinion, and a fifth vote for portions of Justice Breyer's dissent. Justice Kennedy agrees with Chief Justice Roberts's ultimate conclusion that the means chosen by the school districts to achieve their objectives were not narrowly tailored. He takes particular umbrage with what he viewed as the absence of any notion of treating students as individuals rather than tools to achieve demographic balance. However, Justice Kennedy parts company with the Chief Justice on the applicability of *Grutter*. "Diversity, depending on its meaning and definition, is a compelling educational goal a school district may pursue."[72]

Significantly, Justice Kennedy also agrees with the four dissenters that the following "interests" are compelling: (1) encouraging a diverse student body, one aspect of which is its "racial composition"; (2) removing obstacles to "equal educational opportunity" for all students; (3) bringing together students of diverse races and

Grutter, and several other Supreme Court cases dealing with race-conscious admissions policies in higher education, see Chapter 5.

[69] *Id.* at 720.
[70] *Id.* at 726.
[71] *Id.*
[72] *Id.* at 783.

backgrounds; and (4) avoiding racial isolation in schooling. Those interests justify race-conscious educational decisions.[73]

If a school district attempts to achieve these goals through classifications of individual students by their race, that racial classification will be upheld only if it survives strict scrutiny. In other words, it must be narrowly tailored to achieve the stated compelling interest. According to Justice Kennedy, however, some race-conscious programs designed to achieve these compelling interests will not even require strict scrutiny. In a critical passage, he declares:

> School boards may pursue the goal of bringing together students of diverse backgrounds and races through other means including strategic site selection of new schools; drawing attendance zones with general recognition of the demographics of neighborhoods; allocating resources for special programs; recruiting students and faculty in a targeted fashion; and tracking enrollments, performance, and other statistics by race.[74]

These mechanisms are race-conscious but do not lead to a different treatment based on a classification that tells each student he or she is defined by race. Thus, none of the measures Justice Kennedy suggests would trigger strict scrutiny. Instead, Justice Kennedy offers a framework in which educators seeking in good faith to pursue the educational benefits of diversity could act creatively. He continues:

> Executive and legislative branches, which for generations now have considered these types of policies and procedures, should be permitted to employ them with candor and with confidence that a constitutional violation does not occur whenever a decision-maker considers the impact a given approach might have on students of different races. Assigning to each student a personal designation according to a crude system of individual racial classifications is quite a different matter; and the legal analysis changes accordingly.[75]

Justice Kennedy, then, presents a compelling alternative in his concurring opinion. He rejects Chief Justice Roberts' insistence on a color-blind strategy to achieve diversity. Justice Kennedy instead calls for an approach that maintains individual dignity while remaining fully aware of the lingering inequities in American society. His opinion offers a considerably more favorable assessment of the educational benefits of diversity than the view espoused by the other four justices in the majority.

In an unusually lengthy dissent, Justice Breyer details a number of counterarguments to the majority approach. He begins by questioning the premise – accepted uncritically by the majority – that a meaningful difference exists between *de jure* and *de facto* segregation. Indeed, the entirety of the majority approach to *PICS* rests on that dichotomy. For the four dissenters, Justice Breyer observes that, in the case of

---

[73] *Id.* at 797–798.
[74] *Id.* at 789.
[75] *Id.*

Seattle, the line between these two concepts was rather blurry. In fact, the NAACP filed a federal lawsuit against Seattle in 1966 alleging discrimination in its schools.

> The complaint charged that the school board had brought about this segregated system in part by "mak[ing] and enforc[ing]" certain "rules and regulations," in part by "drawing ... boundary lines" and "executing school attendance policies" that would create and maintain "predominantly Negro or non-white schools," and in part by building schools "in such a manner as to restrict the Negro plaintiffs and the class they represent to predominantly Negro or non-white schools."[76]

With this history in mind, Justice Breyer casts serious doubt upon the usefulness of the *de jure* vs. *de facto* paradigm so heavily relied upon by the majority.

Justice Breyer then proceeds to dispute the majority's conclusion that inclusive uses of race-conscious criteria should meet the same judicial review as exclusionary uses of these factors.[77] He further argues that any inquiry into race-conscious state action must necessarily include an investigation into its context. While conceding that an elevated standard of review was appropriate, Justice Breyer criticizes the use of strict scrutiny in the context of "racial limits that seek, not to keep the races apart, but to bring them together."[78]

Even under the application of strict scrutiny, Justice Breyer contends, Seattle and Jefferson County had articulated a compelling interest – and chosen means narrowly tailored to achieve it. The interest, according to Justice Breyer, is "integration" of the public schools. He defines it as "the school districts' interest in eliminating school-by-school racial isolation and increasing the degree to which racial mixture characterizes each of the district's schools and each individual student's public school experience."[79] Justice Breyer further argues that this interest had three compelling elements within it: (1) a remedial element to address historic segregation; (2) an educational element to combat the adverse pedagogical effects of segregated schools; and (3) a democratic element to produce schools reflecting our diverse, pluralistic nation.[80] Justice Breyer disputes the majority's attempts to distinguish between interests in higher education versus elementary and high schools. Channeling the spirit of the *Brown* Court, Justice Breyer notes, "Primary and secondary schools are where the education of this Nation's children begins, where each of us begins to absorb those values we carry with us to the end of our days."[81]

The four-justice minority also concludes that the means chosen by the defendant school districts were narrowly tailored to achieve their stated compelling interest. As Justice Breyer explains:

[76] *Id.* at 809.
[77] *Id.* at 832.
[78] *Id.* at 835, 837.
[79] *Id.* at 838.
[80] *Id.* at 838–840.
[81] *Id.* at 842.

The upshot is that these plans' specific features – (1) their limited and historically diminishing use of race, (2) their strong reliance upon other non-race-conscious elements, (3) their history and the manner in which the districts developed and modified their approach, (4) the comparison with prior plans, and (5) the lack of reasonably evident alternatives – together show that the districts' plans are "narrowly tailored" to achieve their "compelling" goals. In sum, the districts' race-conscious plans satisfy "strict scrutiny" and are therefore lawful.

Justice Breyer ends his dissenting opinion by appealing to the tradition of judicial restraint – allowing the citizenry to find the best path forward within the broad bounds of the Constitution. He concludes, "the Constitution creates a democratic political system through which the people themselves must together find answers. And it is for them to debate how best to educate the Nation's children and how best to administer America's schools to achieve that aim. The Court should leave them to their work."[82]

It is altogether fitting that, in a case in which the pursuit of the educational benefits of diversity did not receive the endorsement of the majority, Justice Breyer's dissent appeals to social constructivism. In his view, the path forward will be found only by citizens working together. This inclusive perspective, coupled with a clear appreciation for diversity, offers an uplifting vision of the power of education.

In light of the various opinions in *PICS*, a school district that would like to create racially diverse learning environments because the district genuinely believes – as the research indicates – that such environments are in the educational best interests of students is at some risk. To take one example *PICS* also declares unconstitutional the school assignment plan employed by the Jefferson County, Kentucky, school district. Jefferson County had been under a federal court order *requiring* it to utilize race-conscious measures to integrate its schools, including individual classifications of students based on race. The court order was lifted in 2001 because of the district's success in achieving racial integration. The district, however, voluntarily continued its student assignment plans after the court order was lifted. The district determined that its sustained effort to desegregate its schools had produced significant educational benefits for all students, and decided to continue the program that it had implemented pursuant to the original court order.

The Supreme Court, however, concludes that the district's voluntary continuation of its race-conscious student assignment program was unconstitutional. In other words, the Equal Protection Clause *required* those strategies until they were successful, and then *prohibited* their continuation. After *PICS*, the Jefferson County school district, which encompasses Louisville, found itself in an unenviable position. After pursuing educationally beneficial policies for decades as required by the courts, the district was told that it may no longer continue those policies voluntarily. Nonetheless, the district responded to *PICS* by declaring its commitment to finding

---

[82] *Id.* at 862.

a constitutionally permissible method of achieving racial integration, including student assignment strategies based on income levels rather than race.[83]

It is clear that "affirmative," race-conscious devices may, and indeed must, be employed to remedy a constitutional violation caused by the maintenance of a dual school system. If so, seemingly, race-conscious decision-making by public officials in their efforts to *avoid* maintaining an unconstitutional dual school system cannot be unconstitutional. Yet, after *PICS*, controlling precedent enshrines this conundrum as the law of the land.

Beyond the practical implications of *PICS*, the opinion raises profound questions about the proper interpretation of both the Equal Protection Clause and *Brown* v. *Board of Education*. Chief Justice Roberts argues that the Equal Protection Clause requires that all governmental decisions and programs be "color blind." He finds in *Brown* the principle that no state may assign children to its schools based on their race. Accordingly, he concludes his opinion by asserting that "[t]he way to stop discrimination on the basis of race is to stop discriminating on the basis of race."[84]

The dissenters, of course, find in the Equal Protection Clause a precise prohibition on government action that discriminates against children because of their race. Calling Chief Justice Roberts's opinion a "cruel distortion of history," the dissenters show that the Equal Protection Clause distinguishes between prohibited efforts to continue racial segregation and lawful efforts to achieve racial integration.[85] Thus, the dissent argues that *Brown* declared unconstitutional the legalized separation and subordination of African American schoolchildren, a constitutional violation remedied by strong, effective, and race-conscious measures designed to achieve racial integration. If racial integration is the remedy to the constitutional violation found in *Brown*, how could *Brown* then be read to declare unconstitutional efforts to achieve such integration? The dissent concludes that the Court's holding threatens the "promise of *Brown*."[86]

EFFECTS OF RECENT SUPREME COURT HOLDINGS ON STUDENT BODY COMPOSITION AND LEARNING OUTCOMES

The Court's recent rejection of challenges to segregation and resegregation has had a significant impact on the racial composition of American schools. American "schools are becoming more segregated in all regions for both African American and Latino students."[87] In particular, the evidence shows that since the early 1990s,

---

[83] See Emily Bazelon, "The Next Kind of Integration," N.Y. *Times*, July 20, 2008, hwww.nytimes.com/2008/07/20/magazine/20integration-t.html?pagewanted=all.
[84] 551 U.S. 748.
[85] *Id.* at 832.
[86] *Id.* at 868.
[87] See Gary Orfield & Chungmei Lee, "*Brown* at 50: King's Dream or Plessy's Nightmare?" Harv. C.R. Project, at 2 (Jan. 2004).

when the Supreme Court began to dilute court-ordered desegregation efforts, "there has been a major increase in segregation."[88] Throughout the nation, "Blacks and Latinos attend schools where two-thirds of the students are Black and Latino and most students are from their own group."[89] Since 1988, the percentage of African American students attending a majority white school has declined from 43.5 percent to 30.2 percent.[90]

There is a stunning link between racial segregation and poverty. While only 15 percent of the intensely segregated white students attend schools with concentrated poverty, 88 percent of the intensely segregated minority students attend schools with concentrated poverty.[91] "Intensely segregated" is generally understood to mean a school in which 90 percent of students are of the same race.[92] Furthermore, minority children in highly segregated minority schools with concentrated poverty

> tend to be less healthy, to have weaker preschool experiences, to have only one parent, to move frequently and have unstable educational experiences, to attend classes taught by less experienced or unqualified teachers, to have friends and classmates with lower levels of achievement, to be in schools with fewer demanding precollegiate courses and more remedial courses, and to have higher teacher turnover. Many of these schools are also deteriorated and lack key resources.[93]

There is significant evidence showing that the academic achievement levels of African American students, as measured by standardized tests, increased for students learning in an integrated educational environment.[94] This offers a powerful support to the consensus among educators that, sadly, was not fully embraced in *PICS*: a diverse learning environment helps all students regardless of race. For reasons relating mainly to funding disparities across districts, minority students stand to bear the brunt of the negative effects associated with resegregation in elementary and high schools.[95] However, studies such as these suggest that students of all races will suffer from the deprivation of a diverse learning environment that inevitably accompanies resegregation.

---

[88] *Id.*
[89] *Id.* at 17.
[90] *Id.* at 21. See also Chemerinsky, Segregation and Resegregation of American Public Education.
[91] *Id.* at 21.
[92] *Id.*
[93] *Id.* at 21–22. *See also* Kevin Carey, "The Funding Gap: Low-Income and Minority Students Still Receive Fewer Dollars, in Many States," *Educ. Trust*, at 6–9 (Fall 2003).
[94] *See* Orfield & Lee, "*Brown* at 50," at 53; Robert Crain & Rita Mahard, *Desegregation Plans That Raise Black Achievement: A Review of the Research*, 35–45 (Santa Monica, CA: Rand Corporation, 1982); William Taylor, "*Brown*, Equal Protection and the Isolation of the Poor," 95 YALE L.J. 1700, 1710–1711 (1986).
[95] For a full treatment of disparities in educational funding – and their disproportionate effect on minority students – see Chapter 6.

CONCLUSION

For fifty-eight years, the "separate but equal" doctrine announced in *Plessy v. Ferguson* permitted *de jure* segregation – or segregation reinforced by the very terms of the law – in the United States. After a heroic, decades-long effort led by advocates such as Charlie Houston and Thurgood Marshall, the *Brown* Court overruled *Plessy* and declared segregation in public schools unconstitutional. It took nearly two hundred years, but at long last the United States had opened the doors of its public schools to all students. The nation could finally implement the vision of the Founders, including Benjamin Rush. All citizens now had the chance to learn alongside one another, making new discoveries by constructing meaningful relationships. In May of 1954, the possibilities seemed endless.

Despite the soaring rhetoric of the unanimous opinion authored by Chief Justice Warren, the implementation of *Brown* has proved uneven at best. The "all deliberate speed" standard for desegregation proclaimed by *Brown II* only encouraged elaborate, bizarre, and, above all, damaging schemes to maintain effectively segregated school systems. While the more direct language and detailed instructions offered in *Swann* helped mitigate the problem, a series of subsequent decisions curtailed the effectiveness of desegregation efforts. *Milliken* barred courts from crafting desegregation plans involving multiple districts absent a nearly impossible showing; due to the pervasive segregation in housing patterns, this made unitary districts practically impossible in many communities. *Freeman* appeared to walk back the necessity to create a unitary district in all respects – signaling a more tolerant approach to ongoing badges and incidents of segregation. *Jenkins* constrained the discretion previously available to district court judges in their attempts to craft desegregation plans.

Most recently, *PICS* signaled a mixed attitude on the part of the Supreme Court toward the benefits of diversity and called for a color-blind approach that would likely have seemed dubious to the *Swann* Court. It also reached the counterintuitive result of prohibiting districts from voluntarily taking measures that the Court had repeatedly imposed as mandatory under the terms of desegregation orders. In the case of Jefferson County, Kentucky, this meant that the very policies deemed constitutionally mandatory for nearly thirty years became unconstitutional the moment the district was declared unitary. *PICS* certainly complicated the application of the principles espoused in *Brown*.

Nearly sixty-five years after *Brown*, advocates for full integration in education are both cheered by the opinion's language and dismayed by its application. The tension in the subsequent cases can be summarized as an ongoing argument over where to draw the line between necessary measures to insure equal opportunity and unnecessary micromanaging in pursuit of indefinite goals. Of course, few observers would draw this line in the exact same place. As we will see, this same tension between accepting the need for equal opportunity and defining the steps necessary to achieve it permeates the debate over the use of race as part of admissions policies in higher education.

5

Voluntary Race-Conscious Admissions Policies in Higher Education

This chapter will analyze voluntary efforts by university officials to more fully integrate the nation's institutions of higher education through the use of race-conscious admissions policies. As the chapter will show, the Supreme Court has declared unconstitutional most efforts to remedy racial segregation, including numerous admissions programs in higher education. Under current law, educational institutions may take race into account in their decision-making for only two reasons. First, a university may consider race in a manner that is narrowly tailored to remedy its own prior proven act of intentional racial segregation. Second, a university may consider race in admissions policies which are narrowly tailored to achieve the educational benefits of student body diversity, broadly conceived.

The Supreme Court has drawn a sharp distinction between desegregation programs designed to remedy specific constitutional violations and race-conscious admissions programs developed to combat generalized societal discrimination.[1] As this chapter will demonstrate, the Court views attempts to address the latter far more suspiciously than efforts to correct the former. In practice, the approach followed by the Court over the past four decades forces universities to tread delicately along a narrow path when implementing a race-conscious admissions policy. Measures that would be encouraged as part of a court-ordered desegregation plan are chastised as unconstitutional in the context of voluntary race-conscious admissions programs in higher education. A similar dynamic was present in the *PICS* opinion discussed in the previous chapter.

Before discussing the Court's seminal *Bakke* decision, a brief overview of the context in which the case arose proves useful. As the 1960s drew to a close, Civil Rights leaders began to shift their focus from the clear, *de jure* discrimination practiced under Jim Crow to the subtle, *de facto* discrimination prevalent throughout the country. Coupled with this was an accompanying emphasis on greater parity between blacks and whites in all areas of American life. In 1965, President Lyndon

---

[1] While "affirmative action" and "race-conscious admissions" are often used interchangeably or conflated, this book will use the former to refer to employment programs and the latter to refer to higher education initiatives.

Johnson delivered a commencement speech to the graduates of Howard University. His address not only illustrated the ongoing shift in emphasis but also foreshadowed the questions that continue to vex Americans today.

> You do not take a person who, for years, has been hobbled by chains and liberate him, bring him up to the starting line of a race and then say, "You are free to compete with all the others," and still justly believe that you have been completely fair.
>
> Thus it is not enough just to open the gates of opportunity. All our citizens must have the ability to walk through those gates.
>
> This is the next and the more profound stage of this battle for civil rights. We seek not just freedom but opportunity. We seek not just legal equity but human ability, not just equality as a right and a theory, but equality as a fact and equality as a result.
>
> For the task is to give 20 million Negroes the same chance as every other American to learn and grow, to work and share in society, to develop their abilities—physical, mental and spiritual, and to pursue their individual happiness.
>
> To this end equal opportunity is essential, but not enough, not enough. Men and women of all races are born with the same range of abilities. But ability is not just the product of birth. Ability is stretched or stunted by the family you live with, and the neighborhood you live in – by the school you go to and the poverty or the richness of your surroundings. It is the product of a hundred unseen forces playing upon the little infant, the child, and the man.[2]

In the half century following Johnson's speech, the United States has struggled to provide equal opportunity, particularly in the realm of education. It has met with still more difficulty in attempting to mitigate the "hundred unseen forces" of which Johnson spoke. The process of removing barriers to equal opportunity which rise not through discriminatory laws but rather through broader societal inequities has proved contentious. It is comparatively easy to persuade the public to repeal laws which discriminate on their very terms; it is much more difficult to convince individuals who, in many cases, have not personally practiced discrimination to support initiatives which could operate to their disadvantage.

Moreover, all these developments have occurred during a time in which the boundless optimism that characterized the immediate postwar period has been largely absent from American public life. The development of race-conscious admissions policies has occurred in an era marked by increasing economic insecurity. A perceived scarcity of meaningful employment and the indisputable skyrocketing of college tuition have combined to create voters who, in many respects, feel more economic pressure than their predecessors who cheered the result in *Brown*. An ever-increasing emphasis on higher education as the sole route to material security – an emphasis not remotely as accentuated during the 1950s and 1960s – has also emerged. Accordingly, a considerable number of Americans view their

---

[2] https://teachingamericanhistory.org/library/document/commencement-address-at-howard-university-to-fulfill-these-rights/ (Accessed May 30, 2019).

children's acceptance at a competitive university as a very serious matter for their children's future wellbeing. As such, any developments that would hamper their children's chances for acceptance – regardless of the rationale behind such developments – can provoke negative reactions.

This context helps explain why the battles fought over race-conscious admissions policies in higher education have sparked such widespread controversy. Opening the schoolhouse doors to every child does not necessarily deprive anyone. Filling limited seats at a university, on the other hand, is more of a zero-sum game. One applicant's success could directly result in another applicant's rejection. In a sense, this outlook demonstrates the ongoing impact of premising an educational system based largely on behaviorist theories. Under this point of view, a benefit accorded to someone else can only result in one's personal detriment. Rather than preparing a citizenry to develop new knowledge by constructing meaningful relationships with one another, behaviorism pits them against each other. It takes people who should be collaborators, colleagues, and friends and makes them competitors, strangers, and adversaries. This tragic misunderstanding of the way human beings learn and live has, unsurprisingly, prevented both this nation and untold millions of its citizens from realizing their full potential.

Labor historian David Hamilton Goddard summarizes this dilemma succinctly. Though his analysis focuses on the employment market, his observations pertain to the dynamic of competitive university admissions equally well. He writes,

> Equal employment opportunity, by contrast (to desegregation), pertained to the allocation of a limited resource – jobs. By attempting to give members of historically disadvantaged groups a better chance to obtain jobs that had traditionally been limited to whites, affirmative action had the potential to alienate large segments of white society that viewed school desegregation and voting rights from a neutral or even a positive standpoint. By attempting to establish true equality of opportunity, affirmative action meant that some whites ... stood to lose the jobs or potential jobs that their skin color had entitled them to in the past. Thus affirmative action was – and continues to be – controversial.[3]

Just as race-conscious admissions policies drew some thematic inspiration from affirmative action in employment, so too did a labor law case set the stage for *Bakke*. In 1971, the Supreme Court handed down its unanimous 8–0 ruling in *Griggs v. Duke Power Co.*[4] Crucially, the Court held that an employer's subjective intent does not matter for the purposes of a Title VII employment discrimination inquiry. Instead, a reviewing court must review the objective effects of the challenged policy.[5] As Chief Justice Burger formulated it, "good intent or absence of discriminatory intent does not redeem employment procedures or testing mechanisms that

---

[3] Ibid. at 3.
[4] 401 U.S. 424. Justice Brennan did not participate in the case.
[5] *Id.* at 432.

operate as 'built-in headwinds' for minority groups and are unrelated to measuring job capacity."[6]

Later, the Court addressed the role of standardized tests in determining employment. The Court cautioned employers that reviewing judges would not permit discrimination in the guise of a test measuring qualities irrelevant to the employer's needs. "What Congress has commanded is that any tests used must measure the person for the job and not the person in the abstract."[7] In other words, the Court called on employers to engage in at least a modicum of individualized review as opposed to designing a system that would produce results based solely on the applicant's race.

Seven years later, the *Bakke* Court would permit colleges to include an applicant's race in its considerations of the applicant's merits. It would, however, summarily reject the use of quotas or mechanical evaluations of an applicant's race. A university, as we will see, can only consider an applicant's race in the context of what that particular student's experiences and background could contribute to the incoming class. To borrow Chief Justice Burger's phrase, universities engaging in race-conscious admissions programs can use race only to measure the applicant for a fit within the university and not the applicant in the abstract.

UNIVERSITY OF CALIFORNIA REGENTS V. BAKKE: DISREGARDING THE BADGES AND INCIDENTS OF SLAVERY

In *Bakke* the Supreme Court addressed for the first time the constitutionality of race-conscious admissions policies in higher education. The case, decided in 1978, concerned a race-conscious admissions plan operated by University of California, Davis Medical School.

UC Davis implemented what it called a "special admissions program." Essentially, the program functioned as a parallel track open only to "disadvantaged" prospective students.[8] Sixteen out of one hundred seats in the class were set aside for applicants from the special admissions program. In practice, applicants from this program could compete for all one hundred seats; their counterparts who did not qualify for the program could compete only for eighty-four seats. The record revealed that, during the year at issue, only racial minorities could participate in the special admissions program.[9]

By a slim five to four majority, the Court deemed strict scrutiny the appropriate standard of review. For the Court, Justice Powell declined UC Davis' invitation to characterize race-conscious admissions programs, which disfavor white applicants on the basis of race, as "benign." He reasoned that the language of the Equal

[6] *Id.*
[7] *Id.* at 436.
[8] 438 U.S. 272.
[9] *Id.* at 276.

Protection Clause of the Fourteenth Amendment applied to all racial distinctions by state actors – regardless of the motivation and regardless of the identities of the favored and disfavored groups.[10] Led by Justice Brennan, a bloc of four justices argued in favor of applying intermediate scrutiny (the standard of review developed for gender discrimination cases) to race-conscious admissions policies.[11] Justice Brennan reasoned that the stigma – or, in other words motive – for drawing racial distinctions determines the standard of review. He concluded that any injury suffered by a white student who was denied admission bore no resemblance to the stigma endured by minorities who suffered under countless examples of discrimination. This qualitative difference in injury, reasoned Justice Brennan, demanded a qualitative difference in judicial review.

The resolution of this crucial threshold question would determine not only the outcome of *Bakke* but also the course of the Court's jurisprudence on race-conscious admissions policies. Where Justice Brennan would have required an "exceedingly persuasive" justification for race-conscious admissions policies, the Court demanded any such policies be narrowly tailored to achieve a compelling state interest. The Brennan approach would have vindicated UC Davis' program and paved the way for a much more robust regime of affirmative action in higher education. Under the Powell approach, however, universities found themselves with far fewer options for crafting more diverse student bodies.

During the litigation, UC Davis proffered four goals (or, constitutionally speaking, "interests") that it sought to pursue through the special admissions program. Specifically, UC Davis sought to: (1) encourage higher minority representation in the medical profession; (2) fight the effects of societal discrimination; (3) increase the number of physicians serving minority communities; and (4) pursue the educational benefits that flow from a diverse student body.[12]

Writing for a divided Court, Justice Powell summarily rejected UC Davis' minority representation argument.[13] He concluded that the Constitution clearly forbade any attempts by higher education institutions to seek a specific racial composition for their class.

Similarly, he reasoned that UC Davis' interest in fighting "societal discrimination" was far too vague to survive strict scrutiny.[14] He concluded that the Court required specific instances of discrimination – demonstrated by judicial, legislative, or administrative findings – in order to justify such a drastic remedy.

In addition, Justice Powell concluded that UC Davis' interest in providing minority communities with more healthcare access was too attenuated to qualify as narrowly tailored.[15] The Court viewed the policy as having no effective

---

[10] *Id.* at 294.
[11] *Id.* at 361.
[12] *Id.* at 306.
[13] *Id.* at 307.
[14] *Id.*
[15] *Id.* at 310.

mechanism to insure students who professed an interest in serving minority communities would, in fact, serve minority communities upon graduating. In rejecting the University's goals of encouraging higher minority representation in the medical profession, combatting the effects of societal discrimination, and increasing the number of physicians serving minority communities, the Supreme Court disregarded the factual reality of racial discrimination throughout society. The Court effectively prohibited efforts to remedy the lingering badges and incidents of slavery.

Only the last of UC Davis' articulated interests – the pursuit of a diverse student body in order to attain the educational benefits of diversity – survived the Court's strict scrutiny inquiry.[16] That interest, of course, serves not just African Americans, but also white students in the educational institution. Although Justice Powell concluded that UC Davis' use of a parallel admissions track with explicitly reserved seats for minorities rendered the program unconstitutional, he accepted that universities could implement a properly structured race-conscious admissions regime. In laying out his vision for a constitutionally permitted race-conscious admissions program, Justice Powell attached the Harvard College Admissions Program as an appendix to his opinion.[17] Extolling the virtues of the Harvard approach, Justice Powell laid out his vision for the pursuit of diversity in higher education.

> It is not an interest in simple ethnic diversity, in which a specified percentage of the student body is in effect guaranteed to be members of selected ethnic groups, with the remaining percentage an undifferentiated aggregation of students. The diversity that furthers a compelling state interest encompasses a far broader array of qualifications and characteristics of which racial or ethnic origin is but a single though important element. . . .[18]
>
> In such an admissions program, race or ethnic background may be deemed a "plus" in a particular applicant's file, yet it does not insulate the individual from comparison with all other candidates for the available seats. . . .[19]
>
> In short, an admissions program operated in this way is flexible enough to consider all pertinent elements of diversity in light of the particular qualifications of each applicant, and to place them on the same footing for consideration, although not necessarily according them the same weight. . . .[20]
>
> This kind of program treats each applicant as an individual in the admissions process. The applicant who loses out on the last available seat to another candidate receiving a "plus" on the basis of ethnic background will not have been foreclosed from all consideration for that seat simply because he was not the right color or had the wrong surname. It would mean only that his combined qualifications, which may have included similar nonobjective factors, did not outweigh those of the other applicant. His qualifications would have been weighed fairly and competitively,

---

[16] Id. at 312.
[17] Id. at 321.
[18] Id. at 315.
[19] Id. at 317.
[20] Id.

and he would have no basis to complain of unequal treatment under the Fourteenth Amendment.[21]

The above paragraphs have, in effect, set the ground rules for race-conscious admissions policies in higher education for the last four decades. Universities may take race into account when determining their applicants' qualifications, but they may do so for the limited purpose of pursuing the educational benefits which flow from a diverse student body. Moreover, they may only do so in a manner in which all quotas, categorical classifications, numerical weights, and sweeping judgments are avoided. Universities may only consider race in the context of an individualized, holistic review akin to the process described in the Harvard admissions policy viewed so favorably by Justice Powell. While subsequent cases would refine the contours of the law in this area, they would all harken back to the basic framework expounded by Justice Powell.

THE IMPLICATIONS OF *BAKKE*

In *Bakke*, Justice Powell and Justice Brennan disagree on what is an acceptable justification for race-based admissions. According to Justice Powell, "the attainment of a diverse student body ... clearly is a constitutionally permissible goal for an institution of higher education. Academic freedom, though not a specifically enumerated constitutional right, long has been viewed as a special concern of the First Amendment."[22] However, Justice Brennan contends that "prior cases unequivocally show that a state government may adopt race-conscious programs if the purpose of such programs is to remove the disparate racial impact [the state's] actions might otherwise have and if there is reason to believe that the disparate impact is itself the product of past discrimination, whether its own or that of society at large."[23]

Justice Powell invalidates the Davis admissions program because some positions were set aside and only minorities could compete for those positions. For Justice Powell, there is no "facial intent to discriminate ... in an admissions program where race or ethnic background is simply [a 'plus'] – to be weighed fairly against other elements – in the selection process."[24] However, the amount of the "plus" factor is directly proportional to the number of minorities admitted because of the race-conscious program. In other words, the larger the target or critical mass, the larger the plus factor. If the plus factor is only a tie breaker between equally qualified candidates, then the only tie would be for the last position to be filled; in any other tie, both applicants would be either accepted or rejected. For the Harvard plan to have any significant impact, the plus factor must be large enough to insure that more minority students are admitted.

[21] *Id.* at 318.
[22] *Id.* at 312.
[23] *Id.* at 369.
[24] *Id.* at 318.

In practice, this limited approach continues to have profound implications for integration in higher education. All institutions seeking to increase minority enrollment must structure their policies around the concept of diversity. Diversity can survive strict scrutiny; considerations of social justice, racial advancement, or demographic balancing cannot. Colleges and universities must also avoid treating applicants as members of racial categories rather than as individuals. As subsequent cases demonstrate, the circumscribed approach mandated in *Bakke* has, if anything, grown even more restrictive in the ensuing years. This erosion of an already narrow precedent has complicated efforts to remove the badges and incidents of slavery and societal discrimination from American life.

During the quarter century following *Bakke*, the Supreme Court issued a series of rulings that were difficult to reconcile. In 1980, the Court upheld a federal statutory program that required the Commerce Department to set aside 10 percent of its grants to minority-owned or minority-controlled businesses.[25] Later, the Court affirmed the constitutionality of affirmative action programs for women.[26] The Court also upheld a governmental policy requiring the promotion of equal numbers of white and African American state police troopers.[27] In *City of Richmond v. J. A. Croson Co.* (1989), however, the Court declared unconstitutional a city program that set aside 30 percent of building contract funds for minority contractors, and in *Adarand Constructors Inc. v. Peña* (1995), the Court seemed to indicate clearly that the only racial affirmative action program that could survive "strict scrutiny" was one tailored to redress specific acts of proven past racial discrimination.[28]

Given this apparently ambiguous case law regarding affirmative action generally and the lack of any controlling authority after *Bakke* regarding race-conscious admissions policies in education, it is not surprising that the lower federal courts clung dearly to language in *Bakke* and ultimately reached conflicting results. In 1996, the Fifth Circuit struck down the University of Texas Law School's race-based admissions policy.[29] In 2002, however, the Sixth Circuit upheld the University of Michigan Law School's "affirmative action" regime.[30]

THE MICHIGAN CASES: POWELL'S NARROW FRAMEWORK BECOMES PRECEDENT

A quarter century after *Bakke*, the Court examined the companion cases of *Grutter* and *Gratz*. Both cases emerged out of policies implemented at the University of Michigan. *Grutter* concerned the admissions policy at the law school, while *Gratz* dealt with the policy used for undergraduates. The differences in the policies

---

[25] See *Fullilove v. Klutznick*, 448 U.S. 448 (1980).
[26] See *Johnson v. Transportation Agency, Santa Clara County*, 480 U.S. 616 (1987).
[27] See *United States v. Paradise*, 480 U.S. 149 (1987).
[28] 488 U.S. 469 and 515 U.S. 200, respectively.
[29] See *Hopwood v. Texas*, 78 F.3d 932 (5th Cir. 1996).
[30] See *Bollinger v. Grutter*, 288 F.3d 732 (6th Cir. 2002).

illuminate the Court's criteria in race-conscious admissions policies cases within higher education. Language from the *Fisher* opinions suggests that, together with *Bakke*, these two cases remain the law of the land.

In *Grutter*, Justice O'Connor begins her analysis by discussing in "detail" Justice Powell's opinion in *Bakke*, declaring that the opinion has provided the model of race-conscious admissions policies followed by public and private educational institutions. Recall that Justice Powell's opinion was not the Court's opinion in *Bakke*. Nonetheless, the lower courts, including the Sixth Circuit, had concluded that they were bound by that opinion because it represented the "narrowest grounds" on which five members of the *Bakke* Court agreed. In *Grutter*, the Supreme Court expressly adopts Powell's approach as the Court's framework: "Today we endorse Justice Powell's view that student body diversity is a compelling state interest that can justify the use of race in university admissions."[31]

The majority rejects the concept implicit in *Croson* and *Adarand* that "the only governmental use of race that can survive strict scrutiny is remedying past discrimination." The Court proceeds to declare that there is a "compelling state interest in student body diversity."[32] The Court is careful to qualify that interest as the "Law School's" interest and as an interest in the "context of higher education."[33]

Writing for the Court, Justice O'Connor places great store in the holistic definition of diversity employed by the University of Michigan Law School.

> The policy aspires to "achieve that diversity which has the potential to enrich everyone's education and thus make a law school class stronger than the sum of its parts." The policy does not restrict the types of diversity contributions eligible for "substantial weight" in the admissions process, but instead recognizes many possible bases for diversity admissions. . . .
>
> The policy does not define diversity "solely in terms of racial and ethnic status." Nor is the policy "insensitive to the competition among all students for admission to the [L]aw [S]chool." Rather, the policy seeks to guide admissions officers in "producing classes both diverse and academically outstanding, classes made up of students who promise to continue the tradition of outstanding contribution by Michigan Graduates to the legal profession."[34] (Internal citations omitted)

It requires no great leap of the imagination to conclude that the administrators of the University of Michigan Law School had thoroughly read and digested Justice Powell's opinion in *Bakke* before crafting their policy. By using the Harvard policy praised by Justice Powell as its template, the Law School positioned itself to comfortably satisfy strict scrutiny once the Court expressly adopted the Powell approach as precedent.

---

[31] 539 U.S. 306, 325.
[32] *Id.*
[33] *Id.* at 342.
[34] *Id.* at 315–516.

The *Grutter* Court alludes to the following "substantial" benefits of a diverse student body: (1) educational benefits; (2) an increase in the "robust" exchange of ideas; (3) cross-racial understanding; (4) breaking down racial stereotypes; (5) livelier, more spirited, enlightening, and interesting classroom discussions; (6) the promotion of learning "outcomes"; (7) better preparation of students to work and interact in an "increasingly diverse" society and workforce; (8) better preparation as professionals in an "increasingly global marketplace"; (9) helping the military to fulfill its very mission of "national security"; (10) facilitating the "diffusion of knowledge and opportunity through public institutions of higher education" to be accessible to all individuals and thereby sustaining our "political and cultural heritage"; (11) fostering the effective participation by members of all racial and ethnic groups which is vital to becoming *one* nation; (12) supporting the training in law school for diverse national leaders and thereby cultivating leaders with legitimacy; and (13) developing attorneys of diverse races and ethnicities who will be able, in turn, to help all members of a "heterogeneous society" succeed.

The Court makes clear that diversity is not just about race, but includes the variety of backgrounds and experiences which students bring to the educational environment. The majority opinion, however, says little of how underrepresented minority applicants, by virtue of their history of underrepresentation, may have qualities that by definition enhance their law school qualifications. Instead, the Court speaks primarily of the state's interest in a diverse student body.

In the years since *Grutter*, the overwhelming weight of empirical research has validated the Court's conclusion that student body diversity is a compelling governmental interest. Student body diversity produces measurable educational benefits for *both* minority and nonminority students, including promoting cross-racial understanding, reducing prejudice and stereotyping, and fostering professional development, civic engagement, and leadership.[35] Moreover, the latest neuroscientific research also demonstrates that student body diversity creates significant improvements in the cognitive abilities of all students, including critical thinking and problem-solving skills.[36] In particular, when a student is exposed to thoughts, ideas, backgrounds, and perspectives that are different from his or her own, that

---

[35] See, e.g., Nida Denson & Mitchell Chang, "Racial Diversity Matters: The Impact of Diversity-Related Student Engagement and Institutional Context," 46 *Am. Educ. Res. J.* 322 (2009); Nida Denson, "Do Curricular and Co-curricular Diversity Activities Influence Racial Bias? A Meta-analysis," 79 *Rev. Educ. Res.* 805 (2009); Thomas Pettigrew & Linda Tropp, "How Does Intergroup Contact Reduce Prejudice? Meta-analytic Test of Three Mediators," 38 *Eur. J. Soc. Psychol.* 922 (2008); Victor Saenz et al., "Factors Influencing Positive Interactions Across Race for African American, Asian American, Latino and White College Students," 48 *Res. Higher Educ.* 1 (2007).

[36] See, e.g., Anthony Antonio et al., "Effects of Racial Diversity on Complex Thinking in College Students," 15 *Psych. Sci.* 507 (2004); Samuel Sommers et al., "Cognitive Effects of Racial Diversity: White Individual Information Processing in Heterogeneous Groups," 44 *J. Experimental Soc. Psychol.* 1129 (2008); Nicholas Bowman, "College Diversity Experiences and Cognitive Development: A Meta-analysis," 80 *Rev. Educ. Res.* 4 (2010).

student experiences cognitive disequilibrium, dissonance, and incongruity.[37] The student's brain then must work hard to process the information, to confront the dissonance, and to accommodate the unusual perspective. Regular encounters with diverse students increase the brain's capacity to process information and to engage in complex, higher-order thinking skills.

As the *Grutter* Court declares, the state must demonstrate that its compelling governmental interest in student body diversity is pursued by means that are "specifically and narrowly framed to accomplish that purpose."[38] The Court indicates that the "hallmarks of a narrowly tailored plan" include the following: (1) race is considered only as a "plus" factor, as part of an individualized, holistic review of each applicant, and not as a part of a "quota" system; (2) race is used in a flexible, nonmechanical way – specifically, a manner in which no quantifiable or numerical weight is automatically assigned to the applicant's race; (3) the institution's attention to numbers and "daily reports" of the racial composition of the admitted class serves its goal of attaining the benefits of student body diversity, rather than the impermissible aims of attaining a fixed percentage of minority students, balancing the class, or matching demographics external to the institution; (4) serious, good-faith consideration is given to workable race-neutral alternatives, but a university need not "(exhaust) every conceivable race neutral alternative"; (5) nonminority applicants are not unduly burdened because they are selected over underrepresented minority applicants where their experiences contribute to diversity; and (6) the criteria are limited in time through sunset provisions or periodic review.[39]

The Court finds that the law school's use of race as a factor, even a "plus" factor, as part of its "truly individualized consideration" of each applicant "bears the hallmarks of a narrowly tailored plan."[40] As long as the law school makes a "highly individualized, holistic review of each applicant's file," giving serious consideration to all the ways an applicant might contribute to a diverse educational environment, a race-conscious admissions policy will apparently satisfy the rigors of strict scrutiny. In *Gratz*, of course, the Supreme Court ruled that the state's undergraduate admissions policy, which automatically distributes twenty points (or one-fifth of the points needed to guarantee admission) to every single underrepresented minority solely based upon race, was not narrowly tailored to achieve educational diversity. The absence of an "individualized assessment" of every applicant and presence of a quantifiable numerical value assigned to the applicant's race as part of the admissions program's point system appear to be the fatal flaws in the undergraduate policy.[41]

---

[37] Richard Crisp & Rhiannon Turner, "Cognitive Adaptations to the Experience of Social and Cultural Diversity," 137 *Psych. Bull.* 242 (2011).
[38] 539 U.S. 306, 333.
[39] *Id.* at 337–342.
[40] *Id.* at 309.
[41] 539 U.S. 244, 274.

The *Grutter* Court declares that the "goal of attaining a critical mass of underrepresented minority students does not transform [a] program into a quota."[42] The Court recognizes that an educational institution may determine that the enrollment of a critical mass of underrepresented minorities is necessary to achieve the educational benefits of student body diversity. The Court describes critical mass as a "meaningful number" and says it requires enough underrepresented minorities that those enrolled do not feel as though they are stereotypical spokespeople for their group. In short, the Court permits institutions to pay some attention to numbers in the context of developing race-conscious admissions policies. Some attention to numbers does not in and of itself constitute a quota. Conceptually, the Court's comfort with an absence of precise metrics – atypical in a strict scrutiny inquiry – ties in well with Justice Powell's holistic, non-demographic view of diversity and his categorical rejection of racial balancing to match state demographics.

The definition of "critical mass" must be linked to the desired educational benefits of student body diversity. The number of underrepresented minorities in an educational environment must be large enough that the interactions among diverse students will occur with sufficient regularity inside and outside of the classroom to further the institution's educational objectives. A precise number is likely impossible to discern, and, in any event, will depend on the educational context. The latest research does show, however, that the educational benefits increase as the number of "contacts" between students of diverse groups increases.[43] In fact, because each "contact" between diverse students expands their cognitive capacities, regular contact among diverse students is critical to their full educational development.[44]

The absence of a meaningful number of diverse students in classrooms and in the educational community increases (1) daily incidents of micro-aggression against racial minorities, and (2) stereotype threat – the academic and emotional harm to isolated minority students who are made to fear that their academic performance will confirm negative stereotypes assigned to their group.[45]

In a portion of its opinion specifically ridiculed by the dissenters, the majority in *Grutter* defers to the educational expertise of the state of Michigan regarding the educational benefits flowing from a diverse student body. The majority relies on its tradition of deferring to local control and to the expertise of educational professionals.

---

[42] 539 U.S. 306, 335–336.
[43] See Thomas Pettigrew & Linda Tropp, "A Meta-analytic Test of Intergroup Contact Theory," 90 *J. Pers. & Soc. Psychol.* 751 (2006).
[44] See Nida Denson & Shirley Zhang, "The Impact of Student Experiences with Diversity on Developing Graduate Attributes," 35 *Higher Educ. Stud.* 529 (2010).
[45] See Derald Sue et al., *Microaggression in Everyday Life: Race, Gender and Sexual Orientation* (Hoboken, NJ: John Wiley & Sons, 2010); Janice McCabe, "Racial and Gender Microaggression on a Predominantly White Campus: Experiences of Black, Latina/o and White Undergraduates," 16 *Race Gender & Class* 133 (2009).

Significantly, the educational benefits created by student body diversity are not credibly undermined by speculation regarding "academic mismatch." The "academic mismatch" argument is based upon the notion that students admitted to "elite" academic institutions because of their race will not be sufficiently prepared to compete at that institution and therefore will not succeed.[46] The most recent evidence, however, has revealed that "the mismatch hypothesis ... is empirically groundless."[47] Minority students who are admitted to educational institutions pursuant to race-conscious admissions programs in fact generally outperform their academic credentials, experience significant academic success, complete their degree requirements, and report overall satisfaction with their educational experience.[48]

The fate of the race-conscious undergraduate admissions program developed by the University of Michigan – and roundly rejected by the Supreme Court in Gratz v. Bollinger – highlights the Court's emphasis on individualized review of applications for hallmarks of diversity, broadly conceived.[49] The majority took particular issue with the undergraduate program's blanket policy of awarding all members of an underrepresented racial minority twenty points (out of 100 needed for admission).[50] This award was automatic under the program, and made without any individualized review of the merits or qualities of any particular applicant who was a member of a racial minority.[51] Coupled with the ambiguous role of the admissions committee in delivering an individualized review for each applicant, this mechanical distribution of bonus points proved fatal for the policy. Writing for the majority, Justice Rehnquist concluded that while Michigan cited a compelling interest in attaining the educational benefits of diversity, its means were not narrowly tailored to that end.[52] Notably, the majority in Gratz joined the majority in Grutter in explicitly adopting Justice Powell's view that the pursuit of the educational benefits that flow from a diverse student body is a compelling interest sufficient to survive strict scrutiny.[53]

Together, the so-called Michigan cases of Grutter and Gratz stand for the proposition that any race-conscious admissions program in higher education must (1)

---

[46] See Richard Sander, "A Systematic Analysis of Affirmative Action in American Law Schools," 57 STAN. L. REV. 1963 (2005).

[47] See Sigal Alon & Marta Tienda, "Assessing the 'Mismatch' Hypothesis: Differences in College Graduation Rates by Institutional Selectivity," 78 Soc. Educ. 294 (2005). See also Katherine Barnes, "Is Affirmative Action Responsible for the Achievement Gap Between Black and White Law Students? A Correlation, A Lesson and an Update," 105 NW. U. L. REV. 791 (2011).

[48] See Mary Fischer & Douglas Massey, "The Effects of Affirmative Action in Higher Education," 36 Soc. Sci. Rev. 531 (2007); Ian Ayers & Richard Brooks, "Does Affirmative Action Reduce the Number of Black Lawyers?," 57 STAN. L. REV. (2005).

[49] 539 U.S. 244 (2003).

[50] Id. at 256.

[51] Id.

[52] Id. at 269.

[53] Id. at 268.

feature an individualized, holistic review of each applicant and (2) take a broad view of diversity which embraces more than an applicant's racial background. Yet, the Michigan cases also serve to complicate the path a university implementing a race-conscious admissions program must walk. On the one hand, both opinions categorically reject the use of quotas or assignment of automatic numerical values to a candidate's race. On the other hand, several justices signal their disdain for the seemingly amorphous, unquantifiable quality of the critical mass concept advanced in *Grutter*. Moreover, further ambiguity arises regarding the nature and limits of the "deference" afforded by reviewing courts to the pedagogical judgment of university administrators. Barely a decade after *Grutter* and *Gratz*, a fact pattern would emerge that compelled the Court to explore these precise areas of ambiguity.

FISHER I AND II: DEFINING THE LIMITS OF DEFERENCE UNDER STRICT SCRUTINY

In *Fisher v. University of Texas* (*Fisher I*), the Supreme Court revisited the constitutionality of race-conscious admissions policies.[54] In an opinion authored by Justice Kennedy, the Court vacated the appellate court's decision upholding the Texas plan and remanded the action for strict judicial scrutiny of whether the plan is narrowly tailored to achieve the educational benefits of student body diversity.

In its cases leading up to *Fisher*, the Supreme Court developed guidelines for judicial scrutiny of race-conscious educational decisions. A court must make sure that the educational institution's interest in achieving the educational benefits of student body diversity is "compelling" and that the means employed by the institution have the "hallmarks" of a narrowly tailored plan to achieve the educational benefits of student body diversity.

Throughout recent race-based admissions cases, the Court has recognized that achieving the educational benefits which flow from student body diversity is a "compelling" governmental interest that could justify an educational institution's consideration of race. Justice Kennedy's opinion in *Fisher* recognizes that "compelling" interest. He writes, the "attainment of a diverse student body ... serves values beyond race alone, including enhanced classroom dialogue and the lessening of racial isolation and stereotypes."[55]

The Court did not overturn *Grutter*. In his separate concurrence, however, Justice Thomas stated that he would overrule *Grutter* and hold that a state's use of race in higher education admissions is categorically prohibited by the Equal Protection Clause. In addition, Justice Scalia wrote a separate concurrence to emphasize the fact that the parties did not ask the Court to reverse *Grutter*, and therefore he was unwilling to do so.

---

[54] 570 U.S. ___ (2013), (Slip Op.).
[55] *Id.* at 6.

In *Fisher*, the Court reaffirms that an educational institution's judgment that student body diversity is essential to its mission, which is based on its "experience and expertise," is entitled to judicial deference even in the context of strict scrutiny.[56] The courts must require the institution to provide a "reasoned, principled explanation" for its educational objectives, and the institution cannot define its objectives by reference to a specified quota, percentage or balance of racial groups. Nonetheless, the courts must still defer to an institution's educated judgment about the level and nature of diversity that is required to produce the educational benefits it seeks.

The *Fisher* Court, however, makes clear that an educational institution is not entitled to any judicial deference on the question of whether the means it has chosen to achieve the educational benefits of diversity are "narrowly tailored." Rather, the institution must demonstrate that its admissions processes have the following hallmarks of narrow-tailoring: (1) each applicant is evaluated as an individual; (2) the race of the applicant is a meaningful, but not a "defining" feature of the application; and (3) the institution has considered workable race-neutral alternatives, and no such alternative would produce the educational benefits of diversity.[57] In order to survive strict scrutiny, the educational institution must demonstrate that "available, workable race-neutral alternatives do not suffice." To meet that burden, however, the institution may show that it conducted a serious, good-faith consideration of race-neutral alternatives, and that those alternatives: (1) were not "workable"; (2) created intolerable "administrative expense"; (3) did not promote the institution's educational objectives as well as race-conscious measures; or (4) did not "achieve sufficient diversity" to realize the educational benefits sought by the institution.[58]

The University of Texas at Austin argued that its race-conscious admissions plan was necessary to achieve a "critical mass" of diverse students in classrooms and programs throughout the University. The University reached the informed judgment that the educational benefits of student body diversity were produced only if there were meaningful numbers of diverse students interacting with each other in the educational environment. Significantly, the Court in *Fisher* did not reject the concept of "critical mass." It thereby left intact the possibility that administrators could reach the pedagogical judgment that the educational benefits of diversity only flow if there is a "critical mass" of diverse students in classrooms, common areas, and departments. An educational institution could meet its strict scrutiny burden by showing that race-conscious decisions are necessary to produce a critical mass of diverse students throughout the institution, which in turn is indispensable to meeting its compelling interest in realizing the educational benefits of diversity. In other words, the institution can meet its burden by demonstrating that none of the alternatives to race-conscious decisions will be "workable" because they will fail to

[56] *Id.* at 9.
[57] *Id.* at 10–11.
[58] *Id.*

produce levels of diversity that are "sufficient" to meet the institution's educational objectives.[59]

After the Supreme Court remanded the case to the Fifth Circuit for a rehearing conducted in accordance with the standards of strict scrutiny, the Fifth Circuit again upheld the University of Texas's (UT's) race-conscious admissions plan. Unsurprisingly, the Court granted certiorari, hearing arguments in late 2015. As in *Fisher I*, Justice Kagan recused herself from involvement in the case. The sudden death of Justice Scalia in February 2016 further reduced the *Fisher II* Court to seven members.

Writing for a four-justice majority, Justice Kennedy begins by recapitulating the principles emphasized in *Fisher I*.

> *Fisher I* set forth three controlling principles relevant to assessing the constitutionality of a public university's affirmative-action program. First, "because racial characteristics so seldom provide a relevant basis for disparate treatment," ... "[r]ace may not be considered [by a university] unless the admissions process can withstand strict scrutiny." Strict scrutiny requires the university to demonstrate with clarity that its "purpose or interest is both constitutionally permissible and substantial, and that its use of the classification is necessary ... to the accomplishment of its purpose."
>
> Second, *Fisher I* confirmed that "the decision to pursue 'the educational benefits that flow from student body diversity' ... is, in substantial measure, an academic judgment to which some, but not complete, judicial deference is proper." A university cannot impose a fixed quota or otherwise "define diversity as 'some specified percentage of a particular group merely because of its race or ethnic origin.'" Once, however, a university gives "a reasoned, principled explanation" for its decision, deference must be given "to the University's conclusion, based on its experience and expertise, that a diverse student body would serve its educational goals."
>
> Third, *Fisher I* clarified that no deference is owed when determining whether the use of race is narrowly tailored to achieve the university's permissible goals. A university, *Fisher I* explained, bears the burden of proving a "nonracial approach" would not promote its interest in the educational benefits of diversity "about as well and at tolerable administrative expense." Though "[n]arrow tailoring does not require exhaustion of every conceivable race-neutral alternative" or "require a university to choose between maintaining a reputation for excellence [and] fulfilling a commitment to provide educational opportunities to members of all racial groups," it does impose "on the university the ultimate burden of demonstrating" that "race-neutral alternatives" that are both "available" and "workable" "do not suffice."[60] (Internal citations omitted)

The Court next explains the mechanics of UT's admissions system. Due to a Texas law passed in response to *Hopwood* (in which the Fifth Circuit struck

---

[59] *Id.* at 11.
[60] 578 U.S. ___ (2016), (Slip Op.), 6–8.

down an earlier race-conscious admissions program at UT), any student graduating in the top ten percent of his or her high school class received automatic admission at UT. The effect of this law was to fill three quarters of the seats at UT without review of any factor other than the student's class rank.[61]

The remaining quarter of seats at UT were filled pursuant to the results of a holistic review, albeit applied in a more mechanical manner than the model Harvard program or the plan upheld in *Grutter*. UT ranked students by combining the scores of their Academic Index (AI) and Personal Achievement Index (PAI).[62] While the AI comprised an applicant's academic metrics, the PAI sought to add a holistic element to the admissions process. The PAI included two equally weighted essays as well as a Personal Achievement Score (PAS). The PAS was comprised of six equally weighted factors. One of these six factors ("Special Circumstances") included an applicant's race as one of seven components. Thus, an applicant's race under the UT plan comprised one-seventh of the Special Circumstances score. The Special Circumstances score made up one-sixth of the PAS. The PAS was one-third of the PAI, and the PAI was one-half of the overall score. Expressed numerically, race impacted, at most, $1/7 \times 1/6 \times 1/3 \times 1/2 = 1/252$ of an applicant's score.

This limited use of race, observes Justice Kennedy, was undertaken after a year-long study embarked on by UT after the *Grutter* decision. Moreover, the Court notes that UT had unusually limited discretion to admit and deny applicants due to the operation of the Top Ten Percent Plan imposed upon it by the Texas Legislature. Perhaps with these factors in mind, Justice Kennedy cautions: "The fact that this case has been litigated on a somewhat artificial basis, furthermore, may limit its value for prospective guidance."[63]

The Court then proceeds to rebut each of petitioner's four arguments. First, the Court concludes that UT articulated its compelling interest with sufficient clarity to survive strict scrutiny.[64] It notes that achieving the educational benefits of diversity cannot be measured solely by numerical metrics such as a rise in minority enrollment. UT's consistently presented goals included developing a robust academic environment characterized by an exchange of varied ideas and exposure to different cultures.[65] For the Court, this places UT within the letter and spirit of *Bakke* and *Grutter*.

Second, the Court rejects petitioner's contention that UT had already achieved a critical mass of minority students.[66] The Court accepts that UT's ongoing attention to the student body composition and undergraduate experience supported its good-faith determination that critical mass had not been reached. Moreover, this

---

[61] *Id.* at 3.
[62] *Id.* at 4.
[63] *Id.* at 10.
[64] *Id.* at 11.
[65] *Id.* at 13.
[66] *Id.* at 15.

monitoring does not cross the line into impermissible racial balancing or a *de facto* quota system. UT, per the Court, manages to tread the narrow path required of institutions considering race in admissions.

Third, the Court emphasizes that the "minimal impact" in minority enrollment traceable to UT's admissions plan is evidence of narrow tailoring rather than a sign of its absence.[67] The small, incremental results of the race-conscious admissions plan offer a powerful rejoinder to any argument that the program was unconstitutionally broad and vague in its approach.

Finally, the Court holds that any alternate measures proposed by petitioner were either attempted by UT, investigated thoroughly by administrators, or would entail sacrificing other types of diversity in favor of narrow racial demographics.[68] Justice Kennedy takes the opportunity to reiterate that the diversity permitted under the line of cases descending from *Bakke* involves far more than mere racial considerations.

> [Petitioner's proposed alternatives] are but examples of the general problem. Class rank is a single metric, and like any single metric, it will capture certain types of people and miss others. That does not imply that students admitted through holistic review are necessarily more capable or more desirable than those admitted through the Top Ten Percent Plan. It merely reflects the fact that privileging one characteristic above all others does not lead to a diverse student body. Indeed, to compel universities to admit students based on class rank alone is in deep tension with the goal of educational diversity as this Court's cases have defined it.[69]

Justice Kennedy concludes the Court's opinion by reiterating the need for a multifaceted and holistic approach to diversity in university admissions. He also reaffirms the special role filled by universities within the American system in forming leaders and democratic citizens.

> For all these reasons, although it may be true that the Top Ten Percent Plan in some instances may provide a path out of poverty for those who excel at schools lacking in resources, the Plan cannot serve as the admissions solution that petitioner suggests. Wherever the balance between percentage plans and holistic review should rest, an effective admissions policy cannot prescribe, realistically, the exclusive use of a percentage plan. In short, none of petitioner's suggested alternatives – nor other proposals considered or discussed in the course of this litigation – have been shown to be "available" and "workable" means through which the University could have met its educational goals, as it understood and defined them in 2008. *Fisher I*, 133 S. Ct., at 2420. The University has thus met its burden of showing that the admissions policy it used at the time it rejected petitioner's application was narrowly tailored.
>
> A university is in large part defined by those intangible "qualities which are incapable of objective measurement but which make for greatness." Sweatt

[67] *Id.* at 15–16.
[68] *Id.* at 17.
[69] *Id.*

v. Painter, 339 U.S. 629, 634 (1950). Considerable deference is owed to a university in defining those intangible characteristics, like student body diversity, that are central to its identity and educational mission. But still, it remains an enduring challenge to our Nation's education system to reconcile the pursuit of diversity with the constitutional promise of equal treatment and dignity.

In striking this sensitive balance, public universities, like the States themselves, can serve as "laboratories for experimentation." United States v. Lopez, 514 U.S. 549, 581 (1995) (Kennedy, J., concurring); see also New State Ice Co. v. Liebmann, 285 U.S. 262, 311 (1932) (Brandeis, J., dissenting). The University of Texas at Austin has a special opportunity to learn and to teach. The University now has at its disposal valuable data about the manner in which different approaches to admissions may foster diversity or instead dilute it. The University must continue to use this data to scrutinize the fairness of its admissions program; to assess whether changing demographics have undermined the need for a race-conscious policy; and to identify the effects, both positive and negative, of the affirmative-action measures it deems necessary.

The Court's affirmance of the University's admissions policy today does not necessarily mean the University may rely on that same policy without refinement. It is the University's ongoing obligation to engage in constant deliberation and continued reflection regarding its admissions policies.[70]

Just as the result in *Fisher II* infuriated opponents of race-conscious admissions policies, the reasoning left proponents of these programs less than satisfied. The Court's opinion is best read as a narrow preservation of a unique admissions scheme. It is not by any means a ringing, issue-settling endorsement of the use of race in admissions. The Court's repeated allusions to the singular attributes of UT's admissions policy as well as its emphasis on the unusual procedural posture of the case and incomplete state of the factual record all serve to muddy the waters. The language of *Fisher II* leaves the door open for arguments in future cases encouraging the Court to disregard *Fisher II* – distinguishing it based upon factual differences – and limit its future applicability. The prospects for *Fisher II* to have the broad reach of *Bakke* look dim.

At the time of writing, the Harvard University admissions policy extolled in *Bakke* is itself the subject of a lawsuit in a federal court within the District of Massachusetts. *Students for Fair Admissions v. Harvard University* alleges impermissible discrimination on the part of Harvard against Asian-Americans. The suit claims these students are systematically underrepresented at Harvard due to manipulation of a metric analogous to UT's "Special Circumstances" factor in order to lower Asian-American students' scores in the admissions process.

The case likely is destined for the Supreme Court. In the three years since *Fisher II*, the composition of the Court has shifted dramatically. While no one can predict the outcome of a particular case with exact precision, there appears to be a five-

[70] *Id.* 19–20.

justice bloc on the Court amenable to either overturning *Bakke* or dramatically limiting its application. Accordingly, the future of race-conscious admissions programs in higher education is by no means secure.

Such programs designed to combat the badges and incidents of segregation and discrimination are under pressure not only in the courts but also at ballot boxes across the country. As we will see, referenda challenging both affirmative action and race-conscious admissions policies have largely met with success in recent years. Since 2013, these efforts have had the backing of a favorable Supreme Court decision as well.

BALLOT INITIATIVES AIMED AT PROHIBITING RACE-CONSCIOUS ADMISSIONS POLICIES

In 1996, California voters passed Proposition 209, a ballot initiative that amends the California constitution to provide that the state "shall not discriminate against, or grant preferential treatment to, any individual or group on the basis of race, sex, color, ethnicity, or national origin in the operation of ... public education." The prohibition includes all California school districts and universities. In 1998, Washington voters passed a virtually identical ballot initiative. The Ninth Circuit upheld these ballot initiatives against constitutional challenges.[71]

In the wake of the Supreme Court's decision in *Grutter* allowing the University of Michigan to consider race as a factor in admissions to law school, the voters in Michigan enacted Proposal 2, which amends the Michigan Constitution to provide: "The University of Michigan ... and any other public college or university, community college, or school district shall not discriminate against, or grant preferential treatment to, any individual or group on the basis of race, sex, color, ethnicity, or national origin in the operation of public employment, public education, or public contracting."[72]

The language of these ballot initiatives appears to prohibit public educational institutions from granting any preferential treatment to any student or applicant "on the basis of" race or gender. By contrast, the Equal Protection Clause permits public educational institutions to give preferential treatment on the basis of race if narrowly tailored to achieve a compelling interest, and permits public educational institutions to give preferential treatment on the basis of gender if supported by an exceedingly persuasive justification. Accordingly, a public educational institution governed by these ballot initiatives may not be able to defend its racial or gender preferences by asserting compelling or persuasive interests such as the educational benefits of student body diversity.

---

[71] See, e.g., *Coalition to Defend Affirmative Action v. Brown*, 674 F.3d 1128 (9th Cir. 2012); *Coalition for Economic Equality v. Wilson*, 122 F.3d 692, 702 (9th Cir. 1997). ("Rather than classifying individuals by race or gender, Proposition 209 *prohibits* the State from classifying individuals by race or gender.")

[72] MICH. CONST. art. 1, §6.

On the other hand, the language of these initiatives prohibits only "preferences" on "the basis of" race or gender. That language does not prohibit preferences based on other characteristics, which may be proxies for race and gender. Justice Kennedy explored these possibilities in his concurrence in *PICS*. For example, a decision to admit an African American applicant to the University of California, Davis Law School for a host of reasons of which race is merely one part can be defended because that decision was not made on the basis of race. Race was not the causal factor, or even a substantial factor, in the decision. This shows that the use of race (or gender) as one of many factors in reaching an admissions decision (or a student assignment decision) does not necessarily run afoul of these ballot initiatives.

SCHUETTE V. BAMN: A BLOW TO RACE-CONSCIOUS ADMISSIONS POLICIES

In *Schuette*, a fractured Supreme Court addresses whether an amendment to the Constitution of the State of Michigan banning the race-conscious admissions policy upheld by the Court in *Grutter* offended the Equal Protection Clause. A six-justice majority holds that the amendment did not violate the Equal Protection Clause – premising their common conclusion on three very different rationales.

The challenged measure, called Proposal 2, appeared as a ballot question in Michigan in 2006. The terms of the amendment prohibited the State of Michigan – including its colleges, universities, and school districts – from discriminating or granting preferential treatment to any person or group on the grounds of race, sex, color, ethnicity, or national origin.[73] The Court emphasizes that *Schuette* does not concern the constitutionality of race-conscious admissions policies; its decision only examines the methods (if any) by which the voters of a state could direct their state government to prohibit such policies.[74]

At this point, the majority diverges dramatically in its reasoning. The author of the "majority" opinion, Justice Kennedy, joins Chief Justice Roberts and Justice Alito in concluding that Proposal 2 did not offend the "political process doctrine" announced in *Hunter*.[75] Under Justice Kennedy's formulation, this doctrine applies only in cases in which there existed a demonstrated, race-based injury which was aggravated by means of state encouragement or participation.[76] Examples of this include situations in which the state transferred power on a particular issue to the voters from an unelected body intended to protect minority rights. In *Hunter*, for instance, Akron voters passed a measure requiring fair housing ordinances to be approved by public referendum rather than an appointed commission.[77] These

---

[73] 572 U.S. ___ (2014), (Slip Op.), 2.
[74] *Id.* at 4.
[75] *Id.* at 11.
[76] *Id.* at 8.
[77] *Id.* at 7.

facts, "established that invidious discrimination would be the necessary result of the procedural restructuring."[78]

In contrast, the bloc led by Justice Kennedy rejects any reading of the political process doctrine that would trigger strict scrutiny when (1) a state action with a "racial focus" exists and (2) the action makes it more difficult for minorities than non-minorities to achieve legislation "in their interest."[79] Justice Kennedy reasons that this test would prove nearly impossible to administer, perpetuate racial stereotypes, and provide a perverse incentive for advocates to couch their initiatives in explicitly racial terms in order to keep issues away from voter referenda.[80]

Justice Kennedy concludes his opinion by noting that, in contrast to the political process doctrine line of cases: "What is at stake here is not whether injury will be inflicted but whether government can be instructed not to follow a course that entails, first, the definition of racial categories and, second, the grant of favored status to persons in some racial categories and not others."[81] Finally, he reiterates, "this case is not about how the debate about racial preferences should be resolved. It is about who may resolve it."[82]

In a typically colorful opinion, Justice Scalia wades into what he calls a "jurisprudential twilight zone between two errant lines of precedent" to "confront a frighteningly bizarre question."[83] Justice Scalia, joined by Justice Thomas, concurs in the result announced in Justice Kennedy's opinion. However, he advocates abandoning the political process doctrine in favor of an alternate approach. He instead calls for the application of the standard announced in *Washington v. Davis*; namely, that plaintiffs must prove intent and causation to sustain a claim for an equal protection violation stemming from a facially neutral act.[84] He underscores that he, "would further hold that a law directing state actors to provide equal protection is (to say the least) facially neutral, and cannot violate the Constitution."[85]

Conversely, Justice Breyer authors a concurring opinion which highlights the limited nature of the *Schuette* holding. Justice Breyer emphasizes that *Schuette* only addresses amendments aimed at invalidating race-conscious admissions programs premised solely upon the diversity interest affirmed in *Grutter*. The holding would thus have no precedential value regarding amendments aimed at invalidating programs intended as a remedy for past discrimination or its direct effects.[86] Justice Breyer also explicates the key factual differences distinguishing *Schuette*

---

[78] *Id.* at 8.
[79] *Id.* at 11.
[80] *Id.* at 12.
[81] *Id.* at 17–18.
[82] *Id.* at 18.
[83] 572 U.S. ___ (2014), (Slip Op.), 1.
[84] *Id.* at 15.
[85] *Id.* at 3.
[86] 572 U.S. ___ (2014), (Slip Op.), 1.

from the political process doctrine cases. He notes that *Schuette* did not involve a reordering of the political process or, in fact, a fundamental change in who made the ultimate decision.[87] He observes that, prior to Proposal 2, authority to set admissions policies legally rested in the hands of an elected university board. In practice – but not in law – the boards delegated this power to "unelected university faculty members and administrators," but remained legally entitled to reassert their authority at any time.[88] Per Justice Breyer, Proposal 2 does not represent a seizure of power so much as an additional directive from the voters who, technically, always held the authority in question. As he explains:

> In [the political process doctrine cases] minorities had participated in the political process and they had won. The majority's subsequent reordering of the political process repealed the minority's successes and made it more difficult for the minority to succeed in the future. The majority thereby diminished the minority's ability to participate meaningfully in the electoral process. But one cannot as easily characterize the movement of the decision-making mechanism at issue here – from an administrative process to an electoral process – as diminishing the minority's ability to participate meaningfully in the *political* process. There is no prior electoral process in which the minority participated.[89] (Emphasis in original)

Justice Breyer concludes by reiterating that the holding in *Schuette* is limited to situations in which (1) decisions made by an administrative body were transferred to a politically responsive one and (2) the decisions pertained to race-conscious admissions programs justified solely by the pursuit of the educational benefits of diversity rather than the need to remedy past intentional discrimination or its direct effects.

Justice Sotomayor offers a vigorous dissent. Joined by Justice Ginsburg, she argues that the Court's decision abandons its responsibility to guard minority rights from unadulterated majority rule. Justice Sotomayor also contends for a more expansive application of the political process doctrine, presents a different reading of the facts than the account proffered by Justice Breyer, and calls for a more explicit reckoning with the badges and incidents of racial injustice in American society.

The dissent begins by noting that the effect of the amendment is to create two parallel processes by which the citizens of Michigan could weigh in on university governance: "one for persons interested in race-sensitive admissions policies and one for everyone else."[90] Justice Sotomayor argues that the guarantees of the Equal Protection Clause cannot be curtailed by the political power of the majority; the courts must instead step in to protect the rights of minorities from such processes. Lamentably, Justice Sotomayor continues, the majority neglects that responsibility

---

[87] *Id.* at 1–2.
[88] *Id.* at 4.
[89] *Id.* at 5.
[90] 572 U.S. ___ (2014), (Slip Op.), 4.

in *Schuette*.[91] The dissent then proceeds to recount the Court's many vindications of minority rights.[92]

Justice Sotomayor next argues for adopting the broad formulation of the political process doctrine rejected by Justice Kennedy.[93] The dissent counters that determining the presence or absence of a "racial focus" in legislation would prove far more administrable than the majority claims. She notes:

> There is no conflict between this Court's pronouncement in *Grutter* and the common-sense reality that race-sensitive admissions policies further a compelling state interest in achieving a diverse student body precisely because they increase minority enrollment, which necessarily benefits minority groups. In other words, constitutionally permissible race-sensitive admissions policies can both serve the compelling interest of obtaining the educational benefits that flow from a diverse student body, and inure to the benefit of racial minorities. There is nothing mutually exclusive about the two.[94]

Justice Sotomayor further criticizes the majority for its insistence upon the intentional infliction of a racially motivated injury as a prerequisite to invoking the political process doctrine. In contrast, the dissent would apply the doctrine in any situation in which the decision-making process for an issue of a racial nature was altered in a way that would place a substantial or undue burden on minorities.[95] Indeed, Justice Sotomayor frames the doctrine as prohibiting the political process from being restructured "in a manner that makes it more difficult for a traditionally excluded group to work through the existing process to seek beneficial policies."[96]

The dissent also challenges Justice Breyer's account of the distribution of power within Michigan universities. Justice Sotomayor disputes Justice Breyer's characterization of the amendment as an additional directive on decision-making rather than a seizure of that power. According to the dissent, the removal of discretion from the elected board members – and accompanying "reordering" of the political process – runs afoul of the political process doctrine.[97] The dissent argues:

> The salient point is this: Although the elected and politically accountable boards may well entrust university officials with certain day-to-day admissions responsibilities, they often weigh in on admissions policies themselves and, at all times, they retain complete supervisory authority over university officials and over all admissions decisions. . . .

---

[91] *Id.* at 6.
[92] *Id.* at 6–10.
[93] *Id.* at 15.
[94] *Id.* at 16.
[95] *Id.* at 15.
[96] *Id.* at 37.
[97] *Id.* at 21.

There is therefore no need to consider "[extending the political process doctrine] to reach situations in which decision-making authority is moved from an administrative body to a political one ... such a scenario is not before us."[98]

Justice Sotomayor devotes the last quarter of her dissent to calling for the Court to explicitly recognize the ongoing effects of racial discrimination and injustice. She condemns the majority's apparent willingness to take a "color-blind" approach. This section of the dissent features language rarely seen in a Supreme Court opinion, and is worth quoting at length.

> My colleagues are of the view that we should leave race out of the picture entirely and let the voters sort it out. We have seen this reasoning before. It is a sentiment out of touch with reality, one not required by our Constitution, and one that has properly been rejected as "not sufficient" to resolve cases of this nature.
>
> Race matters. Race matters in part because of the long history of racial minorities' being denied access to the political process. ...
>
> Race also matters because of persistent racial inequality in society – inequality that cannot be ignored and that has produced stark socioeconomic disparities. ...
>
> And race matters for reasons that really are only skin deep, that cannot be discussed any other way, and that cannot be wished away. Race matters to a young man's view of society when he spends his teenage years watching others tense up as he passes, no matter the neighborhood where he grew up. Race matters to a young woman's sense of self when she states her hometown, and then is pressed, "No, where are your *really* from?", regardless of how many generations her family has been in the country. Race matters to a young person addressed by a stranger in a foreign language, which he does not understand because only English was spoken at home. Race matters because of the slights, the snickers, the silent judgments that reinforce that most crippling of thoughts: "I do not belong here."
>
> In my colleagues' view, examining the racial impact of legislation only perpetuates racial discrimination. This refusal to accept the stark reality that race matters is regrettable. The way to stop discrimination on the basis of race is to speak openly and candidly on the subject of race, and to apply the Constitution with eyes open to the unfortunate effects of centuries of racial discrimination. As members of the judiciary tasked with intervening to carry out the guarantee of equal protection, we ought not sit back and wish away, rather than confront, the racial inequality that exists in our society. It is this view that works harm, by perpetuating the facile notion that what makes race matter is acknowledging the simple truth that race *does* matter.[99] (Emphasis in original; internal citations omitted).

Finally, Justice Sotomayor ends her dissent by incorporating graphic illustrations of the deleterious effects of Proposal 2 (and analogous measures in other states) on minority enrollment. She traces precipitous declines in minority representation at

---

[98] *Id.* at 29.
[99] *Id.* at 44–46.

University of Michigan, UCLA, and University of California, Berkeley.[100] She concludes:

> Colleges and universities must be free to prioritize the goal of diversity. They must be free to immerse their students in a multiracial environment that fosters frequent and meaningful interactions with students of other races, and thereby pushes such students to transcend any assumptions they may hold on the basis of skin color. Without race-sensitive admissions policies, this might well be impossible. The statistics I have described make that fact glaringly obvious. We should not turn a blind eye to something we cannot help but see.[101]

THE OVERWHELMING EDUCATIONAL BENEFITS OF A DIVERSE LEARNING ENVIRONMENT

From *Bakke* to the present, the Supreme Court has held that race-conscious educational policies can be constitutionally justified if they are narrowly tailored to achieve the compelling interest of the educational benefits of student body diversity. In so doing, the Court has brought the empirical question of the educational benefits of student body diversity to constitutional prominence. But that empirical question has been answered. The evidence is clear that a diverse learning environment produces substantial and multi-dimensional educational benefits for all students at all levels of education.

Diversity in backgrounds and perspectives provides tremendous growth and learning.[102] A diverse learning environment produces significant educational benefits for all students, including promoting cross-racial understanding; reducing prejudice, stereotyping, and implicit bias; and fostering collaborative problem-solving.[103] These skills are vital to a student's ultimate ability to find success and wellbeing in increasingly diverse work and social environments.

Moreover, a diverse learning environment advantages students by strengthening their cognitive abilities.[104] We now know that students learn best in small groups.[105] And we also know that the groups that are best for learning are those that are diverse.[106]

When a student is exposed to different thoughts, ideas, perspectives, and backgrounds, the student experiences cognitive dissonance, incongruity, and imbalance.[107] The student's brain then must work hard to process the information, to absorb the dissonance, and to accommodate the unusual

---

[100] Id. at 51–55.
[101] Id. at 57.
[102] Kaufman et al., *The Pre-K Home Companion*, at 73.
[103] Ibid. at 75.
[104] Ibid. at 73.
[105] Ibid.
[106] Ibid. at 74.
[107] Ibid. at 73.

perspective.[108] Regular encounters between people with diverse experiences strengthen a person's brain.[109] These encounters help to develop the mental capacity to engage in higher order thinking skills and complex problem-solving strategies.[110] Diversity thus promotes better problem-solving.[111] Diverse groups of learners consistently outperform otherwise high-achieving groups in solving complex problems.[112] Diverse individuals in a group create a higher level of collective intelligence than groups comprised even of higher achieving individuals.[113] Diversity in the learning environment thereby fosters increased individual and group innovation.[114]

A diverse learning environment also builds the critical cognitive capacity to take another person's perspective.[115] The ability to appreciate, understand, and respect the thoughts, feelings, and intentions of people who seem to be different is particularly challenging. But the pattern of confronting and overcoming the challenge of accommodating different perspectives is the key to learning.[116] The experience enables the student to embrace rather than to fear difference.[117]

In addition, a diverse learning environment creates vital cross-cultural competencies, including the ability to understand and navigate a culture different from one's own.[118] Students who learn in a diverse learning environment grow to be professionals with the cross-cultural competency necessary to compete in a diverse global economy.[119]

Diversity produces greater democratic citizenship outcomes because students grow to understand that differences need not be divisive, appreciate another person's perspective, and become engaged in leadership and civic activities.[120] A diverse learning environment produces students who are better able to resolve conflict without violence.[121]

In fact, the development of interpersonal relationships between students of different races in the educational environment is more effective at promoting the benefits of diversity than any other pedagogical method.[122] Interracial contact leads to stronger interpersonal cognitive skills because students learn to be more careful,

---

[108] Ibid.
[109] Ibid.
[110] Ibid.
[111] Ibid. at 74.
[112] Ibid.
[113] Ibid.
[114] Ibid.
[115] Ibid. at 73.
[116] Ibid. at 74.
[117] Ibid.
[118] Ibid. at 75.
[119] Ibid.
[120] Ibid.
[121] Ibid.
[122] Ibid. at 75–76.

nuanced, and precise in their perceptions of the thoughts, feelings, and intentions of others.[123]

Lack of diversity, on the other hand, facilitates the growth in minority students of stereotype threat, which is a powerful force undermining belief in one's own abilities.[124] Diverse educational environments help to mitigate the harmful effects of implicit bias in all members of the learning community.[125] Because students who have meaningful relationships with diverse peers in a learning environment grow to manage implicit bias, they do not suffer the interference with cognitive processes and executive function that such bias can produce.[126]

Diversity can be a source of great strength in a program as it enhances the learning of all students. In the short term, diversity supports the development of important cognitive skills in young children; in the long run, it can foster far greater social understanding and social equity.

Children who fear difference because they have not had the opportunity to experience it may develop a profound hostility to difference throughout their lives. That hostility can manifest itself in bullying and violence.

Children who learn to embrace difference at an early age, by contrast, are more likely to be healthy and stable adults. They have learned that if their own view of the world is ruptured by an unusual experience, they have the ability to repair that rupture. The rhythm of rupture followed by repair in a child's brain helps that child to persevere, focus, and apply this vital mental process in all of their activities. In other words, a diverse learning environment builds executive function.

CONCLUSION

The line of cases governing the use of race-conscious admissions policies in higher education has emerged as one of the most hotly contested areas in American jurisprudence. For all the bitter arguments and multiple court challenges, Justice Powell's opinion in *Bakke* has remained controlling precedent for forty years. Of the four justifications offered by UC Davis, Justice Powell accepted only one as a compelling interest: the pursuit of the educational benefits which flow from a diverse student body. Diversity, per Justice Powell, encompassed a myriad of factors in which racial background was to be considered as just one of many facets of an applicant's file. The *Grutter* Court confirmed this understanding and further emphasized the need for colleges to engage in a holistic, individualized review, cautioning universities to avoid treating their applicants as undifferentiated members of a racial group.

[123] Ibid. at 76.
[124] Ibid.
[125] Ibid.
[126] Ibid. at 74.

Although discoveries in neuroscience and advances in pedagogy continually confirm the educational benefits of diversity, the Supreme Court appears increasingly skeptical. The *Fisher II* Court upheld a program substantially similar to the one endorsed in *Grutter* – yet openly questioned its precedential value, appearing to limit it to the facts at hand. In light of these developments, it is becoming clear that the Court, as constituted, does not appreciate the pedagogical power of diversity as fully as advocates would prefer. The line of cases governing the use of race in admissions demonstrates the gap between legal reasoning and proven educational expertise. A jurisprudence more fully informed by a thorough understanding of the way in which human beings learn would include embracing the possibilities offered by diversity with greater enthusiasm. It would also facilitate more effective efforts to remove the badges and incidents of slavery, segregation, and discrimination from our society.

While Justice Sotomayor's dissent in *Schuette* calls for a full and frank inventory of racial injustice in higher education, her observations apply in the realm of school funding disparities as well. In the next chapter, we will explore the Supreme Court's approach to this question and examine its continuing ramifications and the badges and incidents of inequity it engenders. We will also revisit the precise status of education as a fundamental right and review the various avenues available to advocates seeking greater equity in American schools.

6

San Antonio, Inequity, and the Human Struggle

For all the soaring language offered in praise of education in *Brown* and its progeny, the Supreme Court never deemed a free public education a fundamental right under the Constitution. In this chapter, we will examine the Supreme Court's explicit answer to this question left unanswered by the *Brown* line of cases. That answer continues to have profound implications for attempts to deliver the equality of opportunity mandated by the Court in *Brown*.

The Supreme Court, however, does not necessarily have the last word on the question of education's status as a fundamental right. Each state in the union has its own constitution and, under our state–federal dichotomy, the highest court in each state is the ultimate authority in all cases that do not implicate a federal question. Thus, the Supreme Court cannot review the rulings of state courts that concern statutory interpretations of a state's constitutional provisions. As we will see, this bedrock principle of American jurisprudence creates a space in which several state courts have extended considerably more robust protection to education than has the federal judiciary.

As we saw while discussing race-conscious admissions policies in higher education, the badges and incidents of racial injustice linger over many questions in education law – even when those questions are discussed in ostensibly race-neutral terms. This is especially true in the context of educational funding. In this chapter, we will explore how funding regimes based on local property taxes have, all too frequently, operated to the detriment of minority students. We will also examine how different jurisprudential approaches at the federal level and across the several states have had considerable impacts on attempts to rectify this imbalance. In addition, we will outline the principal lines of attack open to advocates of more equitable funding arrangements – paying special attention to compelling recent developments in Illinois. All the while, we will bear in mind the basic question of whether these funding mechanisms reflect a proper understanding of the way children learn.

AMERICA'S SCHOOLS AND THEIR STUDENTS

Before examining *Rodriguez*, an overview of the student demographics and funding sources of American education is informative.[1] In the United States, slightly more than 50 million students attend public elementary and secondary schools, about 5.2 million students attend private schools, and approximately 1.5 million school-aged children are homeschooled.[2]

There are about 13,600 public school districts in America, and about 99,000 public schools.[3] Of these public schools, about 5,300 are charter schools.[4] In addition, there are approximately 30,900 private schools in the country.[5] Of these private schools, 68 percent have a religious orientation.[6] Accordingly, these parochial institutions educate 80 percent of the private school students in America.[7]

Slightly more than 70 percent of all students enrolled in private school are white, 9 percent are African American, and 10 percent are Hispanic or Latino, and 5 percent are Asian.[8] The racial composition of America's public schools is 52 percent white, 16 percent black, and 24 percent Latino or Hispanic.[9] In the past decade, the number of white children enrolled in public schools decreased from 28.7 million to 25.6 million, and the percentage of white children in public schools declined from 60 to 52 percent. During the same period, the percentage of African American students has remained flat, while the percentage of Latino or Hispanic children has increased from 17 to 24 percent.[10] The National Center for Education Statistics projects that by 2023, the percentage of white students in public school will

---

[1] Data regarding America's schools and students (their enrollment numbers, costs, etc.) vary depending on the source because of underreporting, definitional problems, and the fact that this field is constantly evolving. Because of that, data cited in this book are accurate but approximate.

[2] William J. Hussar & Tabitha M. Bailey, *Projections of Education Statistics to 2021* (Washington, DC: U.S. Department of Education National Center for Education Statistics, January 2013), http://nces.ed.gov/pubs2013/2013008.pdf; Thomas D. Snyder & Sally A. Dillow, *Digest of Education Statistics 2012* (Washington, DC: U.S. Department of Education National Center for Education Statistics, December 2013), table 40, http://nces.ed.gov/pubs2014/2014015.pdf. The actual number of home-schooled children is difficult to quantify, and some estimates place the number at close to 2 million. www.hslda.org.

[3] Hussar & Bailey, *Digest of Education Statistics 2012*, table 100.

[4] Ibid., table 108.

[5] Stephen P. Broughman & Nancy L. Swaim, *Characteristics of Private Schools in the United States: Results from the 2011–12 Private School Universe Survey* (Washington, DC: U.S. Department of Education National Center for Education Statistics, July 2013), http://nces.ed.gov/pubs2013/2013316.pdf.

[6] Ibid.; W. S. Barnett et al., *The State of Preschool 2012: State Preschool Yearbook* (New Brunswick, NJ: National Institute for Early Education Research, 2012), http://nieer.org/sites/nieer/files/yearbook2012.pdf.

[7] Broughman & Swaim, *Characteristics of Private Schools in the United States*.

[8] Ibid.

[9] *Racial/Ethnic Enrollment in Public Schools* (Washington, DC: U.S. Department of Education National Center for Education Statistics, April 2014), http://nces.ed.gov/programs/coe/indicator_cge.asp.

[10] Ibid.

decrease to 45 percent, while the percentage of Hispanic students will grow to 30 percent.[11]

THE SOURCES OF REVENUE TO SUPPORT AMERICAN EDUCATION

The United States spends a total of about $590 billion per year to educate its students, or about $11,000 per student.[12] That figure is projected to increase to $665 billion by 2021, or about $12,500 per student.[13]

Of the $590 billion spent on education in America, about $141 billion comes from the federal government.[14] The United States Department of Education's appropriation of $67.3 billion in discretionary spending has been used primarily to fund three programs: the Elementary and Secondary Education Act Title I Grants to local school districts to support low income students; the Individuals with Disabilities Education Act state grants to support children with special education needs; and the Pell Grants to support college education. The Department of Education also has utilized its discretionary Title I appropriation to fund approximately $550 million in Race to the Top funds. The Obama administration also requested $750 million in early childhood education development grants, which are offset in part by a significant reduction in impact aid for schools.[15] The federal government's total expenditures on education comprise approximately 4 percent of the total federal budget.[16]

State and local taxes generally make up more than 90 percent of a school district's revenue.[17] Most states produce that local revenue through property taxes, while some states employ income taxes, sales taxes, "sin" taxes, or a combination of taxes.

Property taxes are usually based primarily on a percentage of the assessed valuation of the residential property in a district. Some states redistribute property taxes from property-rich districts to property-poor districts, spread property tax revenue throughout the state, or create a "foundation" level of funding for all districts.

---

[11] Ibid.
[12] Hussar & Bailey, *Projections of Education Statistics to 2021*.
[13] Ibid.
[14] New America Foundation, U.S. Departments of Education, Health & Human Services, Agriculture, Defense, and Veterans Affairs, White House Office of Management and Budget, and Congressional Budget Office, *The Federal Education Budget* (New America Foundation Federal Budget Project, 2014), http://febp.newamerica.net/background-analysis/education-federal-budget.
[15] Ibid.
[16] In fiscal year 2013, the federal government spent $3.5 trillion, making its expenditures of $141 billion on education about 4 percent of the total budget. U.S. Dep't. of Education Budget Tables.
[17] See Common Core of Data (CCD), "National Public Education Financial Survey: 2000–01 through 2010–11," *Digest of Education Statistics 2013* (Washington, DC: U.S. Department of Education, National Center for Education Statistics), table 235.10, http://nces.ed.gov/programs/coe/indicator_cma.asp (calculating that most school districts rely on federal funding for less than 10 percent of their revenue).

In theory, the foundation level represents a legislative judgment about the amount of money that must be allocated to each student for that student to receive a minimally adequate education. In practice, however, the foundation level often is determined based on the availability of residual funds. Where a district's local taxes do not reach that foundation level, some states will allocate statewide funds to make up the difference.

HEAD START FUNDING

In 2014, the federal government spent $6.4 billion on Head Start, and 813,000 three- to five-year-old children were enrolled in Head Start programs.[18] The federal Head Start program provides early learning programs for children in impoverished families. To be eligible for Head Start, families generally must have income at or below the federal poverty level, which is about $23,550 for a family of four.[19] The median annual income of Head Start families is $22,714.[20]

Head Start also serves a diverse group of children – 29 percent identified themselves as African American and 40 percent identified themselves as Hispanic or Latino.[21] Thirty percent of participants are from families in which English is not the primary language, and 25 percent of participants are from families in which Spanish is the primary language spoken at home.[22] The diversity of the Head Start program is a source of great strength, enhancing the learning of all students.[23]

Head Start programs are operated by local school districts, other local governmental agencies, or private organizations that receive a five-year renewable grant from the federal government.[24] In 2014, 1,622 organizations received Head Start grants to provide early childhood education, 1,016 of which were local school districts. The federal government spends about $7,900 per student to provide early childhood education in Head Start programs.[25]

---

[18] *Justification of Estimates for Appropriations Committees* (U.S. Department of Health and Human Services, Fiscal Year 2002–2015), www.hhs.gov/budget/fy2014/secretary-congressional-justification.pdf.

[19] See *2013 Poverty Guidelines* (U.S. Department of Health & Human Services, 2013), http://aspe.hhs.gov/poverty/13poverty.cfm.

[20] See *Head Start Family and Child Experiences Survey* (FACES) (U.S. Department of Health & Human Services Office of Planning, Research & Evaluation, 2011), www.acf.hhs.gov/programs/opre/research/project/head-start-family-and-child-experiences-survey-faces.

[21] *Head Start Program Facts, Fiscal Year 2012* (U.S. Department of Health & Human Services, 2012), https://eclkc.ohs.acf.hhs.gov/hslc/data/factsheets/docs/hs-program-fact-sheet-2012.pdf.

[22] Ibid.

[23] See David L. Kirp, *Improbable Scholars: The Rebirth of a Great American School System and a Strategy for America's Schools* (New York: Oxford University Press, 2013); David L. Kirp, "The Secret to Fixing Bad Schools," *N.Y. Times*, February 9, 2013, www.nytimes.com/2013/02/10/opinion/sunday/the-secret-to-fixing-bad-schools.html?pagewanted=all&_r=0 ("There's abundant evidence showing the lifetime benefits of early education.")

[24] See 2013 Poverty Guidelines.

[25] New America Foundation, The Federal Education Budget.

In 1995, Congress extended Head Start programs to include Early Head Start. The Early Head Start program is designed to support poor mothers and their children from birth to age three.[26] The program provides home visits and center-based services, including pre- and post-natal counseling, nutritional advice, and support for early childhood health and development.[27] Approximately 115,000 children are served by Early Head Start, with a federal funding stream of $1.37 billion.[28] This amounts to just 4 percent of those whose families are economically eligible (compared to Head Start programs, which serve 42 percent of eligible three and four year olds).[29]

RODRIGUEZ: THE SUPREME COURT'S TOLERANCE FOR ADMITTED INEQUALITY IN EDUCATION

The combined federal and local sources of revenue do not provide adequate or equitable educational opportunities. Federal educational mandates are unfunded or underfunded. The bulk of revenue available to support education in America derives from local property taxes. The formulas for allocating local property taxes to educational purposes are based at least in part on the property wealth of a school district. Districts with high property wealth thus receive significantly more resources per child than districts with low property wealth.

This educational finance regime creates wide disparities in the resources available to districts and their children. Because neighborhoods are still generally segregated by race and ethnicity, and most minority children reside in property-poor districts, the disparity in educational funding adversely affects minority children. These overall inequities in educational funding are replicated in the disparities in access to early childhood programs.

In *San Antonio Independent School District v. Rodriguez*,[30] Mexican-American parents of children in elementary and secondary schools challenged the Texas system of funding public schools largely through local property taxes. The Texas educational funding regime at issue in *Rodriguez* is typical of state and local educational finance systems throughout the nation. In Texas – much like school funding mechanisms in all fifty states – poor areas were taxed at a high rate relative to the value of property, but had little to spend on education; wealthier areas could tax at low rates, but still managed to raise ample revenue. In Texas, this difference in tax base grew more pronounced with the advent of industrialization.[31] Eventually, the

---

[26] Powell, "The Head Start Program," 67.
[27] Ibid.
[28] Ibid.
[29] Sara Neufeld, "The Power of Pre-K: Model Early Ed Program in Chicago Lifts Entire Family," *In Plain Sight: Poverty in America*, November 23, 2013, www.nbcnews.com/_news/2013/11/23/21537069-the-power-of-pre-k-model-early-ed-program-in-chicago-lifts-entire-family.
[30] 411 U.S. 1 (1973).
[31] *Id.* at 7–8.

State implemented a supplemental funding regime. Although this "Texas Minimum Foundation School Program" guaranteed a minimum level of funding for each child, that foundation level undisputedly failed to compensate for the dramatic disparities in educational funding among schools in the school district and throughout the state.[32]

Plaintiffs challenged the funding scheme, arguing that it violated the Equal Protection Clause of the Fourteenth Amendment. The Supreme Court, however, rejected the challenge.

The Court first determined the level of judicial scrutiny that should be applied to assess the constitutionality of the funding regime. In order to determine whether any state or federal legislation violates the Equal Protection Clause, the Supreme Court has established different levels of judicial scrutiny. The Court analyzes most legislation by determining only whether the law is rationally related to a legitimate state interest. Under that deferential "rational basis" standard of review, legislation enjoys a strong presumption of constitutionality.

If, however, legislation impinges upon a fundamental constitutional right of a "discrete and insular minority," the Court will "strictly scrutinize" the statute. Under that exacting standard, a statute will be declared unconstitutional unless it is narrowly tailored to achieve a compelling governmental interest.[33] In *San Antonio*, the Supreme Court did not apply strict scrutiny. It determined that the challenged system of educational funding did not discriminate against a suspect class of discrete and insular minorities, and did not impinge upon any fundamental right.[34]

First, the Court reasoned that the plaintiffs could not show that the funding regime worked to the particular disadvantage of a discrete and insular minority. Rather, the regime adversely affected a "large, diverse, and amorphous class, unified only by the common factor of residence in districts that happen to have less taxable wealth than other districts."[35] According to the Court, the plaintiffs did not have traditional indicia of a suspect class: an immutable characteristic, a history of purposeful unequal treatment, or political powerlessness.[36] Moreover, there was no basis in the record to assume that the poorest people all live in the same school district.[37] Nor did Texas's policies result in an absolute deprivation of a minimally adequate education.[38]

Second, the Court reasoned that there is no right to education explicitly or implicitly guaranteed by the United States Constitution. The Court declined to create substantive constitutional rights in order to mandate an overhaul in educational funding. Although education is linked to the exercise of other constitutional

---

[32] *Id.* at 10–14.
[33] See *United States v. Carolene Products Company*, 304 U.S. 144, 152 n.4 (1930).
[34] 411 U.S. 1, 18.
[35] *Id.* at 28.
[36] *Id.*
[37] *Id.* at 23.
[38] *Id.* at 19.

rights such as free speech and voting, the Court also declined to find an implicit right to education in the Constitution.[39] The Court recognized that its past cases had expressed an abiding respect for the vital role of education in a free society. Yet, it concluded that the importance of a service does not determine whether it must be regarded as fundamental for purposes of examination under the Equal Protection Clause.[40]

Having determined that strict scrutiny should not be used to analyze the constitutionality of Texas's funding regime, the Court concluded that the regime satisfied the rational basis test.[41] Under that minimal level of scrutiny, the Court found that Texas's educational regime is rational because it reflects local control over funding for education.[42]

ASSESSING RODRIGUEZ: A CRITICAL ANALYSIS

As the Supreme Court recognizes, Texas concedes that its dual system of financing public education results in grossly unequal allocations of resources to different school districts.[43] The Court concludes that the individuals adversely affected by the Texas system are not a "suspect class" because (1) the system does not operate to the "peculiar" disadvantage of a class defined as "indigent"; (2) the individuals affected are not absolutely deprived of the benefit of education; and (3) the class of individuals who have low taxable wealth do not share the characteristics of insularity, political powerlessness, or a history of unequal treatment, which have typically defined "suspect classes."[44]

The Court ultimately addresses the question whether "education is a fundamental right, in the sense that it is among the rights and liberties protected by the Constitution."[45] After acknowledging the grave significance of education in the lives of Americans, the Court refocuses the inquiry as whether "there is a right to education explicitly or implicitly guaranteed by the Constitution."[46] The Court then finds no explicit or implicit protection for the right to education in the Constitution. Yet the Court hints that the Constitution may implicitly protect against the "absolute denial of educational opportunities" to children.[47]

The Court considers, but ultimately rejects, the notion that the right to education is fundamental because it is indispensable to other constitutionally protected rights, such as the First Amendment right to speech as well as the intelligent utilization of

[39]   Id. at 30, 33–34.
[40]   Id. at 30.
[41]   Id. at 54–55.
[42]   Id. at 49–53.
[43]   Id. at 15–16.
[44]   Id. at 22–28.
[45]   Id. at 29.
[46]   Id. at 33–34.
[47]   Id. at 37.

the right to vote.[48] The Court nowhere mentions *Pierce* or *Meyer* in this context. In *Pierce* and *Meyer*, the Supreme Court recognized the fundamental right of parents to educate their children according to their own conscience. The Court states that education presents a "myriad of intractable economic, social, and even philosophical problems."[49] These "problems" are then used by the Court to justify its decision to refrain from entering an arena traditionally relegated to local control.

The majority also questions the premise that the amount of material resources invested in education has a determinable effect on student outcomes. The Court creates the impression that a divide exists within the academy on the most basic pedagogical questions.[50] As Justice Powell expresses it, "Related to the questioned relationship between cost and quality is the equally unsettled controversy as to the proper goals of a system of public education."[51] The majority presents even these maxims as the subject of an ever-evolving, shifting debate. It implies that any prudential decisions made in response to these supposedly constantly changing best practices should come from local school boards rather than federal courts.

In reaching its conclusion regarding the constitutionality of Texas's educational finance system, the Court also declares that "the history of education since the industrial revolution shows a continual struggle between two forces: the desire by members of society to have educational opportunity for all children, and the desire of each family to provide the best education it can afford for its own children."[52] In this telling declaration, the Supreme Court presumes that there is a natural "struggle" between what is best for the family and what is best for the community. The Court legitimates the undisputed disparities in education by arguing that those disparities are rooted in human nature. It presumes education is a competitive, atomistic enterprise because human nature is competitive and atomistic. This presumption has justified many inequitable educational practices throughout American history.[53]

In a brief concurrence, Justice Stewart describes the Texas funding system as "chaotic and unjust."[54] Though hardly a ringing endorsement of Texas's approach, Justice Stewart joins the judgment of the Court in full. Conversely, in his equally brief dissent, Justice Brennan advocates for the application of strict scrutiny to any classification affecting education.[55]

In dissent, Justice White questions the notion that the Texas funding system could qualify as rational in any accepted sense of the term. He observes, "it provides

[48] *Id.* at 35.
[49] *Id.* at 42.
[50] *Id.* at 43.
[51] *Id.*
[52] *Id.* at 49.
[53] See Chapter 3 for a detailed discussion of this train of thought in American education and behaviorist theory.
[54] 411 U.S. 1, 50.
[55] *Id.* at 63.

a meaningful option to Alamo Heights and like school districts but almost none to Edgewood and those other districts with a low per-pupil real estate tax base."[56] Justice White succinctly exposes the flaws inherent in the exclusive reliance on property taxes for school district revenue.

> As is readily apparent, because of the variance in tax bases between districts, results, in terms of revenues, do not correlate with effort, in terms of tax rate. Thus, Alamo Heights, with a tax base approximately twice the size of Edgewood's base, realized approximately six times as many maintenance dollars as Edgewood by using a tax rate only approximately two and one-half times larger.[57]

This straightforward appeal to common sense and basic math raises questions left largely unanswered by the Court's opinion.

The most detailed and compelling reply to the majority's reasoning, however, came from Justice Thurgood Marshall. While his dissent, of course, is not binding precedent, his singular perspective continues to challenge conventional narratives and inspire reform advocates. Nearly a half century later, his views remain relevant to the debate over educational funding in America.

Justice Marshall begins by emphasizing the implications of the Court's holding:

> The Court today decides, in effect, that a State may constitutionally vary the quality of education which it offers its children in accordance with the amount of taxable wealth located in the school districts within which they reside. The majority's decision represents an abrupt departure from the mainstream of recent state and federal court decisions concerning the unconstitutionality of state educational financing schemes dependent upon taxable local wealth. More unfortunately, though, the majority's holding can only be seen as a retreat from our historic commitment to equality of educational opportunity and as unsupportable acquiescence in a system which deprives children in their earliest years of the chance to reach their full potential as citizens.[58]

Few could have appreciated the degree of this retreat more acutely than the author of these words. Remember, while an attorney, Justice Marshall successfully argued before the Court in *Brown*, and led it closer to calling education a fundamental right than it has ever subsequently ventured. For his part, Justice Marshall expresses no doubt that the funding scheme violates the Equal Protection Clause of the Fourteenth Amendment.[59]

In addition to highlighting the discriminatory effects of the funding system, Justice Marshall also explores what he views as absurdities present in its construction. He quotes one of the developers responsible for designing the mechanism used to predict local funding ability. The developer described its effectiveness as "a little

---

[56] *Id.* at 64.
[57] *Id.* at 65.
[58] *Id.* at 70–71.
[59] *Id.* at 72.

better measure than sheer chance, but not much."[60] Tracing the consequences of this scattershot approach, Justice Marshall observes: "What the Court fails to emphasize is the cruel irony of how much more state aid is being given to property-rich Texas school districts on top of their already substantial local property tax revenues."[61]

Justice Marshall then offers a thought-provoking alternative approach to addressing questions of equity in education. His views question the assumptions underlying the Court's opinion and propose a new path forward for reform advocates.

> I believe the question of discrimination in educational quality must be deemed to be an objective one that looks to what the State provides its children, not to what the children are able to do with what they receive. That a child forced to attend an underfunded school with poorer physical facilities, less experienced teachers, larger classes, and a narrower range of courses than a school with substantially more funds – and thus with greater choice in educational planning – may nevertheless excel is to the credit of the child, not the State. . . . Indeed, who can ever measure for such a child the opportunities lost and the talents wasted for want of a broader, more enriched education?[62]

Instead of recounting the "myriad of problems" in securing educational opportunities referenced by the majority, Justice Marshall speaks in terms of possibilities. In his paradigm, the purpose of education is not to assure a minimal level of competence sufficient to read instructional materials but instead to unlock and develop the natural talents of every student. Relatedly, he continues: "The Equal Protection Clause is not addressed to the minimal sufficiency but rather to the unjustifiable inequalities of state action. . . . In my view, then, it is inequality – not some notion of gross inadequacy – of educational opportunity that raises a question of denial of equal protection of the laws."[63] If, as Justice Marshall clearly believes, education is an exercise in maximizing potential rather than securing bare essentials, his interpretation of the Equal Protection Clause is more suitable to this task than the majority's approach.

A frank engagement with the questions of wealth and poverty also characterizes Justice Marshall's dissent. He criticizes the majority for its unwillingness to directly address this question; Justice Powell, of course, stopped short of viewing wealth as a suspect class. Justice Marshall, on the other hand, argues that doing so is rooted in the Court's prior holdings. He writes, "we have generally gauged the invidiousness of wealth classifications with an awareness of the importance of the interests being affected and the relevance of personal wealth to those interests."[64] Justice Marshall continues, "it must be recognized that while local district wealth may serve other

[60] *Id.* at 79.
[61] *Id.* at 82.
[62] *Id.* at 84.
[63] *Id.* at 89–90.
[64] *Id.* at 122.

interests, it bears no relationship whatsoever to the interest of Texas schoolchildren in the educational opportunity afforded them by the State of Texas."[65] This pithy treatment of an issue labored over by the majority suggests a workable alternative that avoids the numerous pitfalls feared by Justice Powell in the Court's opinion.

Finally, Justice Marshall concludes with a stirring summation of his argument and a rebuke to the majority's deference to the political branches of government:

> The Court seeks solace for its action today in the possibility of legislative reform. The Court's suggestions of legislative redress and experimentation will doubtless be of great comfort to the schoolchildren of Texas's disadvantaged districts, but considering the vested interests of wealthy school districts in the status quo, they are worth little more. The possibility of legislative action is, in all events, no answer to this Court's duty under the Constitution to eliminate unjustified state discrimination. In this case we have been presented with an instance of such discrimination, in a particularly invidious form, against an individual interest of large constitutional and practical importance. To support the demonstrated discrimination in the provision of educational opportunity the State has offered a justification which, on analysis, takes on at best an ephemeral character. Thus, I believe that the wide disparities in taxable district property wealth inherent in the local property tax element of the Texas financing scheme render that scheme violative of the Equal Protection Clause.[66]

Justice Marshall's comprehensive dissent continues to resonate with advocates for increased equity in education. It outlines a framework for school funding standards that, if adopted, would help create a system of public schools more conducive to equal opportunity. It would, in all likelihood, help effectuate the ideals for public education present in the writings of the Founders and earnestly endorsed by social constructivist theorists. Just as importantly, it would combat the badges and incidents of racism and discrimination.

THE LEGACY OF *RODRIGUEZ*

Today, *Rodriguez* remains binding Supreme Court precedent for cases addressing inequities in school funding based on the operation of local property taxes. In 1986, the Court reiterated this principle in its opinion disposing of *Papasan* v. *Allain*.[67] The *Papasan* Court addressed a Mississippi school funding program that treated counties differently based on whether their schools were built on land subject to federal land grant laws in the 1800s. This treatment negatively impacted the funding received by the twenty-three northern Mississippi counties that sat on land ceded to the United States by the Chickasaw Nation in 1832.[68]

---

[65] *Id.*
[66] *Id.* at 132–133.
[67] 478 U.S. 265.
[68] *Id.* at 271.

Since these so-called Chickasaw Cessation counties did not contain schools situated on land allotted to Mississippi by Congressional land grant programs, they received less favorable treatment under the terms of a Mississippi educational trust fund. As a result, the fund paid out approximately $0.63 per pupil in the Chickasaw Cessation counties as opposed to an average of $75.34 across the rest of Mississippi.[69]

This disparity in funding provided the basis of the equal protection claim in *Papasan*.[70] Writing for the majority, Justice White observed that *Rodriguez* and (as we will see later in this chapter) *Plyler* left open the question of whether a minimally adequate education is a fundamental right subject to heightened scrutiny.[71] Justice White then immediately leaves the question open in *Papasan* as well – adopting the *Rodriguez* standard for the case at hand.[72] The majority remanded the case for further proceedings to resolve issues not present in *Rodriguez*. As Justice White explained:

> This case is therefore very different from *Rodriguez*, where the differential financing available to school districts was traceable to school district funds available from local real estate taxation, not to a state decision to divide state resources unequally among school districts. The rationality of the disparity in *Rodriguez*, therefore, which rested on the fact that funding disparities based on differing local wealth were a necessary adjunct of allowing meaningful local control over school funding, does not settle the constitutionality of disparities alleged in this case, and we differ with the Court of Appeals in this respect.[73]

On remand, the Court directed the lower courts to address the following question: Given that the State has title to assets granted to it by the Federal Government for the use of the State's schools, does the Equal Protection Clause permit it to distribute the benefit of these assets unequally among the school districts as it now does?[74]

In dissent, the author of *Rodriguez*, Justice Powell, emphasized that the challenged trust fund accounts for only 1.5 percent of Mississippi's overall educational funding scheme.[75] Local revenues, he continued, only make up 26 percent of funds expended for schools in Mississippi – with nearly three quarters of funds coming from the state and federal governments.[76]

On remand, the parties agreed to an equitable remedy designed to offer an "equivalent substitute" for funding to the Chickasaw Cessation counties.[77] While the litigation did not call *Rodriguez* into serious question, it did result in the

---

[69] *Id.* at 273.
[70] *Id.* at 274.
[71] *Id.* at 275.
[72] *Id.* at 286.
[73] *Id.* at 288.
[74] *Id.* at 289.
[75] *Id.* at 296.
[76] *Id.* at 301.
[77] See Michael J. Kaufman & Sherelyn R. Kaufman, *Education Law, Policy, and Practice* (New York: Wolters Kluwer, 2018), 121.

Supreme Court leaving the door open for arguments claiming that inequitable funding disbursements stemming from a state decision to unequally distribute resources fails the rational basis test.

THE INADEQUATE AND INEQUITABLE FUNDING OF AMERICAN EDUCATION

In most states, school districts receive local revenue in direct proportion to the value of the residential property in the district. As a result, significant disparities occur in the per-pupil revenue allotted to different school districts within the same state. By 1998, the *median* disparity in per-pupil spending between the wealthiest and poorest school districts within a state had grown to nearly $12,000 per student.[78]

Wide disparities also exist in the average per-pupil expenditures between different states. For example, while the national average per-pupil expenditure is $10,834, New Jersey spends $18,485 per student, and Utah spends only $6,849 per student.[79] This disparity in revenue is exacerbated because districts also rely on interest earned on their revenue for additional funds. Districts and states that attract less revenue, of course, also garner less interest income.

These disparities have a racial component as well; districts with mostly white students spend on average approximately $900 more per student than do other districts. As the Education Trust reported, "[s]chool districts that educate the greatest number of low-income and minority students receive substantially less state and local money per student than districts with the fewest such students."[80]

Additionally, findings from the Equity and Excellence Commission, a federal advisory committee chartered by Congress, show:

> While some young Americans – most of them white and affluent – are getting a truly world-class education, those who attend schools in high poverty neighborhoods are getting an education that more closely approximates school in developing nations. In reading, for example, although U.S. children in low-poverty schools rank at the top of the world, those in our highest-poverty schools are performing on a par with children in the world's lowest-achieving countries.[81]

---

[78] See also Quality Counts '98, "Resources Data Table"; Common Core of Data (CCD), School District Finance Survey, F-33; Carey, "The Funding Gap"; Kozol, *Savage Inequalities*.

[79] Ranking of the States 2012 and Estimates of School Statistics 2013 (National Education Association, December 2012), www.nea.org/home/54597.htm.

[80] See "School Board News," Natl. Assn. School Bds., 7. See also Carey, "The Funding Gap," 6. ("The troubling pattern of funding shortfalls repeats itself for school districts educating large numbers of minority students.")

[81] *For Each and Every Child: A Report to the Secretary of the United States Department of Education by the Equity and Excellence Commission* 12 (2013).

The predominant system of financing education from local property taxes is inefficient because it directs the least amount of funds to the students who need them the most. The Report states:

> Twenty-two percent of American schoolchildren live in conditions of poverty. ... Nearly half of today's schoolchildren qualify for free or reduced-price school lunches. The achievement gap between children from high- and low-income families is 30 to 40 percent larger among children born in 2001 than among those born 25 years earlier. Poverty rates are disproportionately high for students of color.[82]

Students who need the greatest amount of effective resources receive the least. In fact, the Supreme Court of New Jersey, in *Abbott IV*, held that the state's system of financing public education, which directed funds to students in accordance with the property wealth of their school districts, was in violation of the state constitution's requirement that the state maintain an "efficient" system of education.[83] The system was not efficient because it allocated the least amount of funding to the students who needed the most funding, and allocated the most amount of funding to the students who needed it the least.[84]

Moreover, as Raj Chetty and John Friedman prove in *Does Local Tax Financing of Public Schools Perpetuate Inequality?*, this prevalent method of financing education through local property taxes also perpetuates intergenerational inequality: low parental income is a determinant of the low quality of a child's school, and the low quality of that child's school is a determinant of that child's low future income.[85]

Finally, as Nobel Prize-winning economist James Heckman has shown, the nation's investment in education is inefficient because it focuses on the wrong age group.[86] The bulk of educational spending is dedicated to secondary and higher education.[87] Those investments are too late in the life of a student to produce an effective rate of return.[88] Bruce Perry notes that the country ramps up the amount of money it devotes to educating children at precisely the wrong time – after the child's brain has stopped developing at a rate that can be shaped by the investments.[89]

Although investments in some programs, such as adolescent mentoring and after-school programs, may produce some modest returns, the greatest returns are

---

[82] Ibid.
[83] *Abbott ex rel. Abbott v. Burke* (*Abbott IV*), 693 A.2d 417, 439 (N.J. 1997).
[84] *Id.* at 431.
[85] Raj Chetty & John Friedman, *Does Local Tax Financing of Public Schools Perpetuate Inequality?* 7 (Harvard Univ. & Nat'l Bureau of Econ. Research), www.rajchetty.com/chettyfiles/proptax_nta.pdf [https://perma.cc/K2YY-CVH2].
[86] See James J. Heckman, *Schools, Skills, and Synapses* 25 (Nat'l Bureau of Econ. Research, Working Paper No. 14064, 2008), www.nber.org/papers/w14064.pdf [https://perma.cc/GD2R-GK3E].
[87] Kaufman et al., *Learning Together* at 117, 247 (citing *The Heckman Equation*, Heckman, https://heckmanequation.org/the-heckman-equation/ [https://perma.cc/N2EP-48XD]).
[88] *The Heckman Equation* at note 101.
[89] Bruce Perry & Annette Jackson, "The Long and Winding Road: From Neuroscience to Policy, Program, Practice," *Insight Magazine*, no. 9, 2014, at 4–8, 9.

produced from investments in early childhood education.[90] According to Heckman, investments in early childhood education produce the most robust returns in the form of reduced grade retention, special education costs, health care costs, criminal involvement costs, prison costs, and family instability costs.[91] These investments also generate higher taxable income and increased home ownership.[92] As such, the nation is currently spending the most money educating children who need the least amount of funds, at a moment in their lives that is the least effective at producing educational growth. In no sense does this arrangement demonstrate a proper understanding of the way children learn.

THE RELATIONSHIP BETWEEN FUNDING AND QUALITY

The school funding decisions raise the fundamental political issue of the relationship between resources and the quality of education. In *Rodriguez*, the Supreme Court stated "one of the major sources of controversy concerns the extent to which there is a demonstrable correlation between educational expenditures and the quality of education."[93] The *Rodriguez* Court assumed that quality was to be measured in student outcome, presumably by standardized achievement test results. Alternatively, quality could be measured by inputs: the educational opportunities given to each child to reach their own potential.[94] Justice Marshall endorsed this approach in his dissent.

Despite Justice Powell's suggestion that there is a split among experts regarding the connection between educational funding and educational quality, the weight of authority clearly supports the connection. In fact, the studies that Justice Powell cites as authority for his perceived dispute among scholars are virtually uniform in their conclusion that the *appropriate* allocation of resources has a beneficial impact on the quality of education under any legitimate definition of "quality."[95]

[90] Ibid.
[91] *The Heckman Equation* at 20.
[92] Kaufman et al., *Learning Together* at 121–124. See generally *Research Summary: The Lifecycle Benefits of an Influential Early Childhood Program*, Heckman, https://heckmanequation.org/resource/research-summary-lifecycle-benefits-influential-early-childhood-program/ [https://perma.cc/W8SR-4DGG].
[93] 411 U.S. 1, 43 (1973).
[94] See, e.g., James Coleman, "The Concept of Equality of Educational Opportunity," 38 *Harv. Educ. Rev.* 7 (1968).
[95] See, e.g., Bruce Baker, *Does Money Matter in Education?*, Albert Shanker Institute, 1–44, www.shankerinstitute.org/sites/shanker/files/moneymatters_edition2.pdf; Geoffrey D. Borman & Maritza Dowling, *Schools and Inequality: A Multilevel Analysis of Coleman's Equality of Educational Opportunity Data*, 100 Teachers College Record 1–40 (2010); Christopher Jencks, *Inequality* (1972); Charles Silverman, *Crisis in the Classroom* (1970); *The Coleman Report*, Office of Education, Equality of Educational Opportunity (1966) (hereinafter *Coleman Report*); Daniel P. Moynihan & Frederick Mosteller, *On Equality of Educational Opportunity* (1972). See also Arthur E. Wise, *Rich Schools, Poor Schools: The Promise of Equal Educational Opportunity* (1968); John E. Coons et al., *Private Wealth and Public Education* (1970).

More recent studies confirm the relationship between funds and quality.[96] Where there is disagreement among scholars regarding the connection between money and quality, that disagreement relates to the method of measuring quality or, more significantly, the role of factors *other* than resources in the quality of education. The *Coleman Report*, for example, offered the controversial finding that "schools bring little influence to bear on a child's achievement that is independent of his background and general social context."[97] As a result, the *Report* observed, "inequalities imposed on children by their home, neighborhood, and peer environment are carried along to become the inequalities with which they confront adult life."[98] Although one of the authors of the *Coleman Report* has since come to accept the idea that educational resources can influence a child's achievement and mobility, the fundamental questions raised by the *Report* have not gone away.[99] Indeed, a recent federal attempt at school reform had the effect of weaponizing questions of funding – particularly in struggling districts.

NO CHILD LEFT BEHIND: POURING GASOLINE ON THE FIRE OF RESOURCE DISPARITY

In 2001, Congress passed the No Child Left Behind Act – a reauthorization of the Elementary and Secondary Education Act (ESEA) discussed in Chapter 4. Touted as a signature legislative achievement for the Bush administration, NCLB sought to revitalize public education in the United States.

Unfortunately, NCLB implemented a regime that reduced learning to standardized test results and implemented the most harmful principles of behaviorist theory. In Chapter 3, we saw how behaviorist pedagogy viewed students as responsive only to a system based on draconian punishments interspersed with occasional rewards for compliance. NCLB, in effect, applied this paradigm to the schools themselves. This created, predictably, a climate that featured scapegoating of teachers, manipulation of testing statistics, and few if any improvements in student outcomes.

Eminent educational scholar Diane Ravitch reconsidered her initial support for NCLB after realizing its practical implications. In *The Death and Life of the Great*

---

[96] Rob Greenwald et al., "The Effect of School Resources on Student Achievement," 66 *Rev. Educ. Res.* 361 (1996); Harold Wenglinsky, "How Money Matters: The Effect of School District Spending on Academic Achievement," 70 *Soc. Educ.* 231 (1997); *Funding for Justice: Money, Equity, and the Future of Public Education* (1997) (hereinafter *Funding for Justice*); Lawrence O. Picus, *Student-Level Finance Data: Wave of the Future* (Clearing House Nov./Dec. 2000); Ronald F. Ferguson, "Paying for Public Education: New Evidence on How and Why Money Matters," 28 *Harv. J. Legis.* 465 (1991).
[97] *Coleman Report* at 325.
[98] Ibid.
[99] See Christopher Jencks & Meredith Phillips, *The Black-White Test Score Gap* (Washington, DC: Brookings Institution Press, 1998).

American School System: How Testing and Choice Are Undermining Education, she offers a scathing critique of NCLB's flawed foundations.[100]

Ravitch describes four principles that animated NCLB: (1) annual tests should be conducted by each state for children in grades three through eight; (2) state governments should make all major decisions regarding school reform; (3) underperforming schools would receive assistance; and (4) students attending consistently underperforming schools could transfer elsewhere.[101]

In addition to this "assistance" however, schools that were viewed as not making the grade also faced significant sanctions. Adequate Yearly Progress (AYP) became the watchword for measuring these schools. Failure to demonstrate AYP, Ravitch explains, resulted in escalating penalties. These included: a mandatory right of transfer for each student; an overhaul of curriculum and/or staff; and, after five consecutive years of AYP deficiency, "restructuring."[102] This ominous term encompassed converting to a charter school, privatizing, or (most frequently) undertaking what the law called "major" changes to "school governance."[103]

Ravitch insightfully notes the harm caused by this attempt to adopt corporate oversight techniques to the classroom and schoolhouse. She writes,

> I started to doubt the entire approach to school reform that NCLB represented. I realized that incentives and sanctions may be right for business organizations, where the bottom line – profit – is the highest priority, but they are not right for schools. . . . I came to realize that the sanctions embedded in NCLB were, in fact, not only ineffective but certain to contribute to the privatization of large chunks of public education.[104]

The "large chunks" included many schools suffering the same shortfalls as the Edgewood District in *Rodriguez*. Rather than infusing such schools with desperately needed resources, NCLB paved the way for what amounted to a hostile takeover in all too many cases. As Ravitch observes, "Superintendents in [areas with limited resources and low test scores] boasted of how many schools they had closed, as if it were a badge of honor rather than an admission of defeat. As 2014 draws nearer, growing numbers of schools across the nation are approaching an abyss."[105]

In sum, NCLB's singular focus on test scores and strategy of demolishing rather than reviving struggling schools condensed the worst features of behaviorism and inflicted them on the nation's students – especially the nation's most vulnerable students. Ravitch concludes:

---

[100] (New York: Basic Books, 2010).
[101] Ibid. at 94.
[102] Ibid. at 97–98.
[103] Ibid. at 98.
[104] Ibid. at 102.
[105] Ibid. at 104.

Although NCLB was surrounded with a great deal of high-flown rhetoric when it was passed, promising a new era of high standards and high accomplishment ... the reality was far different. Its remedies did not work. Its sanctions were ineffective. It did not bring about high standards or high accomplishment. The gains in test scores at the state level were typically the result of teaching students test-taking skills and strategies, rather than broadening and deepening their knowledge of the world and their ability to understand what they have learned....[106]

[T]he market, with its great strengths, is not the appropriate mechanism to supply services that should be distributed equally to people in every neighborhood in every city and town in the nation without regard to their ability to pay or their political power. The market is not the right mechanism to supply police protection or fire protection, nor is it the right mechanism to supply public education.[107]

Less tangibly but equally importantly from a social constructivist perspective, the message sent to children by closing their school due to poor metrics is deeply harmful. An adult left unemployed by the closure of, for example, an underperforming manufacturing plant often faces confusion, anxiety, and a sense of disillusionment on being deemed "unnecessary" or "unwanted" by his former employer. How must children feel when their school is closed for underperformance? Carried to its extreme, the logic of NCLB permits not only teachers but also students to, at least temporarily, be laid off in the same manner as a millworker whose plant has closed. Rather than teaching children to construct knowledge together through meaningful relationships, NCLB treats them, in a sense, as employees who must meet certain demands to keep their current job placements. It must be admitted that the regime implemented by NCLB from 2001 to 2015 – with its wholehearted embrace of behaviorist principles – could never have arisen if the *Rodriguez* Court had recognized education as a fundamental right in 1973.

THE PENDULUM SWINGS: THE EVERY STUDENT SUCCEEDS ACT OF 2015

The Every Student Succeeds Act of 2015 (ESSA) provides the most recent template for the respective roles of the federal and state governments in education.[108] ESSA replaces the No Child Left Behind Act, passed in 2001. It delegates greater responsibility to the states and adjusts the system of evaluating students, teachers, and schools.

Nationwide, the federal government sets wide parameters that all states must observe in developing their standards. These relate to the procedures of data collection and reporting rather than substantive goals. Thus, states have great discretion in

---

[106] Ibid. at 110.
[107] Ibid. at 241.
[108] The material under this heading originally appeared in Michael J. Kaufman & Sherelyn R. Kaufman, Education Law, Policy, and Practice (New York: Wolters Kluwer, 2018).

evaluating students, teachers, and schools. States must continue to administer annual reading and math tests for students in grades three to eight as well as once during high school. They also must test in science once during grades three to five, grades six to nine, and grades ten to twelve. The evaluation can take the form either of a single exam or a series of interim tests which produce an annual result. Portfolios, projects, and performance can also play a part in the assessment scheme.

Although ESSA gives the states some leeway in structuring their assessments, the statute continues the No Child Left Behind Act's insistence on the use of standardized tests as the primary method of accountability. Under ESSA, states must differentiate student performance using at least three categories (Basic, Proficient, Advanced). States can choose how much weight to assign the tests in overall evaluations and are encouraged to use other sources – including documentation and evaluations of general school climate.

States also must develop their own systems for evaluating teacher and school performance within a general framework. For all schools, states must include a substantial "academic achievement indicator" (i.e., proficiency on state tests). For elementary and middle schools, states must add another academic indicator (i.e., student growth) that allows for meaningful school differentiation. For high schools, this same measurement is typically satisfied with graduation rates. States must also measure English Language Proficiency and one other less-weighted indicator of school quality or student success that is valid, reliable, and comparable, such as student engagement. Under ESSA, the federal government no longer evaluates teachers based on student test performance. States, meanwhile, may consider this metric as one of many factors in grading educators.

In terms of assigning grades to schools, states must include at least three levels of differentiation for each indicator and summative rating. They must offer comprehensive support to the lowest performing 5 percent of schools in the state, as well as all high schools that fail to graduate one third or more of their students. States additionally are required to provide targeted support for at least one "consistently underperforming" subgroup as defined by the state. This can include economically disadvantaged students, racial and ethnic groups, students with disabilities, or English Language Learners. Further targeted support is required for any subgroup that performs at the level of the lowest performing 5 percent of schools.

ESSA also includes language that specifies the respective roles of federal and state government in school funding. It provides $15 billion in Title I funds for 2017 – increasing to $16.2 billion by 2020. It prioritizes pilot programs which allow for flexibility in the use of federal funds to achieve more equitable per pupil spending. Of the states, it requires maintenance of effort – though it offers more flexibility than under No Child Left Behind. Now, states need only show that their methodology insures that each school got the same overall amount from the state that it would have received without Title I federal funds. The statute does not require specific, individual cost allocation.

In sum, ESSA moves only slightly away from the scheme of high-stakes standardized testing championed by No Child Left Behind. More positively, the statute requires the states to augment their regime of standardized testing with more authentic, holistic, and multifaceted approaches to assessing students, teachers, and schools. It also includes more generous safeguards to insure that struggling schools receive needed resources from both the federal and state government. This is a welcome change from the punitive approach that held sway under NCLB.

Of course, neither NCLB nor ESSA says anything about a "right" to education. Both statutes operate within the *Rodriguez* framework of avoiding an absolute deprivation of an education. Now, we will examine *Plyler* v. *Doe*, in which the Supreme Court appeared to announce a right to be free from an absolute deprivation of education.

PLYLER V. DOE: THE "RIGHT" TO EDUCATION REVISITED

In *Plyler* v. *Doe*,[109] the Supreme Court addressed a question left unresolved in *Rodriguez*: whether the absolute denial of public education to a class of individuals – namely, undocumented school-age children – offended the Equal Protection Clause of the Fourteenth Amendment.[110] The Court answered in the affirmative.

In an opinion written by Justice Brennan, the majority began by addressing the chaotic, ambiguous situation on the United States–Mexico border. Their appraisal rings familiar to readers examining the case nearly four decades later. Quoting the lower court which first examined the case, Justice Brennan observed, "under current laws and practices, 'the illegal alien of today may well be the legal alien of tomorrow,' and that without an education, these undocumented children, 'already disadvantaged as a result of poverty, lack of English-speaking ability, and undeniable racial prejudices, ... will become permanently locked into the lowest socioeconomic class.'"[111]

With this wrenching reality firmly in mind, the *Plyler* Court proceeded to reject the State of Texas's argument that undocumented immigrants were not "persons within the jurisdiction" of Texas and thus not entitled to equal protection.[112] The Court unambiguously rebuked this line of reasoning, noting "[w]hatever his status under the immigration laws, an alien is surely a 'person' in any ordinary sense of that term."[113] The Court also rejected Texas's contention that the class of persons entitled to equal protection is less inclusive than the class of persons entitled to due process.[114] Justice Brennan instead continued the Court's tradition of viewing

---

[109] 457 U.S. 202 (1982).
[110] *Id.* at 205.
[111] *Id.* at 208 (Internal citations omitted).
[112] *Id.* at 210.
[113] *Id.*
[114] *Id.* at 211.

these two classes as identical.¹¹⁵ He articulated the Court's position in no uncertain terms, observing: "The Equal Protection Clause was intended to work nothing less than the abolition of all caste-based and invidious class-based legislation. That objective is fundamentally at odds with the power the State asserts here to classify persons subject to its laws as nonetheless excepted from its protection."¹¹⁶

The Court then took notice of the uniquely challenging position occupied by the plaintiffs. While in the United States illegally, their young age suggests that – in nearly all cases – they had little say in the decision to enter the country. Justice Brennan's careful treatment of the subject follows:

> Sheer incapability or lax enforcement of the laws barring entry into this country, coupled with the failure to establish an effective bar to the employment of undocumented aliens, has resulted in the creation of a substantial 'shadow population' of illegal migrants – numbering in the millions – within our borders. This situation raises the specter of a permanent caste of undocumented resident aliens, encouraged by some to remain here as a source of cheap labor, but nevertheless denied the benefits that our society makes available to citizens and lawful residents. The existence of such an underclass presents most difficult problems for a Nation that prides itself on adherence to principles of equality under law.
>
> The children who are plaintiffs in these cases are special members of this underclass. Persuasive arguments support the view that a State may withhold its beneficence from those whose very presence within the United States is the product of their own unlawful conduct. These arguments do not apply with the same force to classifications imposing disabilities on the minor *children* of such illegal entrants. ... Even if the State found it expedient to control the conduct of adults by acting against their children, legislation directing the onus of a parent's misconduct against his children does not comport with fundamental conceptions of justice. ...
>
> Of course, undocumented status is not irrelevant to any proper legislative goal. Nor is undocumented status an absolutely immutable characteristic since it is the product of conscious, indeed unlawful, action. But [the Texas law] is directed against children, and imposes its discriminatory burden on the basis of a legal characteristic over which children can have little control. It is thus difficult to conceive of a rational justification for penalizing these children for their presence within the United States."¹¹⁷

Having established the innocence of the deprived class, the majority next addressed the nature of the deprivation. Notably, the *Plyler* Court accepted *Rodriguez* on its terms; it conceded that education is not a constitutionally guaranteed right.¹¹⁸ Yet, it noted that education is distinctive from other government welfare "benefits." The Court concluded, "education has a fundamental role in

---

¹¹⁵ *Id.*
¹¹⁶ *Id.* at 213.
¹¹⁷ *Id.* at 218–220.
¹¹⁸ *Id.* at 221.

maintaining the fabric of our society. We cannot ignore the significant social costs borne by our Nation when select groups are denied the means to absorb the values and skills upon which our social order rests."[119] Here, Justice Brennan echoes an idea first developed by classical philosophers: a democracy worthy of the name must educate its future citizens to be full participants in its governance.

Just as the legal status of the entitlement to education is left less than entirely clear in the opinion, so too is the appropriate standard for review. In one section, Justice Brennan questioned the applicability of the traditional equal protection formulations of suspect classes and fundamental rights. After oscillating throughout the opinion – and insinuating that the Texas statute would struggle to pass rational basis review – Justice Brennan settled on an intermediate level of scrutiny: any denial of public education to an identifiable group of innocent children must be justified by demonstrating that it furthers a substantial state interest.[120]

Using this standard, the *Plyler* Court rejected Texas's three proffered interests as insufficient. First, it rebuffed Texas's argument that it may deny public education to undocumented children in order to attempt to stem the tide of illegal immigration. The Court deemed this policy "ludicrously ineffectual."[121] Second, it characterized Texas's contention that these children impose a special burden on educators and school services as wholly unsupported by the record.[122] Third, the Court found Texas's argument that the children are transient and unlikely to remain within the state as unduly vague and speculative.[123]

Three other justices in the majority authored concurring opinions. Justice Marshall called for the wholesale repudiation of *Rodriguez* – reiterating his view that education is a fundamental right.[124] For his part, Justice Blackmun attempted to reconcile *Plyler* and *Rodriguez*, noting that only in *Plyler* did the facts implicate an absolute denial of education to a class of children.[125] Meanwhile, Justice Powell emphasized the lack of agency of the children in the decision to cross the border illegally, and noted the fundamental injustice of visiting punishment on children for the transgressions of their parents.[126]

Writing for the three dissenters, Justice Burger described the challenged statute as "senseless."[127] However, he framed the issue as whether the state may differentiate between persons lawfully present and not lawfully present for the purposes of "allocating its finite resources."[128] The dissenters concluded by arguing that

[119] *Id.*
[120] *Id.* at 230.
[121] *Id.* at 228.
[122] *Id.* at 229.
[123] *Id.* at 229–230.
[124] *Id.* at 231.
[125] *Id.* at 233.
[126] *Id.* at 240.
[127] *Id.* at 242.
[128] *Id.* at 243.

upholding the statute as constitutional (albeit ill-advised) would force the political branches of government to at last apply the required, long-overdue corrective.[129]

The Supreme Court's educational funding decisions leave many unanswered questions. Nonetheless, the overriding import of these cases is clear. The United States Constitution does not expressly or implicitly create a fundamental right to public education. It may, however, protect against an absolute deprivation of education to a discrete class of citizens. Consequently, the Constitution does not prohibit disparities arising from educational funding regimes which pass the rational basis test. In the wake of the Supreme Court's decisions erecting a deferential approach to disparities in funding, and in light of the unmistakable reality of such disparities in virtually every state, the focus of legal challenges to educational funding regimes has shifted to state constitutions.

THE CONSTITUTIONAL RIGHT TO AN ADEQUATE AND EQUITABLE EDUCATION AT THE STATE LEVEL

All state constitutions contain their own "equal protection" clause, as well as language that requires the establishment of public schools. Nearly half of the states also have constitutional language declaring education to be a fundamental value or goal. A strong minority of states has constitutional language requiring an "efficient" or "thorough" educational system. Under these provisions of the state constitutions, a majority of the state courts have found education to be a fundamental right subject to heightened scrutiny.

Even before *Rodriguez*, the California Supreme Court in *Serrano* had declared education to be a "fundamental interest" warranting strict scrutiny review.[130] Under that standard, California failed to establish that its school financing system, which resulted in disparate per-pupil allocations of resources, was necessary to achieve the interest of local control over education. Accordingly, the *Serrano* Court found the California system to be invalid under the Equal Protection Clause, but did not specify whether its decision was based on the United States or California Constitution.

After the Supreme Court's rejection of the challenge to inequitable educational funding under the federal Equal Protection Clause in *Rodriguez*, however, the California Supreme Court made clear that its prior decision in *Serrano* was based on the California Constitution. In *Serrano II*, the Court declared that although the language of the Equal Protection Clause in the California Constitution was "substantially the equivalent" of the United States Constitution's Equal Protection Clause, the two provisions should not be interpreted in lockstep.[131] To the contrary, the two clauses "are possessed of an independent vitality which, in a given case, may

---

[129] *Id.* at 253.
[130] *Serrano v. Priest*, 5 Cal. 3d 584, 487 P.2d 1241 (Cal. 1971) (*Serrano I*).
[131] 18 Cal.3d 728, 764, 557 P.2d 929, 950 (Cal. 1976).

demand an analysis different from that which would obtain if only federal standards were applicable."[132] Similarly, in Wyoming,[133] Connecticut,[134] and North Dakota,[135] the courts invalidated inequitable educational funding regimes under the Equal Protection Clause in their respective state constitutions.

In addition to revisiting the school funding question under the Equal Protection Clause of their state constitutions, state courts also have sought to define the requirements of an "efficient" system of public education. In *Edgewood Independent School District v. Kirby*,[136] in fact, the Texas Supreme Court explicitly reconsidered the Edgewood School District – the very district at issue in *Rodriguez*. The Court concluded that Texas's statewide system for funding education based on local property taxes, which produced a disparity of resources per student of 700 to 1, was contrary to the Texas Constitution's requirement that the legislature support and maintain an "efficient system of public free schools."[137]

In *Campaign for Fiscal Equity, Inc. v. State of New York*,[138] the New York Court of Appeals[139] concluded that the New York City schools failed to satisfy the New York Constitution's requirement of a "system of free common schools, wherein all the children of the state may be educated."[140] After defining a "sound basic education" as one that affords students the skills and knowledge for "meaningful participation in contemporary society," the court found a "systematic failure" to provide New York City high school students with the constitutionally mandated standard of education.[141] In fact, the court concluded, there existed a "mismatch" between the disproportionately higher needs of the city's students and the disproportionately lower level of statewide funding allocated to meet those needs. The court ordered the governor and the legislature to "ascertain the actual cost" of constitutional compliance and then to revise the state's funding formula to insure necessary resources to provide a "sound basic education" for all public school students in New York City.[142]

In *DeRolph v. Ohio*,[143] the Ohio Supreme Court found disparities in educational funding within the state violative of the Ohio Constitution's guarantee of

---

[132] *Id.*
[133] See *Washakie County School District No. v. Herschler*, 606 P.2d 310 (Wyo. 1980).
[134] See *Horton v. Meskill*, 376 A.2d 359 (Conn. 1977).
[135] See *In the Interest of G.H.*, 218 N.W. 2d 441 (N.D. 1974).
[136] 777 S.W.2d 391 (Tex. 1989).
[137] *Id.* at 394.
[138] 100 N.Y.2d 893 (N.Y. 2003),
[139] Despite the existence of a New York Supreme Court, the Court of Appeals is, in fact, New York's highest court.
[140] N.Y. CONST., Art. XI, §1.
[141] 100 N.Y.2d 893, 905 (N.Y. 2003).
[142] See also *Rose v. The Council for Better Education, Inc.*, 790 S.W.2d 186 (Ky. 1989) (finding that Kentucky's constitutional requirement of an "efficient system of common schools" was violated by maintenance of an underfunded and unequally funded system).
[143] 677 N.E.2d 733 (1997).

a "thorough and efficient" educational system. The Court reasoned that the harm presented by inadequate and inequitable funding should not be left for the General Assembly to remedy. A massive amount of evidence was presented showing the schools were "starved for funds, lacked teachers, buildings, and equipment, and had inferior educational programs, and that their pupils were being deprived of educational opportunity." The Court concluded that Ohio's elementary and secondary public schools are neither thorough nor efficient, thus violating the Ohio Constitution.

Since *Rodriguez*, litigants have challenged school finance systems in forty-five states, claiming primarily that those systems violate language in their state's constitution mandating a minimally adequate level of educational resources for all students. They have been successful in a majority of the cases.[144] Nevertheless, the influence of *Rodriguez* extends to many states.

In one notable example, the Illinois Supreme Court leaned heavily on *Rodriguez* in deciding *Committee for Educational Rights v. Edgar*.[145] Interpreting the Equal Protection Clause of the Illinois Constitution in lockstep with the Fourteenth Amendment, the Illinois Supreme Court declined to find a fundamental right to education. Additionally, the Illinois Supreme Court held that the Illinois Constitution's guarantee of an efficient, high quality education system did not implicate funding questions. It concluded that "efficient" did not embrace questions of equality and that defining "high quality" was not a justiciable question. Only the legislative branch, it held, was competent to resolve questions of educational quality.

---

[144] See, e.g., *Roosevelt Elementary Sch. Dist. No. 66 v. Bishop*, 877 P.2d 806, 814 (Ariz. 1994) (interpreting "general and uniform" to require a finance system that "provide[s] sufficient funds to educate children on substantially equal terms"); *Idaho Sch. for Equal Educ. Opportunity v. Evans*, 850 P.2d 724, 734 (Idaho 1993) (interpreting "thorough" in light of the legislature's educational standards and concluding that the standards' requirements of school facilities, instructional programs, and textbooks are "consistent with our view of thoroughness"); *Abbott v. Burke*, 693 A.2d 417, 425 (N.J. 1997) (interpreting "thorough and efficient" in light of the legislature's education standards); *Robinson v. Cahill*, 287 A.2d 187, 211 (N.J. Super. Ct. Law Div. 1972) (interpreting "thorough" to mean "more than simply adequate or minimal"); *DeRolph v. State*, 677 N.E.2d 733, 741 (Ohio 1997) (interpreting a "thorough and efficient" system as one in which no school district is "starved for funds" or "lack[s] teachers, buildings, or equipment"); *Pauley v. Kelly*, 255 S.E.2d 859, 877 (W. Va. 1979) (defining "thorough and efficient" to require, "as best the state of education expertise allows," a system that prepares students for "useful and happy occupations" and "recreation and citizenship"); *Campbell Cnty. Sch. Dist. v. State*, 907 P.2d 1238, 1258–59 (Wyo. 1995) (defining a "thorough and efficient" system of public schools as one marked by completeness and productivity without waste and that is "reasonably sufficient for the appropriate or suitable teaching/education/learning of the state's school age children"); *Lujan v. Colorado State Board of Educ.*, 649P.2d 1005, 1028 (Colo. 1982) (quoting *Northshore Sch. Dist. No. 417 v. Kinnear*, 530 P.2d 178, 202 (Wash. 1974)). ("A general and uniform system [is] one in which every child in the state has free access to certain minimum and reasonably standardized educational and instructional facilities and opportunities to at least the 12th grade.") See also Michael Rebell, *Courts and Kids: Pursuing Educational Equity Through the State Courts* (University of Chicago Press, 2009).

[145] 174 Ill.2d. 1 (1996)

Although the Illinois Supreme Court has upheld the reasoning and result in *Edgar*,[146] proponents of equitable educational funding have raised significant new challenges to Illinois's school finance regime. In *Carr v. Koch*,[147] individual taxpayers claimed that the education finance system violated Illinois' Equal Protection Clause because residents of property-poor school districts pay an effective property tax rate that is significantly higher than the rate paid by similarly situated taxpayers in property-rich districts. At the same time, per-student spending in the property-poor districts is significantly lower than in property-rich districts. On average, residents of K-8 property-poor school districts incur a tax rate 23 percent higher than residents of property-rich districts. Yet, per-student spending is 28 percent less for students in property-poor districts than in property-rich districts. The Illinois Supreme Court, however, held that the taxpayers lacked standing to challenge the state's finance regime because they had not alleged a direct or threatened injury resulting from the finance system.

LEGAL ARGUMENTS SUPPORTING THE RIGHT TO EQUITABLE ACCESS TO EDUCATIONAL PROGRAMS

In light of the structure of American law, there are four types of legal arguments that can be made to support equitable access to education programs: (1) federal constitutional arguments based on an absolute deprivation of a minimally adequate education; (2) state constitutional arguments based on equity, adequacy, thoroughness, or efficiency; (3) state constitutional arguments based on proper judicial remedies for constitutional violations; and (4) state statutory arguments based on a violation of a state's Civil Rights Act or Human Rights Act.

FEDERAL CONSTITUTIONAL ARGUMENTS BASED ON AN ABSOLUTE DEPRIVATION OF A MINIMALLY ADEQUATE EDUCATION

Although the Supreme Court has definitively held that the Constitution does not include a right to education, the Court in *San Antonio v. Rodriguez*, recognized an implicit right to be free from an absolute deprivation of a minimally adequate education. Moreover, in *Plyler* and *Papasan*, the Supreme Court reaffirmed the existence of such a constitutional right to be free from an absolute denial by the government of access to a minimally adequate level of education. As we have seen, this remains difficult to prove.

---

[146] See *Lewis E. v. Spagnolo*, 710 N.E.2d 798 (Ill. 1999).
[147] 960 N.E.2d 640 (Ill. 2011).

STATE CONSTITUTIONAL ARGUMENTS BASED ON EQUITY AND ADEQUACY

Additionally, litigants can continue to turn to state courts to achieve increased access to education programs by relying on the language in state constitutions. A majority of state courts have recognized state constitutional rights to equity and adequacy in educational opportunities.

THE UNCONSTITUTIONAL DENIAL OF ACCESS TO ADEQUATE EDUCATION AT THE STATE LEVEL

As we have seen, a majority of state courts have interpreted the education clauses in their states' respective constitutions to guarantee students the right to an adequate education, and to guarantee the funding necessary to provide that adequate education. The state constitutional right to an adequate education thus could support a claim that the state's failure to provide access to education is a denial of the right to an adequate education.[148] In the school finance area, adequacy cases generally involve: (1) defining the goals of an adequate education, and (2) determining the resources necessary to reach those goals.[149] These cases require the articulation of concrete outcome goals and some demonstration that a particular input would assist in reaching those goals.

To determine whether or not to recognize a right to equal educational opportunity, courts first determine whether education is a fundamental right or whether a school funding system discriminates on the basis of wealth. If the court concludes that education is a fundamental right and/or that a suspect class is implicated, it applies strict scrutiny. Then, the inquiry becomes whether existing inequalities in funding or programs are necessary to satisfy a compelling state interest. If strict scrutiny is not triggered, courts apply the rational basis test. Generally speaking, strict scrutiny leads to a finding of unconstitutionality and rational basis results in a finding of constitutionality for the challenged practice.

STATE STATUTORY ARGUMENTS BASED ON A VIOLATION OF A STATE'S CIVIL RIGHTS OR HUMAN RIGHTS ACT

Litigants can use their state's Civil Rights Act or Human Rights Act to argue that a lack of access to education has a disparate impact on minority children. This emerging area of litigation offers intriguing possibilities. For example, in August 2008, the Chicago Urban League filed a lawsuit against the State of Illinois and the Illinois State Board of Education to have the State of Illinois' current public

---

[148] James E. Ryan, "A Constitutional Right to Preschool," 94 CAL. L. REV. 49 (2006), 75.
[149] Id.

school funding scheme declared unconstitutional and in violation of the Illinois Civil Rights Act of 2003.

The complaint alleged that (1) the State of Illinois has deprived African American, Latino, and other minority children of a high quality education by discriminating against families based on race; (2) the State of Illinois' funding scheme has a discriminatory impact on minority students; and (3) the funding scheme creates inadequate educational opportunity for thousands of public school children.[150]

Specifically, the Chicago Urban League asserted that the State's public school funding scheme: (1) disparately impacts racial and ethnic minority students who attend Majority-Minority Districts in violation of the Illinois Civil Rights Act of 2003; (2) violates the Uniformity of Taxation provision of the Illinois Constitution; (3) violates Plaintiffs' right to attend "high quality educational institutions" guaranteed by the Education Article under the Illinois Constitution; and (4) violates Plaintiffs' right to equal protection under the Illinois Constitution.[151] The court rejected these arguments except for the claim under the Illinois Civil Rights Act of 2003.

The foundation for plaintiffs' viable claim under the Illinois Civil Rights Act of 2003 is that Illinois is specifically charged with the obligation to provide for the establishment of high quality educational institutions and services under the Illinois Constitution, Article X, Section 1.[152] The Education Committee of the Sixth Illinois Constitutional Convention's report on the proposed Education Article of the Illinois Constitution states that "[t]he opportunity for an education where the state has undertaken to provide it, is a right which must be made available to all on equal terms."

The plaintiffs alleged, however, that Illinois' funding scheme has a discriminatory disparate impact on minority students who attend school in poor districts. The plaintiffs pled facts showing that the school funding system has the effect of subjecting minority students to discrimination because they attend schools in "Majority-Minority Districts."[153]

The plaintiffs further alleged that, because defendants' system rests too heavily on local property taxes, students who attend schools in property-poor communities do not receive an equal educational opportunity.[154] Thus, defendants' conduct has the effect of subjecting minority students to discrimination because of their race.[155] The

---

[150] Chicago Urban League Verified Complaint. 2008; Doc no. 08CH30490. http://schoolfunding.info/wp-content/uploads/2017/01/ILComplaint.pdf.
[151] Chicago Urban League News Release, "Urban League Achieves Major Milestone in Education Funding Lawsuit," April 16, 2009, www.thechicagourbanleague.org/site/default.aspx?PageID=342.
[152] *Chicago Urban League Verified Complaint*, 27.
[153] *Chicago Urban League, et al. v. State of Illinois, et al.* Memorandum Opinion, No. 08 CH 30490, 4, www.scribd.com/doc/21445238/Chicago-Urban-League-et-al-v-Illinois-State-Board-of-Education-4-15-09.
[154] *Id.*
[155] *Chicago Urban League Verified Complaint*, 27.

court found that the complaint provided a straightforward challenge to the alleged disparate impact produced by defendants' adoption, implementation, enactment, and enforcement of the school funding system and was therefore viable.[156]

In 2017, the Chicago Urban League reached a settlement with the Illinois State Board of Education (ISBE). The terms of the agreement require ISBE to distribute general state aid in a manner that takes into account the unique needs of Majority-Minority Districts. The agreement applies to years in which Illinois appropriates a general state aid package sufficient to cover less than 95 percent of all district claims for aid.[157] In such years, ISBE may not cut aid to Majority-Minority Districts pursuant to a "proration" method in which the Majority-Minority Districts would face cuts at the same rate as all Illinois districts.[158] Instead, ISBE must use its discretion to formulate a funding management method that takes into account the special needs and circumstances of Majority-Minority Districts.[159] In exchange, the Chicago Urban League dropped its lawsuit. The agreement, which runs until 2027, safeguards Majority-Minority Districts from the full brunt of any shortfalls in state appropriations that may arise during the next decade.

CONCLUSION

Despite all the compliments it pays education, the Supreme Court holds unequivocally in *Rodriguez* that it is not a fundamental right guaranteed by the Constitution. While *Plyler* and *Papasan* both qualify this holding somewhat, neither offers a substantial challenge to it. As a result of the deferential standard of review applied to educational funding, a demonstrably unequal and often unjust system of funding holds sway throughout most of the country. This inequitable funding perpetuates the badges and incidents of racial discrimination.

At the state level, the respective constitutions of nearly all states explicitly commit the state to providing a free public education system. Lawsuits have resulted in a substantial number of states overhauling their funding systems to achieve more equitable disbursements of revenue. These lawsuits have, in many cases, spurred an honest judicial grappling with realities largely avoided by the *Rodriguez* Court.

In an era in which income inequality has increased, advocates for equity in educational funding will likely focus their efforts at the state rather than federal level. In addition to challenges in the courts, such advocates must also bear in mind the importance of state and federal legislatures in determining the future of educational funding.

Considerations of racial justice have informed our discussions of equal opportunity, higher education, and inequitable funding in the past three chapters. Yet,

---

[156] *Chicago Urban League Memorandum Opinion*, 5.
[157] *Chicago Urban League Settlement*, 3.
[158] *Id.* at 4.
[159] *Id.*

despite this inescapable context, most of the key precedents in these areas address the issues on an ostensibly race-neutral basis. While the badges and incidents of racial discrimination are ever in the background of the binding precedents, they seldom take center stage.

For the next two chapters, we will investigate areas of education law specifically intended to aid two groups often excluded from educational opportunities. First, we will delve into the history of protections against gender discrimination – particularly in higher education. Next, we will look at efforts to integrate students with special needs into a mainstream educational environment – especially at the elementary level. As we will see, both groups have borne badges and incidents of their own.

7

Gender Discrimination in Education

This chapter will begin by presenting the historical context in which Title IX of the 1972 Education Act arose – tracing its origins to the broader struggle for civil rights in the 1960s. Next, it will recount the development of Title IX through the decades as critical Supreme Court decisions refined its scope and clarified its implications for students and institutions alike. In addition, we will explore the landmark case of *United States* v. *Virginia* – to date the most significant application of the Equal Protection Clause in the context of gender discrimination in education.

Finally, we will conclude the chapter by examining the shifting landscape of Title IX enforcement, juxtaposing the approaches taken by the Obama and Trump administrations. We will also demonstrate how, despite the great strides made under Title IX, all too many women face unacceptable degrees of sexual assault, harassment, and discrimination. Against this backdrop, we will demonstrate the role a pedagogy steeped in social constructivist thought can play in combatting and, eventually, defeating this scourge. A democracy meant to fulfill the ideals of the Founders cannot afford to discount the contributions of half its citizens. As we will see, an equitable application of Title IX, the Equal Protection Clause, and social constructivist pedagogy will help remove the badges and incidents of gender discrimination.

TITLE IX: HISTORICAL CONTEXT

Much like the race-conscious admissions policies in higher education discussed in Chapter 5, Title IX originated in the Civil Rights Movement of the 1960s. Advocates soon realized that the arguments against discrimination on the basis of race applied with equal force to discrimination on the basis of sex. Indeed, historian Joshua B. Freeman notes, "The passage of the 1964 Civil Rights Act encouraged women to press for equality and greater opportunity at work, at a time when their labor force participation was continuing to rise."[1] Feeding off the momentum of this increased

---

[1] Joshua B. Freeman, *American Empire: The Rise of a Global Power, the Democratic Revolution at Home 1945–2000* (New York: Viking, 2012), 262.

emphasis on societal equality, the feminist movement began to assert itself as a palpable force in American politics.[2] Groups such as the National Organization for Women (NOW) and the Women's Liberation Movement succeeded in changing the discourse on women's rights in a remarkably short period of time. "In 1962, two out of three women polled did not consider themselves victims of discrimination. By 1970, half did," observes Freeman.[3]

Perhaps realizing the energy unleashed by the women's movement could register in the voting booth, bipartisan majorities supported the major pieces of legislation to combat sex-based discrimination.[4] The most consequential and far-reaching of these bills was Title IX of the 1972 Education Act. As we will see throughout this chapter, Title IX explicitly conditions the continued receipt of federal funds on recipients' compliance with the command to eliminate sexual discrimination in their institutions.[5] Its language is simple, direct, and far-reaching. Title IX states:

> No person in the United States shall, on the basis of sex, be excluded from participation in, be denied the benefits of, or be subject to discrimination under any education program or activity receiving Federal financial assistance.[6]

This broad command touches every aspect of education, impacting academics, athletics, and student discipline at all educational institutions accepting federal aid, as well as student body composition at public institutions of higher learning. Title IX has proved especially impactful at the university level.

While the nearly half century of Title IX's existence has featured a number of divisive conflicts surrounding its use and interpretation, women's rights legislation was seen as entirely uncontroversial by both the House and the Senate in 1972. As Freeman ironically notes: "Support for (the Equal Rights Amendment) came from an extraordinarily broad spectrum of national figures from actress Jane Fonda ... to Richard Nixon and Strom Thurmond."[7] Given the many battles over the appropriate scope and usage of Title IX, it is revealing to discover that the basic premise of Title IX enjoyed such an extraordinarily wide consensus at its inception.

THE PARAMETERS OF TITLE IX: BROAD SCOPE, JUDICIAL PRECEDENTS, AND ADMINISTRATIVE REMEDIES

In the Education Amendments of 1972,[8] Congress included Title IX's directive preventing gender-based discrimination in federally

---

[2] Ibid. at 262–265.
[3] Ibid. at 264.
[4] Ibid.
[5] Ibid.
[6] United States Department of Justice, "Equal Access to Education: Forty Years of Title IX" (June 23, 2012), 1.
[7] Ibid.
[8] 20 U.S.C. §§1681–1683.

funded schools.[9] Title IX provides that students attending "educational institutions" that "receiv[e] Federal financial assistance" shall not be "excluded from participation in, be denied the benefits of, or be subjected to discrimination under any education program or activity" because of their sex.[10] Section (c) of the statute defines an "educational institution" to include both public and private schools, from preschools to graduate schools.[11] While the language of the statute may seem clear, the actual scope of Title IX has been the subject of much debate among scholars and the courts.[12]

First, what does it mean to "receiv[e]" federal funding? In *Grove City College v. Bell*,[13] the Supreme Court examined the statute's language, congressional intent, and previous judicial constructions to conclude that any money originally disbursed by the federal government and subsequently collected by an educational institution could constitute "recei[pt of] Federal financial assistance" for purposes of Title IX.[14]

The *Grove City* Court considered the argument that, as a consequence of Title IX's broadly construed financial assistance clause, federal aid awarded to one student should subject an entire college to the Title IX requirements simply because the federal financial assistance would eventually reach the school's general operating budget.[15] Under this construction, the entire college would be the "educational program or activity" subject to regulation. That interpretation would effectively require students to attend a private college without the benefit of federal financial aid, or subject the college, which might otherwise be exempt from Title IX oversight, to disciplinary action by the Office of Civil Rights (OCR) of the Department of Education.

The majority held that such a construction is contrary to the "program-specific" language of the Act.[16] The Court therefore limited the application of Title IX to the particular department that receives the federal monies – in Grove City's case, the specific financial aid program.[17]

Nonetheless, in direct response to the *Grove City* ruling, Congress passed the Civil Rights Restoration Act of 1987, which "restore[d] the prior consistent and

---

[9] 20 U.S.C. §1681(a) (2002). See also Maryann Ahranjani, "Mary Daly v. Boston College: The Impermissibility of Single-Sex Classrooms Within a Private University," 9 Am. U. J. Gender Soc. Pol'y & L., 179, 188 (2001) (hereinafter Ahranjani).
[10] 20 U.S.C. §1681(a).
[11] 20 U.S.C. §1681(c).
[12] See Ahranjani, at 188; Julie M. Amstein, "United States v. Virginia: The Case of Coeducation at Virginia Military Institute," 3 Am. U. J. Gender Soc. Pol'y & L. 69 (1999).
[13] 465 U.S. 555 (1984).
[14] Id. at 568, n.18, quoting Sex Discrimination Regulations: Hearings Before the Subcomm. on Postsecondary Education of the House Comm. on Education and Labor, 94th Cong., 1st Sess. 482 (1975) (1975 Hearings) ("assistance that the Government furnishes, that goes directly or indirectly to an institution, is Government aid within the meaning of Title IX").
[15] Id. at 571–573.
[16] Id. at 570.
[17] Id. at 573–574.

long-standing executive branch interpretation of broad, institution-wide application" of Title IX requirements.[18] Specifically, because the educational institution is the intended recipient of the federal money, it is subject to Title IX requirements. Congress thereby expanded Title IX's reach to include nearly every higher educational institution in the country (both public and private) because, on average, federal funds comprise 43 percent of the revenue received by private universities. In doing so, Congress essentially adopted (and vindicated) the argument advanced by Justice Brennan in his dissenting opinion.[19]

If compliance with Title IX proves too onerous, the institutions are free to "terminate [their] participation in the federal grant program and thus avoid the requirements of Title IX."[20] While Title IX may be described as a "contractual relationship with Congress," the statute's funding mechanism allows Congress to implement substantive educational policies.[21]

In order to receive government funds, institutions are required by Title IX to submit a Certificate of Assurance, indicating that their programs and activities treat all students equally with respect to gender.[22] Each particular funding agency issues the terms of an educational institution's endowment according to Title IX's official interpretation, and cautions that failing to comply with the policy will cause funds to be revoked.[23] Generally, institutions must not discriminate between male and female admissions, athletic programs, access to financial aid, counseling, or campus housing.[24]

Title IX's regulations, however, allow an educational institution to maintain separate athletic teams for men and women where selection is based upon competitive skill or where the teams participate in a contact sport.[25]

The Supreme Court has made clear that individuals may bring a private right of action for damages against an educational institution for violating Title IX.[26] In *Cannon*, the Court inferred from the language, intent, and structure of Title IX a private remedy under federal law for Title IX violations.[27] Because Title IX binds

---

[18] Pub. L. No. 100–259, 1988 S. 557. ("Certain aspects of recent decisions and opinions of the Supreme Court have unduly narrowed or cast doubt upon the broad application of title IX of the Education Amendments of 1972.")

[19] *Grove City*, 465 U.S. 555, 581. Also, see, e.g., U.S. Department of Education, NCES, Current-Fund Revenue of Private Degree-Granting Institutions, by Source: 1980–81 to 1995–96, table 331, http://nces.ed.gov/pubs2003/digest02/tables/dt331.asp.

[20] 20 U.S.C. §1681(a)(5).

[21] See Allison Herren Lee, Title IX, "Equal Protection, and the Richter Scale: Will VMI's Vibration Topple Single-Sex Education?," 7 *Tex. J. Women & L.* 37, 69 (1997) (hereinafter Lee).

[22] 28 C.F.R. §54.115.

[23] Lee, at 69.

[24] *Id.* See also *Mercer v. Duke University*, 190 F.3d 643 (4th Cir. 1999).

[25] 34 C.F.R. §106.41(b). See *Horner v. Kentucky High School Athletic Assn.*, 206 F.3d 685 (6th Cir. 2000) (athletic association's refusal to sanction separate girls' fastpitch softball team did not violate Title IX where girls were given opportunities to compete for spots on the boys' team).

[26] *Cannon v. University of Chicago*, 441 U.S. 677, 717 (1979).

[27] *Id.* at 708.

both public and private institutions, a private right of action extends to both types of institutions as well. The *Cannon* Court found support for a private remedy in the plain language of the statute: it specifically confers a remedy to that class of people wronged by an act of gender discrimination.[28] Additionally, Congress intended to treat Title IX the same as Title VI of the Civil Rights Act of 1964, which itself implied a private right of action.[29] Furthermore, Title IX was originally drafted as an amendment to Title VI until it had been sufficiently modified to require treatment as an independent provision.[30] In fact, Title VI's legislative history so convincingly implied a private remedy that the Supreme Court could "no[t] hesitat[e] [to] conclud[e]" that such a right be allowed.[31]

Furthermore, the Court found that a private remedy was consistent with Title IX's goals of eliminating the appearance of federal support for illegal discrimination and providing victims with recourse against discriminatory schools.[32] Finally, the Court concluded that a private remedy under federal law does not interfere with the states' rights to pursue alternative remedies for two reasons: (1) the federal government historically protects citizens from discrimination and (2) the federal action arises under a statute that regulates recipients of federal money.[33]

In *Franklin v. Gwinnett County Public Schools*,[34] the Court reaffirmed the existence of an implied private right of action under Title IX and held that monetary damages are available to victims of Title IX violations. In *Franklin*, the plaintiff, a tenth-grader, sought monetary damages against the school district, alleging that she was the victim of "continual sexual harassment" by the district's sports coach. Reasoning that Congress enacted Title IX against a backdrop of traditional damages remedies and declined to amend Title IX to reject a private remedy after the Court implied such a remedy in *Cannon*, the Supreme Court held that the plaintiff was entitled to pursue a claim for damages against the district.

In its most recent Title IX decisions, the Supreme Court has assumed the existence of a private remedy, and has defined the contours of that remedy. In *Gebser v. Lago Vista Independent School District*,[35] the Court established the elements of a Title IX claim involving sexual harassment of a student by a teacher. Writing for a five-justice majority, Justice O'Connor adopted a "deliberate indifference" standard for Title IX claims in tort for teacher-on-student harassment. "We conclude that damages may not be recovered in those circumstances unless an official of the school district who at a minimum has authority to institute corrective

---

[28] *Id.* at 694.
[29] *Id.* at 694–696 (see, e.g., pp. 695–696, noting that the only difference between Title IX and Title VI was that the word "sex" replaced the words "race, color, or national origin").
[30] *Id.* at 694, 703.
[31] *Id.* at 703, n.34.
[32] *Id.* at 704.
[33] *Id.* at 704, 708.
[34] 503 U.S. 60 (1992).
[35] 524 U.S. 274 (1998).

measures on the district's behalf has actual notice of, and is deliberately indifferent to, the teacher's misconduct."[36] The Court equated "official of the school district" in this formulation with "appropriate person" under the terms of Title IX.[37] In practice, this means that actual notice to an administrator rather than a rank and file teacher generally will be required to sustain a Title IX civil action for damages under *Gebser*.

The *Gebser* Court declined to adopt the more plaintiff-friendly standards of *respondeat superior* liability or constructive notice liability.[38] It reasoned that given the emphasis on actual notice as part of Title IX's menu of administrative remedies for violations, imposing civil tort liability absent actual notice would depart impermissibly from congressional intent.[39]

In dissent, Justice Stevens noted that by requiring actual notice coupled with deliberate indifference to that notice, the majority created an incentive for school boards and officials to insulate themselves from potentially adverse reports.[40] More plainly, it could encourage unscrupulous officials to seek out ways to maintain plausible deniability. Justice Ginsburg, meanwhile, joined Justice Stevens in full but wrote separately to emphasize that she would permit school districts to raise affirmative defenses based on the existence of an effective sexual harassment policy compliant with the requirements of Title IX.[41]

In *Davis v. Monroe County Board of Education*,[42] the Court adopted the *Gebser* standard as controlling for a private action under Title IX involving sexual harassment of a student by another student. Writing for another (though differently comprised) five-justice majority, Justice O'Connor concluded that a plaintiff may recover damages from a school district under Title IX for harassment suffered at the hands of another student

> when the funding recipient acts with deliberate indifference to known acts of harassment in its programs or activities. Moreover, we conclude that such an action will lie only for harassment that is so severe, pervasive, and objectively offensive that it effectively bars the victim's access to an educational opportunity or benefit.[43]

The plaintiff in *Davis* endured horrible mistreatment at the hands of her fifth grade classmate which, in several instances, appeared from the Court's description to escalate into sexual battery.[44] Indeed, the majority noted that the harassing classmate pled guilty to a charge of sexual battery arising from his abusive behavior toward the plaintiff.[45] The plaintiff's grades declined and her mental health

---

[36] *Id.* at 277.
[37] *Id.* at 290.
[38] *Id.* at 282.
[39] *Id.* at 285, 287–288.
[40] *Id.* at 300–301.
[41] *Id.* at 307.
[42] 526 U.S. 629 (1999).
[43] *Id.* at 633.
[44] *Id.* at 633–634
[45] *Id.* at 634.

deteriorated to the point that she composed a suicide note.[46] Thankfully, the plaintiff recovered and did not act upon the note. It was clear, however, that the degree of abuse she endured had extremely troubling repercussions for her wellbeing.

Despite the plaintiff's repeated requests for assistance – coupled with reports from multiple female classmates who suffered similar violations committed by the same perpetrator – the school administration did nothing to intervene. It took three months of repeated complaints for the plaintiff to be granted a seat change in her classroom.[47] This pattern of conduct, reasoned the Court, sufficed to entitle the plaintiff to make her case for damages under the deliberate indifference standard to a jury.[48]

The Court also signaled that, in cases of student-on-student harassment, a plaintiff would need to show more egregious abuses and lackluster responses to prevail than she would for cases of teacher-on-student harassment.[49] The majority accepted that while schools have supervision over students, the nature of classroom interactions, the immaturity of the potential wrongdoers, and the Court's tradition of accepting the good faith of educators all necessitated a heavy factual inquiry before determining liability in such cases. The Court thus set a relatively low bar for districts to avoid liability, simply requiring – in accordance with Title IX – that officials merely respond "to known peer harassment in a manner that is not clearly unreasonable."[50]

Writing for the four dissenting justices (who, ironically, formed with Justice O'Connor the five-justice majority in *Gebser*), Justice Kennedy questioned the wisdom of applying the standard for teacher-perpetrated harassment to similar acts committed by students, foreseeing a deluge of litigation. He also viewed the *Davis* holding as an inappropriate expansion of federal power into the state responsibility of educating and disciplining children. In addition, he specifically noted the possibility for collisions between Title IX civil claims and procedural rights under IDEA and Due Process hearings for alleged perpetrators.[51] In sum, he envisaged a future in which every instance of harassment with sexual overtones between students could provoke multiple lawsuits from both the complainant and the accused.[52] He argued against putting school districts in this position. The majority opinion in *Davis* responds to the dissent's warnings about the expanded scope of Title IX remedies by making clear that peer sexual harassment must be more "severe, pervasive, and objectively offensive" than gender-based teasing or offensive name calling.

---

[46] *Id.*
[47] *Id.* at 635.
[48] *Id.* at 651.
[49] *Id.* at 653.
[50] *Id.* at 649.
[51] *Id.* at 665–666, 682–683.
[52] We will explore the tension between maintaining safe school environments and observing due process safeguards in Chapter 9.

Under the "deliberate indifference" standard created by *Davis*, a school district is faced with difficult choices in reacting to parental complaints about gender-based teasing in the classroom. A policy prohibiting such behavior alone is not likely sufficient to establish an educational institution's lack of "deliberate indifference." And surely a school district cannot avoid liability by being so inept that it never gains knowledge or actual notice of pervasive sexual harassment.[53] In *Wills* v. *Brown University*,[54] the First Circuit found deliberate indifference in the university's failure to take "timely and reasonable measures to end the harassment."[55]

Title IX prohibits three independent forms of conduct based upon "sex": (1) exclusion from participation in; (2) denial of the benefits of; *and* (3) subjection to discrimination under any education program or activity. In concluding that the level of harassment must be "so severe, pervasive, and objectively offensive" that it denies the victim access to educational benefits provided by the school, the Court in *Davis* argues that Title IX prohibits conduct that denies students educational benefits based upon gender. Yet, while Title IX clearly prohibits such conduct, it also independently prohibits schools from subjecting students to discrimination based upon gender.

In fact, the Court acknowledges that the Department of Education's Office for Civil Rights Guidelines provide that student-on-student harassment falls within the scope of Title IX's proscriptions.[56] If, as the Court argues, sexual harassment is a form of gender discrimination, proof of sexual harassment should alone be sufficient to make out a Title IX claim. There is no persuasive statutory basis for the position that the sexual harassment must *also* deny the victim access to educational benefits. However, as we will see, the Court's more restrictive approach has informed an overhaul of Title IX policy undertaken by the Trump administration.

Title IX prohibits discrimination in admitting students to *public* colleges; unless the private colleges receive federal funds, they are generally exempt from oversight. Yet, it is worth noting – as the *Grove City* Court understood – that federal financial aid grants reach most private colleges. Given the skyrocketing cost of college attendance, many if not most private colleges operate on a model which depends upon federal funds to subsidize tuition. As such, the federal footprint in private education and, accordingly, the range of schools subject to Title IX is quite expansive. However, courts decline to

---

[53] See, e.g., *Massey* v. *Akron City Board of Education*, 82 F. Supp. 2d 735 (N.D. Ohio 2000) (no deliberate indifference when school district was unaware of inappropriate sexual contact between teacher and student); *Doe* v. *Dallas Independent School District*, 153 F.3d 211, 219 (5th Cir. 1998) (merely "inept" actions by school do not constitute deliberate indifference).
[54] 184 F.3d 20 (1st Cir. 1999).
[55] *Id.*
[56] See Department of Education, Office of Civil Rights, Sexual Harassment Guidance: Harassment of Students by School Employees, Other Students, or Third Parties, 62 Fed. Reg. 12034, 12039–12040 (2001) (OCR Title IX Guidelines); see also Department of Education, Office for Civil Rights, "Dear Colleague Letter" on Sexual Violence in Schools (2011); Department of Education, Racial Incidents and Harassment Against Students at Educational Institutions, 59 Fed. Reg. 11448, 11449 (1994).

apply the Equal Protection Clause to private colleges because constitutional challenges impose limitations only on governmental actors.[57]

Conscious of this growing importance and applicability of Title IX, the Department of Justice released a fortieth anniversary retrospective in 2012 in which it summarized the legislation's impact. Title IX, the Department of Justice observed, covered nearly 70 million students in 2011.[58] In addition, in the four decades of Title IX, educational attainment for women surpassed that of men in nearly every observable metric.[59]

The report emphasized that the salutary effects of Title IX go far beyond women in the classroom. It concluded:

> Because education is linked to other benefits, such as participation in the labor force, increased earnings, better health and increased access to healthcare, the benefits of Title IX extend far beyond those realized in school. Additionally, the benefits of Title IX reach beyond those realized by women. By prohibiting schools from treating students differently on the basis of sex, Title IX allows both men and women to equally take advantage of any course of study regardless of gender stereotypes about traditionally "male" or "female" coursework or professions. Title IX's protections against harassment also apply to both sexes and schools must take action to prevent sex-based harassment that interferes with the education of both males and females....
>
> The equal educational opportunities for which the Department advocates will better prepare women for success in the workplace and society at large, and will enable them to take on leadership roles in the public and private sectors. Additionally, as women achieve increased visibility in positions of leadership, more young women will benefit from these inspiring female role models. As equality for women in education and in the workplace progresses, gender gaps throughout society, such as those related to earnings, will continue to wane.[60]

INTERMEDIATE SCRUTINY: KEY MILESTONES IN EQUAL PROTECTION JURISPRUDENCE FOR DISCRIMINATION ON THE BASIS OF SEX

In *Craig v. Boren*,[61] the Supreme Court concluded that "[c]lassifications by gender must serve important governmental objectives and must be substantially related to achievement of those objectives."[62] Although the Court refused to apply the rigorous strict scrutiny standard it has used to analyze racial classifications, it nonetheless

---

[57] As we will see, this means *US v. Virginia* has no immediate effect on the viability of private single-sex educational institutions. However, commentators have raised the possibility that the opinion's reasoning could eventually reach these schools.
[58] U. S. Department of Justice, "Equal Access to Education," 1.
[59] Ibid. at 2–3.
[60] Ibid. at 4, 13.
[61] 429 U.S. 190, 197 (1976).
[62] *Id.* at 199, 210.

determined that gender discrimination is offensive enough to warrant a more searching analysis than that given to laws that do not distinguish based upon race or gender.

As we will see, intermediate scrutiny is gender-neutral in the sense that it treats discrimination against men and women with equal suspicion. Indeed, the facts in *Craig* involved discrimination against men, not women. The challenged Oklahoma statute prohibited the sale of beer with a certain alcohol content to males between the ages of 18 and 21 while allowing females of the same age to purchase it. Decided just three years after *Rodriguez*, this suit seeking equal access to alcohol triggered a more searching judicial review than a claim seeking equity in educational funding.

In *Mississippi University for Women v. Hogan*,[63] the Court later reaffirmed that a statute that classifies people based upon gender can survive an equal protection challenge only if there is an "exceedingly persuasive justification" for the classification. In *Hogan*, the Court struck down a Mississippi statute that excluded males from enrolling in a state-supported professional nursing school. The state's primary justification for its exclusion of men from its nursing program was that it "compensates for discrimination against women and, therefore, constitutes educational affirmative action."[64] The Court declared that in "limited circumstances, a gender-based classification favoring one sex can be justified if it intentionally and directly assists members of the sex that is disproportionately burdened."[65] The class benefited by the state's regime, however, must be shown to "actually suffer a disadvantage related to the classification."[66] In *Hogan* the state failed to persuade the Court that its actual purpose was to "compensate for discriminatory barriers faced by women" because women typically are overrepresented in the nursing profession.[67] Nor could the state establish that its gender-based classification was sufficiently related to its purported compensatory objective.[68]

In 1996, the Supreme Court addressed whether the Equal Protection Clause prohibits a state from offering educational opportunities to men while denying them to women. Led by Justice Ginsburg, a 7–1 majority answered in the affirmative.[69]

In *United States v. Virginia*,[70] Virginia sought to maintain the all-male student body of Virginia Military Institute (VMI). A publicly funded military academy, VMI was noted for its commitment to producing civic leaders, devoted alumni network, and reliance on the so-called "adversative" method of pedagogy.[71] This method – based on the practices in place throughout English boarding schools during the 19th

---

[63] 458 U.S. 718, 724 (1982).
[64] *Id.* at 727.
[65] *Id.* at 728.
[66] *Id.*
[67] *Id.* at 728–731.
[68] *Id.*
[69] Justice Thomas recused himself from the case.
[70] 518 U.S. 515 (1996).
[71] *Id.* at 520.

century – entailed constant surveillance of the students, an emphasis on persevering through physical and mental duress, and strict, militaristic discipline.[72] These unique features, Virginia maintained, rendered VMI unsuitable for educating men and women side by side. Virginia thus argued that admitting women would necessarily mean abandoning the adversarial method. As such, Virginia claimed, VMI could not simultaneously admit women and maintain its unique character as an institution.

Following an initial unfavorable ruling at the appellate level, Virginia established the Virginia Women's Leadership Institute (VWIL).[73] Publicly funded but housed at a private college, VWIL purported to offer a means by which women could approximate a VMI education.[74] VWIL, however, differed from VMI in key areas. Justice Ginsburg noted: "In lieu of VMI's adversarial method, the VWIL Task Force favored 'a cooperative method which reinforces self-esteem.'"[75] Additionally, the record established that the breadth and depth of courses at VWIL paled in comparison to the offerings at VMI.[76] Although VMI's vaunted alumni network agreed to open its doors to VWIL graduates, the Court expressed skepticism that this could compensate for the clear difference between a VWIL degree and a VMI degree.[77] Nevertheless, the Fourth Circuit held that women at VWIL could obtain "substantively comparable benefits" to men at VMI.[78] It thus permitted Virginia to continue barring women from VMI.[79]

Justice Ginsburg framed the Court's task as a two-part inquiry:

> First, does Virginia's exclusion of women from the educational opportunities provided by VMI – extraordinary opportunities for military training and civilian leadership development – deny to women "capable of all of the individual activities required of VMI cadets," the equal protection of the laws guaranteed by the Fourteenth Amendment? Second, if VMI's "unique" situation – as Virginia's sole single-sex public institution of higher education – offends the Constitution's equal protection principle, what is the remedial requirement?[80] (Internal citations omitted)

For the Court, Justice Ginsburg articulated the intermediate scrutiny standard as requiring an "exceedingly persuasive justification" by the government for its disparate treatment based on gender.[81] Justice Ginsburg emphasized that, to meet this exacting standard, state actors could not simply recite stereotypes about traditional

---

[72] *Id.*
[73] *Id.* at 526.
[74] *Id.*
[75] *Id.* at 527.
[76] *Id.*
[77] *Id.*
[78] *Id.* at 529.
[79] *Id.* at 530.
[80] *Id.* at 530–531.
[81] *Id.* at 531.

gender roles as justification.[82] Applied to the facts at hand, this meant that Virginia could not defend its practices at VMI by claiming that most women would not find the environment at the school appealing. The inquiry, the Court underlined, was not whether women generally would gravitate toward VMI; rather, it was whether those women who were willing and able to succeed at VMI were being denied the chance to do so in violation of the Equal Protection Clause of the Fourteenth Amendment.

The Court proceeded to reject Virginia's two arguments for continuing to bar women from attending VMI.[83] First, Virginia claimed that single-sex education provides valuable pedagogical benefits and contributes to the diversity of educational options offered by the state. The Court roundly rejected the diversity rationale, noting that the record contained no evidence that a commitment to diversity informed the formation of the school. Indeed, the diversity line of argument did not appear until well into the litigation.[84] Similarly, Justice Ginsburg noted that the pedagogical benefits of single-sex education for some students was not contested in the litigation.[85] The presence or absence of those benefits, however, was not germane to the question of an equal protection violation.

Second, Virginia argued that the admission of women to VMI would "destroy" the unique character of the program.[86] Justice Ginsburg responded by observing: "The notion that admission of women would downgrade VMI's stature, destroy the adversative system and, with it, even the school, is a judgment hardly proved, a prediction hardly different from other (rationalizations) once routinely used to deny rights or opportunities."[87]

Having established that VMI's all male student body constituted an equal protection violation, the Court turned its attention to fashioning a remedy. Embarking on a lengthy exposition of the differences between VMI and VWIL, Justice Ginsburg characterized VWIL as "different in kind from VMI and unequal in tangible and intangible facilities."[88] She then directly questioned one of Virginia's key premises in electing to establish VWIL:

> As earlier stated ... generalizations about "the way women are," estimates of what is appropriate for *most women*, no longer justify denying opportunity to women whose talent and capacity place them outside the average description. Notably, Virginia never asserted that VMI's method of education suits *most men*. ...
>
> By that reasoning, VMI's ... program would be inappropriate for men in general or *as a group*.[89] (Emphasis in original)

[82] Id. at 533.
[83] Id. at 536.
[84] Id. at 539.
[85] Id. at 536.
[86] Id. at 540.
[87] Id. at 542–543.
[88] Id. at 547.
[89] Id. at 550.

In an insightful comparison, Justice Ginsburg next proceeded to compare the "separate but equal" rationalizations advanced by Virginia regarding VMI and VWIL with *Sweatt*.[90] On the surface, both cases concerned a lack of substantial equality in the opportunities offered. More deeply – as Justice Ginsburg explored in her conclusion – both cases demonstrated the sad reality that prejudices led state actors to immediately write off the potential contributions of large segments of the population. As we have seen, this bigoted tendency counters not only the tenets of social constructivism but also the principles of the Founders.

Finally, Justice Ginsburg concluded by more fully explicating the stakes of *United States v. Virginia*. At a glance, the case involved discrimination against women by a small, insular military academy in one state. Moreover, in all likelihood, only a relatively small number of women (not to mention men) would have any interest in spending their college years under barracks conditions. As such, the temptation existed to view this case as a pedantic dispute with little practical implication. Justice Ginsburg, however, eloquently rejected this reading of *United States v. Virginia*, concluding:

> A prime part of the history of our Constitution, historian Richard Morris recounted, is the story of the extension of constitutional rights and protections to people once ignored or excluded. VMI's story continued as our comprehension of "We the People" expanded. There is no reason to believe that the admission of women capable of all the activities required of VMI cadets would destroy the Institute rather than enhance its capacity to serve the "more perfect Union."[91] (Internal citations omitted)

Concurring in the judgment, Chief Justice Rehnquist wrote separately to criticize the ambiguity in the standard used. He noted that in previous gender discrimination cases, the Court had settled on the "important governmental objective" standard yet adopted the formulation of "exceedingly persuasive justification" in the case at hand.[92] He would have used more consistent language to facilitate clarity in future cases. The Chief Justice also emphasized that, in his view, if Virginia had shown a "genuine effort" to build VWIL into a comparable alternative to VMI, this effort would likely have cured the equal protection violation – allowing VMI to continue barring women.[93]

The Chief Justice proposed the following standard:

> It is not the "exclusion of women" that violates the Equal Protection Clause, but the maintenance of an all-men school without providing any – much less a comparable – institution for women.

---

[90] *Id.* at 554. See Chapter 4 for a detailed discussion of *Sweatt*.
[91] *Id.* at 557–558.
[92] *Id.* at 559.
[93] *Id.* at 563.

> Accordingly, the remedy should not necessarily require either the admission of women to VMI or the creation of a VMI clone for women. An adequate remedy in my opinion might be a demonstration by Virginia that its interest in educating men in a single-sex environment is matched by its interest in educating women in a single-sex institution. . . .
>
> It would be a sufficient remedy, I think, if the two institutions offered the same quality of education and were of the same overall caliber.

In a lengthy dissent, Justice Scalia extolled the virtues of VMI and criticized the Court's reasoning, arguing that the majority opinion relied on political judgments more than established precedent.[94]

The "intermediate" scrutiny applied to gender classifications may lead to anomalous results, particularly when juxtaposed with the "strict" scrutiny applied to racial classifications. In *Freeman* and *Jenkins*, the Supreme Court indicated that a federal court has no power to require school districts to take affirmative steps to maintain a desegregated condition, even where that condition was the source of an original, proven constitutional violation. In *Hogan* and *Virginia*, the Court seems to permit state remedial plans that employ affirmative action to remedy past discrimination and perhaps to achieve the "public good" of diversity. In fact, the language of these opinions suggests that so long as the state can establish that it has a sincere belief that women have been disadvantaged in a particular context, the state can take affirmative, gender-based compensatory steps even absent any proven constitutional violation. As such, the lesser scrutiny applied to gender discrimination seems to allow for greater use of gender-conscious remedies.

Professor Christopher Pyle, however, argues that it is anomalous to subject public colleges to constitutional oversight, but to immunize the ostensibly private colleges that receive nearly as much state funding as public colleges.[95] He contends that women's colleges should justify their exclusionary policies just as the male academies did in *Virginia*. Pyle suggests that *Virginia* may actually lead women's colleges to believe that they are beyond the reach of its holding because the Court implies that the academy discriminated for some "invidious" purpose, preserving an all-male tradition at women's expense, while women's colleges exclude men for a "benign" purpose.[96] Nevertheless, he emphasizes that women's colleges should be aware that the real issue in *Virginia* was whether the institutions improperly relied on outdated stereotypes in "exclud[ing] all members of one sex in order to achieve a legitimate educational end," suggesting that women's colleges are now still permitted to rely on illegitimate generalizations.[97]

---

[94] *Id.* at 566, et seq.
[95] Christopher H. Pyle, "Women's Colleges: Is Segregation by Sex Still Justifiable after *United States v. Virginia*?," 77 B.U. L. Rev. 209, 226–227 (1997).
[96] *Id.* at 217.
[97] *Id.*

To that end, Pyle ultimately concludes that, in theory, *Virginia* created a "skeptical scrutiny" standard, which is somewhere between intermediate scrutiny and strict scrutiny, and does not appear to treat women's colleges and male academies equally.[98] The Court demands an "exceedingly persuasive justification" for denying admission to members of one gender; however, it appears that women's colleges may indeed rely on generalizations about men's and women's education styles and preferences to support their justification, while male academies cannot.[99] Pyle speculates that as this standard is applied in the future, the Court will not, in fact, allow women's colleges to rely on such evidence to make their arguments for segregation.[100] He suggests that women's colleges affirmatively address their discrimination issues *now* in order to avoid future litigation.[101]

RECENT DEVELOPMENTS IN TITLE IX ENFORCEMENT

On April 4, 2011, the Office for Civil Rights (OCR) of the Department of Education issued a "Dear Colleague Letter" which altered the landscape of Title IX enforcement. The Letter announced a much-expanded role for OCR in ensuring institutional compliance with Title IX. It also promulgated expansive definitions of misconduct and mandated sweeping reforms at universities across the country.

Broadly speaking, OCR's focus with respect to Title IX during the Obama administration was on prevention of sexual violence, protection for survivors, and deterrence for wrongdoers. To that end, the Dear Colleague Letter of April 2011 announced guidelines for institutions that emphasized the need for a thorough investigation any time a complaint of sexual misconduct arose. It also held institutions responsible for convening Title IX hearings whenever an investigation was merited. As we will see, the Dear Colleague Letter set parameters for hearings designed to make a potentially traumatic experience as complainant-friendly as possible under the circumstances.[102] Overall, the Obama-era initiative sought to combat what multiple reports suggested was a disturbing level of sexual violence on campuses nationwide.

To that end, the Dear Colleague Letter defined "sexual violence" to include not only sexual assault but also sexual battery and sexual coercion.[103] The Letter also cast a wide net in its definition of sexual harassment, namely: "unwelcome (verbal, nonverbal, or physical) conduct of a sexual nature."[104] Any conduct that met this

---

[98] *Id.* at 230–233.
[99] *Id.* at 231–232.
[100] *Id.* at 271.
[101] *Id.*
[102] In Title IX terms, "Complainant" refers to the student who reported being the target of sexual violence and/or harassment. "Respondent" refers to the student accused of such conduct. "Recipient" refers to the educational body receiving funding under Title IX.
[103] Department of Education, Office for Civil Rights, "Dear Colleague Letter," 1–2.
[104] Ibid. at 3.

definition, the Letter emphasized, violated Title IX and triggered a mandatory investigation as well as, if appropriate, a grievance hearing.

The Dear Colleague Letter cited a 2007 study that concluded approximately 20 percent of women were victims of a completed or attempted sexual assault during their college years.[105] This unsettling statistic functioned as a guidepost for the Letter's directives regarding the scope of an investigation under Title IX as well as the ground rules for grievance hearings.

Regarding investigations, the Dear Colleague Letter mandated recipients to undertake inquiries into alleged Title IX violations whenever they had actual or constructive knowledge of the alleged violation.[106] Merely referring the matter to law enforcement would not satisfy this standard; the recipient-institution still had to conduct its own investigation.[107] In the event of a conflict between a complainant's wishes and the institution's obligation to investigate, the Letter clarified that the obligation to investigate should carry the day.[108] That said, it encouraged recipient-institutions to accommodate the complainant's desire for anonymity or confidentiality whenever possible – even to the point of concealing the complainant's identity from the respondent to the extent practicable. The Letter also discouraged the use of mediation for sexual harassment complaints and categorically rejected the practice in cases involving sexual violence.[109]

Although the Dear Colleague Letter rejected the complainant's wishes as the guiding principle of the investigative process, it sought to create a hearing environment as comfortable as possible for the complainant. The template put forth by the Letter attempted to make the hearing appear more administrative than adversarial in nature and rejected the trappings of courtroom procedure. It also explicitly endorsed the preponderance of the evidence standard (more likely than not) and rejected the clear and convincing evidence standard, the use of which would have resulted in fewer findings of culpability on the part of respondents.[110] The remainder of the Letter emphasized the need to provide ongoing support services to complainants – particularly survivors of sexual assault – even after the investigation and hearing concluded.

The Dear Colleague Letter promulgated by the Obama administration received widespread plaudits. Undoubtedly, it shone a spotlight on the unacceptable levels of sexual predation found in American colleges and universities. It also made the protections of Title IX more visible to the public – Americans had previously associated the statute with equity in athletic programs.

[105] Ibid. at 2.
[106] Ibid. at 4.
[107] Ibid.
[108] Ibid. at 5.
[109] Ibid. at 8.
[110] Ibid. at 11.

Perhaps inevitably, the increased visibility of Title IX also provoked a pronounced backlash in some circles. A number of universities even faced lawsuits from disgruntled students who had faced discipline pursuant to Title IX hearings, alleging their due process rights were violated. In September 2017, the Trump administration announced its intent to rescind the Dear Colleague Letter of April 2011, and shortly thereafter proposed new rules for Title IX.[111]

The Trump administration took a different focus in its overhaul of Title IX policy. It emphasized flexibility for complainants, deference to institutions, and due process for respondents. While the practical implications of these alterations remain the subject of fierce debate, an examination of the rules on their own terms is a necessary first step to evaluating them.

Crucially, the rules adopt considerably more narrow definitions of sexual harassment and actual knowledge than the Dear Colleague Letter of April 2011. Drawing on the Supreme Court's decisions in *Gebser* and *Davis*, OCR now defines sexual harassment as, "unwelcome conduct on the basis of sex that is so severe, pervasive, and objectively offensive that it effectively denies a person equal access to the recipient's education program or activity; or sexual assault."[112] This marks a dramatic departure from the prior definition of sexual harassment used by the Obama administration. The rules also dispense with the constructive knowledge provision, requiring actual knowledge on the part of the recipient-institution.[113]

OCR combines these definitions in its new standard for institutional response. It states that recipients with actual knowledge of sexual harassment must respond "in a manner that is not deliberately indifferent."[114] Deliberate indifference, OCR explains, means a response "clearly unreasonable in light of the known circumstances."[115] In practice, this permits recipient-institutions tremendous discretion in determining how to respond to reports of sexual harassment. Relatedly, the rules offer a safe harbor to recipients that insulates them from enforcement action from OCR provided they follow basic guidelines. As long as recipients initiate grievance procedures in response to (1) a formal complaint or (2) actual knowledge of multiple reports of misconduct by a single respondent, recipients will automatically satisfy the deliberate indifference standard and be insulated from OCR liability.[116] In addition, institutions that provide complainants with written notice of their right to pursue a formal complaint can also avail themselves of the safe harbor provision should the complainant elect not to proceed with a formal grievance process and instead accept other substitute supportive measures offered by the institution.[117] In effect, this means a complainant who is fully informed of all options

---

[111] Department of Education, Office for Civil Rights Q&A on Campus Sexual Misconduct (2017), 1.
[112] Department of Education, Notice of Proposed Rulemaking to Amend 34 CFR Part 106 (2018), 18.
[113] Ibid.
[114] Ibid.
[115] Ibid.
[116] Ibid. at 32–33.
[117] Ibid. at 34.

and knowingly declines a formal process cannot retroactively accuse the institution of deliberate indifference.

The rules also separate the obligation to respond to known reports of sexual harassment from the requirement to investigate formal complaints of sexual harassment.[118] In other words, a report no longer automatically triggers a formal investigation; the complainant has some sway over the path a process follows. Coupled with the considerably more restrictive definition of sexual harassment under the new rules, this will in all likelihood decrease the number of formal complaints.

The Trump administration also places a greater emphasis on protections for the respondent (i.e., the accused) than the Dear Colleague Letter of April 2011. The new rules prohibit recipient-institutions from removing a respondent from programs or activities absent an individualized risk and safety analysis as well as notice to the respondent of an immediate right to appeal any removal.[119] The rules raise the possibility that an unjustified removal of a respondent under these circumstances might itself violate Title IX.[120]

Most dramatically, the new rules completely overhaul the template for formal hearings under Title IX. Under the new rules, both parties must receive written notice of the procedure and the respondent must receive information to permit a reasonable response – including the name of the complainant and a specific description of the alleged incident, to the extent both are known.[121] Both parties must also have equal access to the evidence in advance of the hearing, with sufficient time to prepare meaningfully for the proceedings. The rules mandate that the respondent be permitted, either personally or through representatives, to cross-examine any witnesses – including the complainant – at a live hearing.[122] The parameters of cross-examination mirror the provisions of the Federal Rules of Evidence – which permit significant latitude for parties to inquire into the witness's (and, in this context, potentially the complainant's) sexual behavior or predisposition.[123] Crucially, the rules mandate that should a witness, including the complainant, refuse cross-examination, the decision-maker cannot rely on any statement by said witness in reaching a conclusion.[124] While the rules allow for cross-examination via a video link to keep the parties in separate rooms, OCR nonetheless dictates that a traumatized complainant's testimony play no role in the outcome of the case if he or she refuses cross-examination. In sum, the new rules strip away any residue of an administrative hearing. They instead import most features of a civil trial into the context of Title IX complaints.

[118] Ibid. at 15–16.
[119] Ibid. at 38.
[120] Ibid. at 40.
[121] Ibid. at 48.
[122] Ibid. at 52.
[123] Ibid.
[124] Ibid.

Although the new rules still permit recipient-institutions to employ the preponderance of the evidence standard for Title IX hearings, they may only do so if they use the same standard for other non-sexual instances of misconduct that could still result in the same sanction.[125] Presumably, this would include expellable offenses such as plagiarism, fighting, or cheating on a test. However, recipients may use the clear and convincing evidence standard for sexual misconduct even if they employ the preponderance standard in all other instances.[126] OCR appears throughout the rules to endorse this latter template.

In sum, the new rules promulgated by the Trump administration take a far more deferential approach to the decisions of recipient-institutions in formulating responses to sexual violence and sexual harassment. While such a move will no doubt satisfy many who believed the previous guidelines overreached, it may also create an incentive for some institutions to avail themselves of plausible deniability – just as Justice Stevens warned in his dissent in *Gebser*. Coupled with the much more restrictive definition of conduct that qualifies as a violation of Title IX, it is fair to conclude that these new rules constitute a pronounced disengagement on the part of the government with the problem of sexual harassment and sexual violence.

In addition, the new rules appear at odds with the premise of Title IX. While the language of the statute is, of course, gender neutral, it is beyond dispute that Title IX was developed with an eye toward facilitating more opportunities for women in all aspects of education. Given that the overwhelming majority of targets of sexual harassment and sexual violence are women, it would seem that a regulatory regime that loosens enforcement of procedures meant to combat these ills departs from the very purpose of Title IX. Whether intended or not, these new rules will likely force women to scale obstacles that had been mitigated (though not entirely removed) through increased enforcement of Title IX. As we will see, the available evidence suggests that now is not the time to dismantle Title IX's protections.

THE ONGOING SIGNIFICANCE OF TITLE IX AND THE ROLE OF SOCIAL CONSTRUCTIVISM IN ACHIEVING GENDER EQUITY

Based on a survey of 1,965 students, the American Association of University Women (the AAUW) reported in 2013 that 56 percent of girls surveyed in public school grades seven through eleven acknowledged that they had experienced unwelcome peer sexual advances in school during the 2011–2012 school year.[127] According to the United States Department of Education, "by the time girls graduate from high school, more than one in ten will have been physically forced to have sexual intercourse in or out of school."[128] Sexual harassment by texting, e-mail,

[125] Ibid. at 60–61.
[126] Ibid. at 63.
[127] American Association of University Women, Crossing the Line: Sexual Harassment at School (2013).
[128] Department of Education, Office for Civil Rights, "Dear Colleague Letter."

Facebook, and other forms of electronic communications affected 36 percent of girls surveyed.[129] Although most of the experiences involved expressions or gestures, 13 percent of the girls reported being touched in an unwanted sexual way.[130]

The AAUW Report presents the available research regarding curriculum and instructional materials in American classrooms and finds evidence of pervasive gender bias. Textbooks still generally exclude women, stereotype members of both sexes, depict the subordination of women, isolate materials regarding women, slight contemporary policy issues related to women and falsely portray the history of women.[131] In the classroom as well, evidence indicates that teacher–student interactions are characterized by double standards for men and women, condescension toward women, tokenism, denial of achieved status or authority to women, backlashes against successful women, and strategies that attempt to separate successful women from others in their gender group.[132] The AAUW Report also concludes: "research spanning the past twenty years consistently reveals that males receive more teacher attention than do females" from preschool through college.[133]

Without doubt, the nearly half century since the passage of Title IX has witnessed tremendous gains for American women according to every metric. Participation in the workforce, relative earnings, educational attainment, and representation in diverse arenas have all increased dramatically. Many, perhaps even most, of the official barriers to women's participation in all aspects of national life have crumbled in the past five decades. In a sense, the status of gender equity in American life neatly parallels that of race; *de jure* discrimination is increasingly unacceptable and largely consigned to the past.

Much like racial discrimination, however, all is not well regarding gender equity in the United States. Tragically, *de facto* discrimination on the basis of sex remains the order of the day far too often. Recent years have featured a deluge of horrifying revelations exposing pervasive sexual assault, harassment, and discrimination across an array of industries and institutions. The environments in which predators acted with apparent impunity include: Hollywood studios, institutions of higher education, corporate boardrooms, media outlets, Olympic training facilities, religious organizations, and even the United States Congress. These revelations have exposed a number of previously beloved cultural icons as calculating serial abusers. While many have rightly lost their positions and prestige as a result of their offenses, others have maintained and even continued their rise despite compelling evidence of wrongdoing.

---

[129] Ibid.
[130] Ibid. See also *How Schools Shortchange Girls*, AAUW Educational Foundation and National Education Association, 106–112, 114–126 (1995) (hereinafter AAUW Report).
[131] See AAUW Report at 106–112, 114–127.
[132] Ibid.
[133] Ibid.

Feminist scholar Barbara J. Berg offers a number of grim observations while surveying the contemporary scene. She paints a picture of a society with deficiencies that extend far beyond failing to offer equity in education. She writes: "A striking 80 percent of ten-year-old girls are on diets, because dieting, the girls say, makes them feel better about themselves. And adolescent girls ... list dropping ten to fifteen pounds as a more important goal than future success in love or work."[134] In addition, she denounces the widespread violence and debasing imagery bombarding American television sets, noting that leading programs "seem to be competing ... with one another in coming up with ever more grotesque ways of slaughtering women."[135] Given that this dramatized mistreatment of women on television occurs nearly exclusively at the hands of men, the message received by some impressionable young minds is not hard to fathom.

Berg concludes her scathing assessment with a prescient observation regarding the impulse toward acquisition, competition, and monetary success that pervades American society. Not coincidentally, these impulses are the byproducts of a behaviorist, consequentialist education system. Berg's analysis does not deal with pedagogy, yet her conclusions are nonetheless telling: "It is a peculiarity of our consumer-obsessed society that we've come to equate commercialization with freedom. In reality we're encouraged to desire consumer products along with the images used to sell them and, finally, to become these images ourselves."[136]

Social constructivism holds that human beings learn by building knowledge together through meaningful relationships – between both ideas and people. As such, a truly social constructivist education focuses not only on technical proficiency but also interpersonal competency. A great deal of the ongoing mistreatment on the basis of sex – be it sexual assault, harassment, or discrimination – is traceable to a failure on the part of the perpetrator to treat the survivor as a valued, respected member of the community. Effective social constructivist pedagogy, with its emphasis on perspective taking, role-playing, empathy, and kindness, offers a defense against this mistreatment. A child educated in accordance with social constructivist theory – surrounded by supportive parents, guardians, and teachers, is exceedingly unlikely to exhibit the harmful behaviors detailed by Berg and others.

Other benefits would also emerge in the realm of gender equity as a result of an increased emphasis on social constructivist principles in education. One of the main flashpoints in the area of gender equity today is the debate over the extent, if any, to which men and women learn differently. Social constructivist pedagogy avoids this problem altogether. By placing students at points on a continuum rather than in rigid categories as well as celebrating diversity, social constructivism offers a better way forward. Essentially, it does not assume that gender equates with a particular

---

[134] Barbara J. Berg, *Sexism in America: Alive, Well, and Ruining Our Future* (Chicago: Lawrence Hill Books, 2009), 268.
[135] Ibid. at 254.
[136] Ibid. at 301.

learning style or preordained role. Yet, to the extent differences correlating with gender arise in a social constructivist classroom, such differences are celebrated and treated as opportunities for learning. Students enjoy the freedom to explore and develop their unique talents, and gender differences become an aspect of diversity to be celebrated rather than a crude instrument to divide classrooms. This process has the additional benefit of dispelling stereotypes and generalizations that could otherwise arise. As children increasingly see their classmates as unique, irreplaceable individuals rather than members of a gender (or, for that matter, race), stereotypes crumble before their eyes.

CONCLUSION

While the language of Title IX is simple and straightforward, its command is broad and extensive. Alongside Justice Ginsburg's landmark opinion in *United States* v. *Virginia*, it stands as the strongest legal protection against gender inequity – in both education and society at large – in effect today. Although the protections of Title IX have undoubtedly changed the lives of millions of American women for the better, many advocates for gender equity believe its full promise remains unfulfilled. They lament the limitations read into the statute by the Supreme Court as well as the pronounced de-emphasis on executive-branch enforcement of Title IX violations on display in recent years. Coupled with the sickening revelations of widespread sexual assault and misconduct across a bevy of American institutions, the state of the union with respect to gender equity is far from healthy. The badges and incidents of gender discrimination clearly remain.

In light of this sad reality, it becomes clear that law alone is not sufficient to solve the problem; education must form part of the solution. A social constructivist approach that recognizes human beings learn by constructing knowledge together through meaningful relationships offers great promise in rectifying the problem of gender inequity. Indeed, this pedagogy presents the most effective way to ensure that our democracy does not fall into the tragic and self-destructive trap of preventing half its citizens from contributing fully.

Social constructivist educational practices also promise to more fully embrace another traditionally marginalized group of learners: special education students. In the next chapter, we will explore the history of the nation's treatment of these students – an uplifting path from marginalization to increasing inclusion.

8

Special Education and Inclusion

As we have emphasized throughout the book, a truly democratic education system cannot exclude any group of students. It must welcome and celebrate every potential contribution – irrespective of from where or from whom it may come. We have explored the tragic histories of exclusion and marginalization based on race and gender; now we will turn our attention to efforts to expand the inclusion of students with disabilities. If, as this book and the overwhelming weight of research suggests, human beings learn by constructing knowledge together through meaningful relationships, no education system worthy of the name can systematically deny children that opportunity. This holds true even if providing that opportunity may require an increased, individually tailored effort.

Over the past several decades, American society has become a far kinder and gentler place in its treatment of disabled citizens. This has also proved increasingly true with respect to students with disabilities. This chapter will discuss the key cases and statutes governing the education of children with special needs. It will devote particular attention to the Individuals with Disabilities Education Act (IDEA) and its centerpiece, the Individualized Education Program (IEP). The chapter will examine the Supreme Court's three main forays into the law governing special education – all of which implicate rights under IDEA and the exact requirements of a proper IEP. Next, the chapter will discuss a school district's obligations under IDEA and address the familiar theme of funding shortfalls. The chapter will conclude with a celebration of the emerging concept of neurodiversity. This concept demonstrates that different styles of learning and processing the world need not be reflexively considered disadvantages or disabilities. Instead, these can offer unique benefits and – in the hands of expert teachers – can enrich the learning process for students of all abilities and learning styles. Neurodiversity shows that an emphasis on inclusion effectively rebukes the zero-sum approach inherent in behaviorism and fosters an educational system that more fully develops the democratic citizens of tomorrow. It removes the badges and incidents of discrimination from students with disabilities.

EARLY CASES AND LEGISLATIVE EFFORTS

In *P.A.R.C. v. Commonwealth of Pennsylvania*,[1] the federal district court addressed the then-systemic practice of excluding students with educational disabilities from regular public school classrooms. The Court declared that there must be a presumption that, among the alternative programs of education and training required by statute to be available, placement in a regular public school class is preferable to placement in a special public school class and placement in a special public school class is preferable to placement in any other type of program of education and training.

In *Mills v. Board of Education of District of Columbia*,[2] as well, the court adopted a presumption that among the alternative programs of education, placement in a regular public school class with appropriate ancillary services is preferable to placement in a special school class.

These two cases and a national political campaign for better educational services, spurred Congress to pass three major federal statutes: The Rehabilitation Act of 1973 (RHA), the Individuals with Disabilities Education Act (IDEA; originally passed in 1975 under the name Education for all Handicapped Children Act), and the Americans with Disabilities Act of 1990 (ADA).

Special education legislation, including the Individuals with Disabilities Education Act, requires the states, as a condition attached to the receipt of federal funds, to insure that their young children with educational disabilities receive free and appropriate special education and related services in the least restrictive educational environment.

Section 504 of the Rehabilitation Act states: "No otherwise qualified individual with disabilities in the United States . . ., shall solely by reason of his disabilities, be excluded from participation in, be denied the benefits of, or be subjected to discrimination under any program, or activity receiving Federal financial assistance."[3]

The four purposes of the Individuals with Disabilities Education Act are: (1) to provide all children with disabilities a free appropriate public education that emphasizes special education and related services designed to meet their unique needs; (2) to assist states in implementing a system of early intervention services for infants and toddlers with disabilities; (3) to insure that educators and parents have the necessary tools to improve educational results for children with disabilities; and (4) to assess and insure the effectiveness of efforts to educate children with disabilities.[4]

---

[1] 334 F.Supp. 1257 (E.D. Pa. 1971).
[2] 348 F.Supp. 866 (D.C. 1972).
[3] Rehabilitation Act of 1973, Section 504(a)-(d).
[4] Individuals with Disabilities Education Act, Section 601(d)(1)(A)-(4).

The Individuals with Disabilities Education Act states that children with disabilities are to be educated to the maximum extent with children who do not have disabilities. This statutory regime gives to public school districts an obligation to provide special education services to children, beginning at three years old. IDEA also obliges states to make active attempts to find and test children who may be eligible for special services starting at age three. Many practitioners refer to this as the state's "child find" obligation.

Congress requires that all eligible children receive an Individualized Education Program (IEP) that includes a statement describing how the child's disability affects his or her involvement and progress in the general curriculum and a statement of goals and objectives related to enabling the child to achieve progress in the general curriculum. The statement of services in the IEP must also include a statement of the supplemental aids and services that will be provided for the child and a statement of the program modifications and supports for school personnel that will be provided for the child to progress in the general curriculum and to participate in extracurricular and nonacademic activities. An "Individualized Education Program" or IEP is a written statement for a child with a disability that is developed, reviewed, and revised. An Individual Education Program is a student's "curriculum" for the year, matching up the child's needs with an individualized, appropriate program. An IEP informs the parents of the measures the school district will take to assist the child in meeting the child's annual goals. The IEP is thus a legal obligation for the school to the child for whom the IEP is written. After a child is determined eligible for special education services, a team of school professionals and parents must meet within thirty calendar days to develop an IEP.

The Americans with Disabilities Act (ADA) of 1990 extended civil rights similar to those of the Civil Rights Act of 1964 to people with disabilities. The Act prohibits discrimination on the basis of disability in private sector employment, services rendered by state and local governments, places of public accommodations, transportation, and telecommunications systems. While it does not directly address special education law, the ADA reflects the increasing commitment of American society to better assist citizens with special needs.

The ADA and RHA both require educational institutions to make reasonable accommodations for students with educational disabilities. The Supreme Court in *Southeastern Comm. College* v. *Davis*,[5] however, held that the duty does not rise to requiring a substantial modification, "of an existing program, nor are schools required to create an undue financial or administrative burden."

In *Davis*, the Supreme Court concluded that an "otherwise qualified" person is one who meets all requirements for licensure in spite of his handicap, not except for his handicap. Davis, who had a serious hearing disability, wished to enter a registered nurse educational program. The Court agreed with the trial court that

---

[5] 442 U.S. 397 (1979).

Davis' handicap prevented her from safely performing in both her training program and her desired profession. The Court determined that in such circumstances, the Rehabilitation Act does not impose an obligation to lower or substantially modify an educational institution's standards to accommodate a disabled person.

ROWLEY AND ENDREW F.: DEFINING THE PROCEDURAL AND SUBSTANTIVE GUARANTEES OF AN IEP

The Individuals with Disabilities Education Act (IDEA) requires public schools to provide a Free, Appropriate Public Education (FAPE) to students with disabilities. In *Board of Ed. v. Rowley*,[6] the Court defines FAPE as services that provide students with "some educational benefit." This standard permeates nearly every aspect of special education because it is the standard against which services are measured. For thirty-five years, *Rowley* remained the foundational case in the sphere of IEP litigation.

In *Rowley*, the parents of deaf first grader Amy Rowley filed a lawsuit when the Hendrick Hudson School District declined to provide their daughter with a sign-language interpreter in all academic classes.[7] Citing Amy's "above-average" progress, the District argued that provisions already in place (including use of a sound amplification system as well as weekly access to a tutor and speech therapist) fulfilled its responsibility to provide Amy with a FAPE.[8] The District conceded, however, that Amy would derive a substantial additional benefit from the assistance of a sign-language interpreter.[9]

The Court held that the requirements of IDEA to provide a free appropriate public education were satisfied by the provision of "personalized instruction with sufficient support services to permit the child to benefit educationally from that instruction."[10] The Court further stated that the IEP must be formulated in accordance with the requirements of IDEA. The standard for assessing the IEP is: reasonably calculated to achieve some benefit – no guarantee the child will achieve the goals is required.[11] Since Amy was performing better than average and was receiving personalized instruction that was reasonably calculated to meet her educational needs, the Court held that a sign-language interpreter was not required.[12]

Justice Blackmun concurred in the result, but offered an alternative approach. He questioned "whether Amy's program, *viewed as a whole* offered her an opportunity to

---

[6] 458 US 176 (1982).
[7] *Id.* at 184.
[8] *Id.*
[9] *Id.*
[10] *Id.* at 189.
[11] *Id.*
[12] *Id.* at 210.

understand and participate in the classroom that was substantially equal to that given her non-handicapped classmates"[13] (Emphasis in original).

Justice White authored a dissenting opinion. Joined by Justice Brennan and Justice Marshall, he took issue with the Court's definition of opportunity. Under Justice White's more expansive view, the Court should have required a showing that Amy had an equal opportunity to learn at the same level as her non-handicapped peers to the extent possible. Given that she understood less than half of the classroom dialogue, the standard could not be satisfied on these facts.[14] In addition, Justice White called for a considerably more robust judicial review than the standard adopted by the majority. The dissent emphasized that reviewing courts were competent to judge the "appropriateness" of the services offered to a student under an IEP, and should not defer entirely to the educational expertise of a school district.[15]

The *Rowley* Court bases its opinion on premises remarkably similar to those expressed by the majority in *Rodriguez*.[16] The majority emphasizes opportunity over outcome and process over substance. Indeed, it seems to suggest that the procedural safeguards accompanying an IEP effectively guarantee substantive rights.[17] Just as the school funding system at issue in *Rodriguez* survived because it did not impose an absolute deprivation of education on its students, Amy Rowley's IEP satisfied judicial review because it provided her "some" benefit.[18] The Court thus unfortunately once again adopted a utilitarian approach to education; it viewed the IEP more as a means of avoiding disaster rather than an opportunity to lead a child toward her full potential. Given Amy Rowley's excellent progress under the more limited IEP, it is intriguing to consider how well she could have performed under an IEP calibrated to unlock her talents.

A free and appropriate public education includes special education and related services. While *Rowley* defined an appropriate education, it did not define the requirements under the "related services" provisions of IDEA and the Rehabilitation Act of 1973. In *Irving Independent School District* v. *Tatro*,[19] the Supreme Court recognized that a free appropriate public education includes supplemental and medical services that enable a child to remain at school during the day. In *Cedar Rapids Community Sch. Dist.* v. *Garret F.*,[20] the Supreme Court held that a student who needs assistance with his ventilator throughout the school day is entitled to nursing services under the related services requirement of IDEA.

---

[13] *Id.* at 211.
[14] *Id.* at 215.
[15] *Id.* at 218.
[16] *Id.* at 200.
[17] *Id.* at 198–199, 206.
[18] *Id.* at 196.
[19] 468 U.S. 883 (1984).
[20] 526 U.S. 66 (1999).

In 2017, the Court elaborated on the principles announced in *Rowley* when it decided *Endrew F. v. Douglas County School District*.[21] The parents of an autistic child from Colorado (Endrew) sued the Douglas County School District for the cost of enrolling Endrew in a private school. While attending the private school – which specializes in educating children with autism – Endrew thrived and made marked progress in both intellectual and behavioral terms.[22] This contrasted with his experience in the Douglas County School District. Allegedly, the district made no effort to recalibrate Endrew's IEP on a yearly basis. Endrew's parents claimed that his goals from year to year were often substantially the same. In light of these deficiencies, Endrew's parents contended that the Douglas County School District failed to provide their son a "free and appropriate education" in accordance with IDEA.[23] If Endrew's parents could demonstrate that a violation of IDEA had occurred, the Douglas County School District would be liable to them for Endrew's private school tuition.

In their appeal to the Supreme Court, Endrew's parents placed great weight on the level of detail required for an IEP under IDEA. They thus argued that requiring such an intricate process to produce only the "more than de minimis" benefit adopted by the Tenth Circuit contravenes the legislative intent undergirding IDEA. They contended that "appropriate" in the context of IDEA should be interpreted by the Court to mean that a district must offer children who receive services under an IEP a "substantially equal opportunity" to learn alongside their general education classmates. This standard alone, they claimed, would avert the hollow goals set in Endrew's IEPs.

The Douglas County School District, meanwhile, responded by arguing essentially that the process of creating an IEP mandated by IDEA yields substance in and of itself. They noted that the intricacies of the IEP meeting and ample procedural safeguards enshrined in IDEA almost automatically produce the substantive benefit contemplated by Congress. So long as procedures are observed, the district claimed, satisfaction of IDEA would nearly always follow. Douglas County added that IDEA functions as a contract between the federal government and the states – exchanging compliance with the statute's standards for increased funding. As such, it argued that a sudden change in standard would require states to carry a burden they never contemplated at the time of formation. The district advocated continued adherence to the *Rowley* reading of "appropriate," suggesting the "substantially equal opportunity" standard would be unworkable and lead to rampant litigation.

Writing for a unanimous Court, Chief Justice Roberts rejects the Tenth Circuit standard of "merely more than *de minimus*" benefit as inconsistent with the language of IDEA.[24] The Court then proceeds to limit *Rowley* to fact patterns in which

[21] *Endrew F. v. Douglas County School District* 580 U.S. ___ (2017), (Slip Op.).
[22] *Id.* at 7.
[23] *Id.* at 8.
[24] *Id.* at 14.

a student eligible for an IEP learns in a general education classroom.[25] Chief Justice Roberts enthusiastically endorses the principle of mainstreaming, or placing a special education student in a general education environment whenever feasible.[26] The Court offers the following substantive guidance for IEP content – guidance noticeably more student-friendly than the template offered in *Rowley*:

> *Rowley* had no need to provide concrete guidance with respect to a child who is not fully integrated in the regular classroom and not able to achieve on grade level. That case concerned a young girl who was progressing smoothly through the regular curriculum. If that is not a reasonable prospect for a child, his IEP need not aim for grade-level advancement. But his educational program must be appropriately ambitious in light of his circumstances, just as advancement from grade to grade is appropriately ambitious for most children in the regular classroom. The goals may differ, but every child should have the chance to meet challenging objectives.
>
> Of course this describes a general standard, not a formula. But whatever else can be said about it, this standard is markedly more demanding than the "merely more than *de minimus*" test applied by the Tenth Circuit. It cannot be the case that the Act typically aims for grade-level advancement for children with disabilities who can be educated in the regular classroom, but is satisfied with barely more than *de minimus* progress for those who cannot.[27]

Chief Justice Roberts concludes by outlining instructions for reviewing courts.

> The adequacy of a given IEP turns on the unique circumstances of the child for whom it was created. . . . A reviewing court may fairly expect (school districts) to be able to offer a cogent and responsive explanation for their decisions that shows the IEP is reasonably calculated to enable the child to make progress appropriate in light of his circumstances.[28]

In many important respects, *Endrew F.* marks a new beginning for advocates calling for substantive rights in IEPs. The new standard for services ("reasonably calculated to enable the child to make progress appropriate in light of his circumstances") demonstrates the Court's awareness that every single child can grow and learn. While it did not explicitly repudiate the approach in *Rowley*, *Endrew F.* emphasizes that mere procedural compliance does not satisfy IDEA. Rather, IDEA guarantees to every student with disabilities the substantive right to attempt genuine educational goals – and to have the necessary resources to make this attempt. *Endrew F.* does not resort to broad language about the special need for education in democracies, but it clearly embodies this principle. Just as a proper democracy allows all its citizens to participate and have their say, so does *Endrew F.* attempt to insure that school districts allow all their students to contribute and

[25] *Id.* at 12–14.
[26] *Id.* at 12–13.
[27] *Id.* at 14.
[28] *Id.* at 15–16.

have a genuine chance to improve their abilities. In sum, it is an opinion that would have made Founders like Jefferson, Franklin, Madison, and Rush proud.

THE LEAST RESTRICTIVE ENVIRONMENT

The IDEA provides that states and thus districts,

> must assure that to the maximum extent appropriate that children with disabilities are educated with children that are not disabled, and that special classes, separate schooling or any other removal of children with disabilities from the regular education environment occurs only when the nature or severity of the disability is such that education in regular classes with the use of supplementary aids and services cannot be achieved satisfactorily.[29]

This is commonly referred to as educating a child with disabilities in the least restrictive environment (LRE).

The federal courts are split on the proper test for determining the school district's obligations, but all of the courts consider the following factors: (1) the educational benefits of a "mainstream" placement; (2) the nonacademic benefits of a "mainstream" placement; (3) the effect the disabled student would have on the teacher and students in the regular education environment; and (4) the cost of the "mainstream" placement, including supplemental services.

When a public school district is unable to provide a disabled student with an appropriate education within its own facilities, the district is required to locate and pay for an appropriate alternative placement. In analyzing the issue of alternative placements, the Supreme Court in a combination of two cases, *Burlington v. Dept. of Ed, Massachusetts*,[30] and *Florence County School Dist. v. Carter*,[31] requires school districts to develop an appropriate IEP and to provide an alternative placement if necessary to meet the IEP's objectives. Districts must fund private placements if the district itself is not able to provide the appropriate education for the disabled student.

In addition, there are procedural protections, such as the right to "stay put." In *Honig, California Superintendent of Public Instruction v. Doe*,[32] the Supreme Court held that school districts may not remove students with disabilities from their educational placement during the process of reviewing those placements.[33] Writing for a six-justice majority, Justice Brennan framed the question facing the Court as "whether (despite the language of IDEA), state or local school authorities may nevertheless unilaterally exclude disabled children from the classroom for dangerous or disruptive conduct growing out of their disabilities."[34] In concluding

---

[29] Individuals with Disabilities Education Act, Section 612(a)(5)(A).
[30] 471 U.S. 359 (1984).
[31] 510 U.S. 7 (1993).
[32] 484 U.S. 305 (1988).
[33] *Id.* at 323.
[34] *Id.* at 308.

that such an action is not permitted by IDEA, Justice Brennan reiterated that the statute confers "an enforceable substantive right to public education," for all students within its scope.[35] While announced in a limited context, *Honig* marked another occasion in which the Court uses language often reserved for constitutionally protected fundamental rights while discussing education. Yet, *Honig* did not pursue this avenue any further.

The *Honig* Court rejected two arguments calling on it to read an implicit dangerousness exception into the "stay-put" provisions of IDEA. It first declined to assume that Congress viewed this authority as so obvious it needed no explicit mention.[36] Next, it dismissed the suggestion that Congress accidentally forgot to include such language.[37] Justice Brennan characterized these arguments as "essentially inconsistent assumptions."[38]

The majority spent the balance of the opinion surveying the various options available to schools to protect their students without resorting to a unilateral, indefinite removal.[39] It noted that districts have every right to remove a student for ten days without offering a due process hearing. This period, the Court observed, would allow for a valuable window in which the school and the student's family could try to reach a mutually acceptable solution with which to move forward. The Court also emphasized that, in genuinely dangerous instances, school districts could seek an equitable injunction from a district court temporarily barring a child from attending school. In such a proceeding, Justice Brennan phrased the appropriate standard of review as, "a presumption in favor of the child's current educational placement which school officials can overcome only by showing that maintaining the child in his or her current placement is substantially likely to result in injury either to himself or herself, or to others."[40]

Finally, the Court concluded by reiterating that a suspension in excess of ten days constitutes a change in placement under IDEA.[41] It also left undisturbed the Ninth Circuit's holding permitting district courts to order a state to provide educational services to a child with an IEP when the child's local educational agency fails in this regard.[42]

An additional procedural protection with broader application than the suite of safeguards announced in *Honig* is the right to a due process hearing. Under IDEA, if parents believe that the school district's IEP for their child is not "appropriate," they have the right to request an "impartial due process hearing." In *Shaffer* v. *Weast*,[43]

[35] *Id.* at 310.
[36] *Id.* at 323.
[37] *Id.*
[38] *Id.*
[39] *Id.* at 325–328.
[40] *Id.* at 328.
[41] *Id.* at 329.
[42] *Id.*
[43] 546 U.S. 49 (2005).

the Supreme Court held that the burden of proof at the due process hearing rests with the party seeking relief, which in most cases will be the parents challenging the district's proposed IEP.

THE DUTY TO PROVIDE SPECIAL EDUCATION AND RELATED SERVICES TO CHILDREN BEGINNING AT AGE THREE

IDEA generally requires public school districts, and private schools that contract with public schools, to provide special education services to children beginning at age three. In particular, free and appropriate pre-K programs must be given to children between the ages of three and five, if those children have one or more of the disabilities identified in IDEA.[44] School districts may also use pre-K funds to provide special education services to two year-olds who will become three during the school year.[45]

The disabilities identified in IDEA include physical, educational, learning, or cognitive disabilities that necessitate special education and/or related services.[46] Specifically, school districts have an obligation to provide or to contract with a third-party to provide special education and related services to all three to five year-old children who reside within the district who have: "intellectual disabilities, hearing impairments (including deafness), speech or language impairments, visual impairments (including blindness), serious emotional disturbance (referred to as "emotional disturbance"), orthopedic impairments, autism, traumatic brain injury, other health impairments, or specific learning disabilities; and who, by reason thereof, need special education and related services."[47]

In addition, states have discretion to provide a free appropriate public education to all pre-K children who have "developmental delays." These include delays in physical, cognitive, communication, social, emotional, and adaptive development. If a state decides to serve children with such developmental delays, it must provide to them the full range of services and protections required by IDEA. Accordingly, these children must receive a free and appropriate special education and related services in the least restrictive environment.

The local school district must provide special education and related services to all children protected by IDEA by including them in one of their own district-run pre-K programs, or by financing the child's education in an appropriate local Head Start program, community-based program, or private program.

IDEA also requires early intervention services for children from birth to age three.[48] These children must be served by multiple public and private agencies

---

[44] 20 U.S.C. § 1401(3) (A) (i).
[45] 34 CFR § 300.323(b).
[46] 20 U.S.C. § 1401(3).
[47] Individuals with Disabilities Education Act, Section 602 (3)(A)(i)-(ii).
[48] 20 U.S.C. § 1431, et seq.

that coordinate services pursuant to the dictates of a mandatory "individualized family service plan." To the maximum extent appropriate, these children must be served in their "natural environment" such as in their homes, or in community programs for typically developing children of their age. Moreover, states and school districts must establish procedures for insuring that such children are identified and will make a smooth transition from the early intervention programs to pre-K services and ultimately to elementary school.

In enacting and consistently reauthorizing legislation that encourages states to provide special education services to all eligible three and four year olds, Congress expressly recognized that there was an "urgent and substantial need" for early childhood education for these children. Congress specifically found that early childhood education not only enhanced the "development of infants and toddlers with disabilities," it also reduced "the educational costs to our society, including our Nation's schools, by minimizing the need for special education and related services after infants and toddlers with disabilities reach school age."[49] This congressional finding has been further confirmed by the research of leading scholars such as James Heckman, among many others.

Children with disabilities who attend appropriate pre-K programs in fact make dramatic and lasting advances in their educational, social, and emotional development. The evidence also is clear that children with disabilities who are included in educational environments with their typically developing peers significantly outperform such children who are not so-included in all domains of development, particularly social skills, executive function, language, and cognition.[50]

With appropriate supportive services, the inclusion of children with disabilities in the regular pre-K environment significantly increases the educational and social development of all children in that environment.[51] Despite these proven benefits and the IDEA requirement that three- to five-year-old children with disabilities learn in the least restrictive environments, only one-third of these children throughout the country are included in educational environments with their typically developing peers.[52]

---

[49] Individuals with Disabilities Education Act, Section 631(a)(1)-(2).
[50] Annette Holahan & Virginia Costenbader, "A Comparison of Developmental Gains for Preschool Children with Disabilities Inclusive and Self-Contained Classrooms," *Topics in Early Childhood Special Education* 20(4) (2000): 224–225; Samuel L. Odom, "Preschool Inclusion: What We Know and Where We Go from Here," *Topics in Early Childhood Special Education* 20(1) (2000): 20–27.
[51] Education Law Center, "Pre-K Policy Brief Series: Including Children with Disabilities in State Pre-K Programs," February 2010, 3, n. 19.
[52] U.S. Dep't of Education, Office of Special Education Programs: "Part B, Individuals with Disabilities Education Act, Implementation of FAPE Requirements," July 30, 2005.

SPECIAL EDUCATION FUNDING

Under the Individuals with Disabilities Education Improvement Act, about 750,000 children between the ages of three and five receive special education and related services.[53] Pursuant to its power under the Spending Clause, Congress appropriates the funds through state grant programs to those states that demonstrate compliance with federal requirements. In Part B, the statute authorizes grants to states and local educational agencies to fund special education for children aged three to five.[54] In fiscal year 2014, $11.47 billion was allocated to provide funding for all special education programs for children aged three to twenty-one.[55]

The level of funding provided to each state is based on an elaborate formula. The federal government guarantees to each state at least the same amount of funds that the state received for fiscal year 1999. The 1999 Part B appropriation was $5 billion.[56] The federal funds that are appropriated above the 1999 level are distributed to the states based on their relative share of children within the age range served by IDEA (85 percent of the remainder) and their relative share of children within that age range who are living in poverty (15 percent of the remainder).

States may keep up to 10 percent of the allocated funds for administrative and other state level expenses before distributing the rest to local school districts. Congress also has established a maximum contribution to any particular state of 40 percent of that state's average per-pupil expenses.

School districts spend about 1.9 times more to educate a child with special needs than they do to educate other children.[57] Yet, in 2014, the average per-student federal dollars distributed for special education services to all children with disabilities was only $1,743, and the average per-pupil federal dollars distributed for three to five year olds receiving special education services was only $471. Even if most school districts combine those funds to serve particular children, the total amount of funds falls short of providing adequate funding.

The total average amount per pupil distributed by the federal government is about $2,200. The total cost of providing services to a child receiving special education is 1.9 times the average per student expenditure of $10,034, or approximately $20,585. The federal contribution of 40 percent of that amount would be about $8,234. The federal allocation of $2,200 per student, therefore, provides only a small fraction of the amount of funding that Congress itself requires under its IDEA funding regime.

The extent to which the early childhood mandates of IDEA are underfunded also is demonstrated by the aggregate funding gap. If IDEA were fully funded, the states would receive from the federal government at least 40 percent of the overall cost of educating all of its children with disabilities. In fiscal year 2014, however, federal

---

[53] Ibid.
[54] See §619, Part B.
[55] New America Foundation, The Federal Education Budget.
[56] Ibid.
[57] Ibid.

funding only covered 16 percent of those costs.⁵⁸ Under Part B, full funding would have sent $28.65 billion to the states. Yet, the states only received $11.48 billion. The $17.17 billion shortfall must then be absorbed by the states and local school districts. Indeed, since 2010, the annual Part B appropriation for special education services has been consistently less than half of even the amount of funds that Congress requires of itself to provide full funding.

NEURODIVERSITY AND THE COMPELLING POSSIBILITIES OF INCLUSIVE EDUCATION PRACTICES

As Steve Silberman describes in his brilliant book, *NeuroTribes: The Legacy of Autism and the Future of Neurodiversity*, the recognition of neurodiversity correctly reframes diagnoses such as ADHD or autism spectrum disorder as differences in learning strategies along a natural continuum.⁵⁹ All learning takes place on that continuum. Silberman demonstrates that

> [o]ne way to understand neurodiversity is to think in terms of *human operating systems* instead of diagnostic labels like *dyslexia* and *ADHD*. The brain is, above all, a marvelously adaptive organism, adept at maximizing its chances of success even in the face of daunting limitations . . . Not all the features of atypical human operating systems are bugs. By autistic standards, the "normal" brain is easily distractible, is obsessively social, and suffers from a deficit of attention to detail and routine. Thus people on the spectrum experience the neurotypical world as relentlessly unpredictable and chaotic, perpetually turned up too loud, and full of people who have little respect for personal space.⁶⁰

Accordingly, educators who are attuned to the most recent brain research can appreciate and build upon great strengths in each of the different approaches to learning. Students with learning differences, therefore, should not only be accommodated but also celebrated.

"Accommodating" these learning differences is often presented as a nearly insurmountable task that wearies teachers and deprives neurotypical students of valuable instructional time. To the contrary, a skilled teacher can navigate this potential conflict with proper support and a bit of creativity. In *Behavior Solutions for the Inclusive Classroom*, Beth Aune, Beth Burt, and Peter Gennaro compile an invaluable guidebook for educators.⁶¹ The book details a number of common situations that, if approached without caution, could lead to disruption and frayed nerves for students and teachers. Rather than applying mechanical, punitive tactics, the book suggests that educators instead seek to redirect the unique strengths and energies of their students in a more productive direction.

⁵⁸ New America Foundation, The Federal Education Budget.
⁵⁹ (New York: Avery, 2015).
⁶⁰ Ibid. at 471.
⁶¹ (Arlington, TX: Future Horizons, 2010).

For example, a student with difficulty focusing or staying seated should be redirected toward running an errand for a teacher, given a manual task within the classroom, or simply allowed a short break to stretch his legs.[62] Any of these brief detours will allow the overenergetic student to settle down and return to the lesson without detracting from his classmates' instructional time. A student exhibiting emotional distress can be allowed to recollect herself in a quiet, calm environment or reminded of a favorite story or memory.[63] A student engaged in a temper outburst can be allowed the choice of multiple options to calm down (i.e., take a walk or take deep breaths) or can be steered toward an area of the room less likely to result in confrontation.[64] This approach encourages a teacher to think creatively and seek solutions that are most appropriate in light of the student's unique profile.

Incidentally, it bears noting that many of the techniques outlined in *Behavior Solutions for the Inclusive Classroom* apply just as readily to neurotypical students. Over the course of a long school year, nearly every student in a class will have a day or two in which they are the child in need of a teacher's special attention or care. While students with special needs may experience these situations with greater frequency and intensity, it must be remembered that even the most "normal" children are capable of disruption or misbehavior. As such, the best learning environments treat any behaviors exhibited by special education students as perhaps different in degree but certainly not in kind from their general education classmates. Accommodating the unique needs of students with disabilities requires the exact same practice of empathy and kindness as tolerating the quirks of general education students over a long year together. In an atmosphere of mutual respect and good will, there are few classroom obstacles that cannot be overcome.

In *IEP and Inclusion Tips for Parents and Teachers*,[65] Anne I. Eason and Kathleen Whitbread present a compelling case for educating special needs students in general education settings. They write:

> There is a strong research base to support the education of children with disabilities alongside their nondisabled peers. Although separate classes, with lower student to teacher ratios, controlled environments, and specially trained staff would seem to offer benefits to a child with a disability, research fails to demonstrate the effectiveness of such programs. There is mounting evidence that, other than a smaller class size, "there is little that is special about the special education system," and that the negative effects of separating children with disabilities from their peers far outweigh any benefit to smaller classes.
>
> Students with disabilities in inclusive classrooms show academic gains in a number of areas, including improved performance on standardized tests, mastery of IEP goals, grades, on-task behavior and motivation to learn. Moreover, placement

---

[62] Ibid. at 22–26.
[63] Ibid. at 42–46.
[64] Ibid. at 122–124, 129.
[65] (Verona, WI: Attainment Company, 2006).

in inclusive classrooms does not interfere with the academic performance of students without disabilities with respect to the amount of allocated time and engaged instructional time, the rate of interruption to planned activities and student achievement on test scores and report card grades.[66] (Internal citations omitted)

Eason and Whitbread also emphasize the importance of developing friendships for children with special needs.[67] In their view, a clear plan to insure full socialization is an indispensable part of any IEP. In earlier chapters, we discussed the importance of friendships across racial groups in breaking down harmful stereotypes and increasing trust and cohesion. The exact same principles hold true in bridging any gaps – real or perceived – between special education students and their general education peers. There is no more effective tool to accomplish this than having students of all ability levels live and learn together on a daily basis in small classrooms guided by a compassionate and creative teacher.

Such an approach not only boosts children with special needs but also teaches general education students valuable lessons about perseverance and compassion. A particularly inspiring example of the possibilities offered by inclusive education methods comes from the accomplishments of special education students at Forest Hills Northern High School in Grand Rapids, Michigan.[68] The book recounts the efforts of a special education teacher and football coach, Mike Kersjes, to take his students to NASA's Space Camp in Huntsville, Alabama. Despite facing pushback from both Space Camp staff and school district officials, Kersjes and his students became the first special education class to participate in the program. Space Camp, generally viewed as an exercise in training scientifically gifted students for future careers in NASA, had never previously made any attempt to include special needs children.

Kersjes' class not only survived Space Camp but thrived in it. In fact, his class won three group awards for their excellence during the weeklong program.[69] One student even received an award naming him the outstanding camper of the week. In a moving scene, he cut the ribbon on which his medal hung so that he could give a piece to each of his teachers and classmates – enabling them to share in the award.[70] This remarkable display of generosity and friendship underscores a key principle of inclusion. Bringing students of different abilities together is not merely a favor to the less-skilled. To the contrary, no student could fail to be improved by having the opportunity to spend time observing the attitude displayed by Kersjes' class.

---

[66] Ibid. at 12.
[67] Ibid. at 53.
[68] Mike Kersjes with Joe Layden, *A Smile as Big as the Moon: A Teacher, His Class, and Their Unforgettable Journey* (New York: St. Martin's Press, 2002).
[69] Ibid. at 256–266.
[70] Ibid. at 269–270.

The book's final scene offers a beautiful vision of the possibilities of inclusive education. Kersjes writes:

> The plane touched down neatly, smoothly, and we taxied back up the runway to the terminal. Robynn and I remained in our seats ... (watching) as they went about their business, indistinguishable from the rest of the passengers. There was nothing in the way they spoke, moved, or behaved that betrayed their status as special education students. They seemed like normal kids. Good kids. ...
>
> I could hear something, a slight hum that grew into a rumble ... the faint sounds of laughter, shouting ... the sound of loved ones being welcomed home. Then something else, something I recognized from years of football, a wonderful sound, the sound you hear when you're a coach, trailing your players, walking from the locker room to the field, through the hallways, and out into the Friday night air, where the crowd waits for you with open arms.
>
> A sound every kid should hear at least once in his life. A sound our kids had never heard before, at least not directed solely at them. Not like this.
>
> > Clapping ... cheering ... whistling ...
> > The sound of ... *acceptance*.[71]

CONCLUSION

Without doubt, American society has made a genuine effort to more fully welcome and value those citizens with disabilities or learning differences. In the realm of education, this struggle is best exemplified by IDEA and its guarantee of a free, appropriate public education facilitated by an IEP. The Supreme Court has followed the trend of the nation as a whole, beginning with a minimalist approach to IDEA in *Rowley* that expanded in *Honig* and grew significantly in *Endrew F.*

Despite the considerable progress of the past few decades, school districts continue to suffer from funding shortfalls. In this fiscally tight environment, the temptation to view the disbursement of educational resources as a zero-sum game frequently proves too difficult to overcome. Sadly, relations between families of special needs students and school districts often are characterized by suspicion and anger rather than trust and cooperation.

Even so, ongoing advances in neuroscience and the tireless efforts of visionary educators and advocates are illuminating the exciting possibilities of inclusive approaches to education. In this paradigm, both special education and general education students have much to learn and teach each other. Their abilities, strengths, and weaknesses may be different but they are nonetheless equal partners entirely capable of contributing and enriching the classroom with their presence. A social constructivist approach to education fosters and reinforces this mindset.

---

[71] Ibid. at 274.

This encouraging trend offers a powerful safeguard against the tragic tendency to relegate special needs students to the periphery of school and society. It combats the badges and incidents of unjustified stigma. It fulfills the promise of IDEA and facilitates an environment in which children can more effectively construct knowledge together by building meaningful relationships.

In the next chapter, we will examine another area in which all too many children are dismissed as incapable of improvement or growth. Student disciplinary practices – particularly exclusionary discipline methods – often parallel the same tendency to marginalize which Congress sought to combat with the passage of IDEA. If the future health of democracy depends upon young citizens constructing knowledge together through meaningful relationships, then the nation's school system cannot afford to discount a single child. Yet, as we have seen and will see in the context of exclusionary discipline, this is a far too common occurrence.

9

Civil Rights in the Educational Environment and Student Discipline

Throughout most of the book, we have explored efforts to include groups that have historically been prevented from enjoying full access to education in America. These groups, of course, were treated in this manner not because of anything they did but instead suffered the badges and incidents of discrimination. While Chapter 9 continues to discuss these concerns, it also investigates the treatment of students who have done something wrong – whether a criminal offense or a disciplinary infraction. Nevertheless, we will see that even wrongdoers should, whenever possible, remain valued members of the school community. All too often, the punishments meted out on students who misbehave are unduly harsh and exacerbated by racial bias and other instances of discrimination. In an era tragically characterized by heartbreaking acts of mass violence in schools, many officials are tempted to replace education with incarceration. The badges and incidents of slavery continue in the school-to-prison pipeline and in the dramatic disparities in school discipline and exclusion based on race.

In this chapter, we will begin by investigating the key Supreme Court precedents controlling student discipline. The deference shown by the Court has, in effect, given school officials free reign in this arena. Next, we will trace the federal government's evolving views on the efficacy of zero tolerance policies and exclusionary discipline techniques. We will explore ESSA's ambiguous treatment of these policies and the Obama administration's efforts to limit and scrutinize their use. In addition, we will analyze a renewed federal initiative for school safety announced in the aftermath of the Marjory Stoneman Douglas High School shooting on February 14, 2018. This initiative, we will see, appears to include a renewed embrace of exclusionary discipline. Finally, we will examine how this approach fuels the school-to-prison pipeline and explain how a social constructivist education requires an emphasis on restorative justice.

DUE PROCESS GOES TO SCHOOL: GOSS V. LOPEZ AND THE FRAMEWORK OF EXCLUSIONARY DISCIPLINE

In *Goss v.Lopez*, the Supreme Court held that students do not leave their due process rights at the schoolhouse door. Writing for the majority, Justice White made clear that the Due Process Clause of the Fourteenth Amendment applies to disciplinary removals of students.[1]

The case arose when a number of high school and junior high school students in Columbus, Ohio, found themselves summarily suspended without a hearing after a period of student unrest. Indeed, one plaintiff testified that, "at least 75 other students were suspended from his school on the same day."[2] The record demonstrated that school officials did not engage in even a modicum of individualized fact finding with regard to the suspended students. Significantly, the widespread chaos surrounding the incidents that led to the suspensions allowed for the possibility that at least some of the disciplined students were simply in the wrong place at the wrong time. Without a hearing, there was every chance that innocent bystanders were caught in the disciplinary dragnet.

Justice White began his analysis by noting that the students' entitlement to public education under the Ohio Constitution created a protected liberty and property interest under the Due Process Clause of the Fourteenth Amendment.[3] The Court also observed that severe reputational harm could attach to an extended suspension from school.[4] Accordingly, the Court held that any suspension from school required at least some degree of due process.[5]

In determining precisely how much process was "due," the Court emphasized that deference to administrators should guide the application of its holding. As Justice White explained,

> At the very minimum, therefore, students facing suspension and the consequent interference with a protected property interest must be given *some* kind of notice and afforded *some* kind of hearing. . . .
>
> It also appears from our cases that the timing and content of the notice and the nature of the hearing will depend on appropriate accommodation of the competing interests involved. . . . The student's interest is to avoid unfair or mistaken exclusion from the educational process, with all of its unfortunate consequences. The Due Process Clause will not shield him from suspensions properly imposed, but it disserves both his interest and the interest of the State if his suspension is in fact unwarranted. The concern would be mostly academic if the disciplinary process were a totally accurate, unerring process, never mistaken and never unfair. Unfortunately, that is not the case, and no one suggests that it is. Disciplinarians, although proceeding in utmost good faith, frequently act on the reports and advice of others; and the controlling facts and the nature of the conduct under challenge are often disputed. The risk of error is not at all trivial, and it should be guarded against if that may be done without

---

[1] 419 U.S. 567 (1975).
[2] *Id.* at 570.
[3] *Id.* at 572–574.
[4] *Id.* at 575.
[5] *Id.* at 576.

prohibitive cost or interference with the educational process.⁶ (Internal citations omitted; emphasis in original)

For suspensions of ten days or less, the Court simply required oral or written notice to the student explaining the basis of the accusation as well as a chance to offer his or her version of events.⁷ A formal hearing was unnecessary, reasoned the Court; even a simple conversation would satisfy due process in this context. The majority noted, however, "[s]tudents whose presence poses a continuing danger to persons or property or an ongoing threat of disrupting the academic process may be immediately removed from school. In such cases, the necessary notice and rudimentary hearing should follow as soon as practicable."⁸ Already, the Court laid the groundwork for the widespread use of exclusionary discipline by creating such a broad and deferential exception to its demand for due process prior to removing a student.

The Court concluded by reiterating its deference to school officials in disciplinary matters, noting that "an informal give-and-take between student and disciplinarian" would suffice in nearly all cases.⁹ It left open the possibility that a suspension lasting longer than ten days may require more formal procedures.¹⁰

In dissent, Justice Powell expressed skepticism that an absence of ten days or fewer constituted an "educational injury" given the length of the school year.¹¹ He offered a more compelling criticism by observing that the Court's opinion placed teachers and students in a more adversarial, litigious posture rather than the traditional mentor, quasi-parental relationship.¹² He observed: "We have relied for generations upon the experience, good faith, and dedication of those who staff our public schools, and the nonadversary means of airing grievances that always have been available to pupils and their parents."¹³

Justice Powell's observation that effective relationships solve more problems than procedures borrowed from litigation tracks quite well with social constructivist pedagogy. Whether those relationships would obviate the need for due process protections in an imperfect world is another question. Yet, he certainly raised points worth considering in the project of building a school system more in tune with the principles of social constructivism. While it is unclear whether Justice Powell appreciated the implications of his critique, it remains a truly insightful observation.

Goss continues to control the degree of procedural safeguards required when school officials seek to suspend a student for less than ten days. A decade later, the

---

⁶ *Id.* at 579–580.
⁷ *Id.* at 581.
⁸ *Id.* at 582–583.
⁹ *Id.* at 584.
¹⁰ *Id.*
¹¹ *Id.* at 589.
¹² *Id.* at 593–594.
¹³ *Id.* at 595.

NEW JERSEY V. T.L.O.: THE LIMITS OF THE FOURTH AMENDMENT IN SCHOOLS

Just as he did in *Goss*, Justice White wrote for the Court in *T.L.O.*, holding that the Fourth Amendment applies in the school setting.[14] However – much like its treatment of due process in *Goss* – the Court made clear that students do not enjoy the full scope of protection offered under traditional Fourth Amendment jurisprudence.

The underlying incident involved in the case occurred when T.L.O., a fourteen-year-old high school freshman in New Jersey, was caught smoking cigarettes with a classmate in the bathroom by a teacher.[15] The teacher then brought both students to the principal's office, whereupon Assistant Vice Principal Theodore Choplick began interrogating the students.[16] Although T.L.O.'s classmate admitted smoking, T.L.O. denied the accusation.[17] Assistant Vice Principal Choplick then demanded to see T.L.O.'s purse; after opening the purse, he found a pack of cigarettes, removed them, and berated T.L.O. for lying to him.[18] Having established that T.L.O. was likely smoking, he then resumed his search of the purse, finding evidence of the use and sale of marijuana.[19] The case then ran its course through the juvenile justice system in New Jersey, eventually requiring the Court to determine whether the Fourth Amendment applied in schools and, if so, whether the search of T.L.O.'s purse violated the Fourth Amendment.

In its analysis, the majority adopted the standard governing so-called "stop and frisk" searches by law enforcement personnel. Specifically, the Court announced that in the school setting, the Fourth Amendment standard was not probable cause but instead the more deferential "reasonable suspicion" inquiry – typically articulated as "reasonableness, under all the circumstances, of the search."[20] In effect, this grants tremendous discretion to administrators.

Elaborating on the standard further, Justice White explained,

> Under ordinary circumstances, a search of a student by a teacher or other school official will be "justified at its inception" when there are reasonable grounds for suspecting that the search will turn up evidence that the student has violated or is

---

[14] 469 U.S. 325 (1985), 333.
[15] *Id.* at 328.
[16] *Id.*
[17] *Id.*
[18] *Id.*
[19] *Id.*
[20] *Id.* at 341.

violating either the law or the rules of the school. Such a search will be permissible in its scope when the measures adopted are reasonably related to the objectives of the search and not excessively intrusive in light of the age and sex of the student and the nature of the infraction.[21]

Applying this rule, the Court concluded that Assistant Vice Principal Choplick's search of T.L.O.'s purse did not violate the Fourth Amendment. Justice White's analysis follows:

> (The teacher's) report gave Mr. Choplick reason to suspect that T.L.O. was carrying cigarettes with her; and if she did have cigarettes, her purse was the obvious place in which to find them. . . .
> The discovery of the rolling papers concededly gave rise to a reasonable suspicion that T.L.O. was carrying marihuana (sic) as well as cigarettes in her purse. This suspicion justified further exploration of T.L.O's purse, which turned up more evidence of drug-related activities. . . . In short, we cannot conclude that the search for marihuana was unreasonable in any respect.[22]

In effect, according to the majority, one thing led to another. The search of T.L.O.'s purse satisfied the reasonable suspicion standard under the Fourth Amendment.

Justice Powell concurred in the opinion, but wrote separately to once again emphasize how the Court's analysis could upset the traditional relationship between teachers and students by turning allies into adversaries.[23] Justice Blackmun also wrote separately to explain that the reasonable suspicion standard is the exception to traditional Fourth Amendment analysis and not the typical rule.[24]

In dissent, Justice Brennan agreed that the Fourth Amendment applied in the school setting and that educators should not have to satisfy the usual requirement of a search warrant.[25] However, he argued that the probable cause standard should still control.[26] Under the probable cause inquiry, he continued, the search of T.L.O.'s purse clearly violated the Fourth Amendment.[27]

Justice Stevens offered a dissent that presciently viewed the Court's opinion as further opening the door to exclusionary discipline. He criticized the majority for imposing a standard that, in his view, permitted searches of "students suspected of violating only the most trivial school regulations and guidelines for behavior."[28] As he phrased it, "a search for curlers and sunglasses in order to enforce the school dress code is apparently just as important as a search for evidence of heroin addiction or

---

[21] Id. at 342.
[22] Id. at 345–347.
[23] Id. at 350.
[24] Id. at 351–352.
[25] Id. at 357.
[26] Id.
[27] Id. at 369.
[28] Id. at 371.

violent gang activity."[29] Justice Stevens' concerns anticipated the rise of zero tolerance disciplinary policies quite accurately.

Instead of the extensive deference allowed by the majority, Justice Stevens would have permitted school officials to search a student or their personal effects, "when they have reason to believe that the search will uncover *evidence that the student is violating the law or engaging in conduct that is seriously disruptive of school order, or the educational process*"[30] (Emphasis in original). This standard, Justice Stevens explained, would insure that invasive searches occurred only in situations of sufficient gravity rather than in response to the countless *de minimus* rule violations that occur throughout any given school day.[31]

Moreover, the discretion permitted by the majority, if abused, could set a harmful example for the nation's schoolchildren and budding democratic citizens. Justice Stevens concluded,

> The schoolroom is the first opportunity most citizens have to experience the power of government. Through it passes every citizen and public official, from schoolteachers to policemen and prison guards. The values they learn there, they take with them in life. One of our most cherished ideals is the one contained in the Fourth Amendment: that the government may not intrude on the personal privacy of its citizens without a warrant or compelling circumstance. The Court's decision today is a curious moral for the Nation's youth. Although the search of T.L.O.'s purse does not trouble today's majority, I submit that ... "none who acts under color of law is beyond reach of the Constitution."[32]

Today, *T.L.O.* remains controlling precedent for searches and seizures of students and their effects that take place on school grounds. Its impact continues to reach far. In subsequent years, the Court has used the *T.L.O.* framework to conclude that a highly invasive body search of a thirteen-year-old girl was unconstitutional.[33] However, the Court has upheld both random and blanket drug testing policies for high school student athletes.[34]

United States v. Lopez

In *Lopez*, the Court struck down the Gun Free Schools Zones Act of 1990 on the grounds that the statute exceeded Congress' authority to legislate pursuant to the

---

[29] *Id.* at 377.
[30] *Id.* at 378.
[31] *Id.* at 382.
[32] *Id.* at 385–386.
[33] See *Safford Unified School District #1* v. *Redding* 557 U.S. 364 (2009).
[34] See *Vernonia School District 47 J* v. *Acton* 515 U.S. 646 (1995) and *Board of Education of Independent School District No. 92 of Pottawatomie County* v. *Earls* 536 U.S. 822 (2002) respectively.

Commerce Clause.³⁵ The Act made it a federal crime to possess a gun in a school or within 1,000 feet of a school.

Writing for the Court, Chief Justice Rehnquist recounted the three permissible avenues of regulation under the Commerce Clause: the channels of interstate commerce, the instrumentalities of interstate commerce, and activities having a substantial relation to interstate commerce.³⁶ Naturally, a statute dealing with gun possession in and around schools could only fit in the third category. *Lopez* marked the first time that the "substantial" qualifier was explicitly adopted by the Court.³⁷ This made it significantly more likely that congressional action under the Commerce Clause would not survive judicial review.

Chief Justice Rehnquist characterized the Act as "a criminal statute that by its terms has nothing to do with 'commerce' or any sort of economic enterprise, however broadly one might define those terms."³⁸ The Court accordingly rejected the Justice Department's argument that (1) the costs of violent crime had a substantial effect on commerce and (2) areas substantially affected by violent crime would, in effect, be removed from participating in interstate commerce.³⁹ The Court also denounced the contention that the presence of guns in schools derailed the educational process sufficiently to create a substantial effect on interstate commerce by preventing the formation of a fully educated citizenry.⁴⁰ The majority viewed all of these arguments as broad enough to encompass federal intrusion into any area of national life and, consequently, as far beyond the scope of any rational reading of the Commerce Clause.

In his concurrence, Justice Kennedy embarked upon a ponderous exploration of Commerce Clause jurisprudence. He concluded: "In a sense any conduct in this interdependent world of ours has an ultimate commercial origin or consequence, but we have not yet said the commerce power may reach so far."⁴¹

Justice Thomas also concurred, writing separately to advocate for a reading of the Commerce Clause that more closely accorded with the economic conditions familiar to the Founders in the late 1700s. He called for a more thorough reexamination of Commerce Clause jurisprudence at a later date.⁴²

In a brief but incisive dissent, Justice Stevens noted that guns are "articles of commerce" under any sensible definition.⁴³ He also offered an updated interpretation of the Commerce Clause in the context of the 1990s, writing: "The market for the possession of handguns by school-age children is, distressingly, substantial.

---

35   514 U.S. 549 (1995), 551.
36   *Id.* at 558–559.
37   *Id.*
38   *Id.* at 561.
39   *Id.* at 563–564.
40   *Id.* at 564.
41   *Id.* at 580.
42   *Id.* at 602.
43   *Id.*

Whether or not the national interest in eliminating that market would have justified federal legislation in 1789, it surely does today."[44]

Justice Souter also dissented, focusing heavily on the inherent contradiction of allowing the Court to define "commercial" while at the same time purporting to engage in rational basis review.[45] This strain of analysis would result in the policy preferences of particular blocs of justices guiding the outcome of Commerce Clause cases, argued Justice Souter. He admonished the majority that the only appropriate question based upon precedent was "whether the legislative judgment is within the realm of reason."[46] Justice Souter also noted that this standard of "rational possibility" did not even require Congress to produce a record of legislative findings explaining its reasoning.[47] Any rational basis that existed for Congress' passage of the Act, Justice Souter reminded the Court, should have salvaged it under traditional Commerce Clause jurisprudence.

Justice Breyer presented a particularly comprehensive dissent. He began by countering the majority approach, offering three principles of Commerce Clause cases. First, Congress can regulate local activities that have a significant effect on interstate commerce.[48] Second, Congress can measure the cumulative rather than individual impact of such activities.[49] Third, Congress is entitled to a "degree of leeway in determining the existence of a significant factual connection between the regulated activity and interstate commerce."[50] With these three principles in mind, Justice Breyer employed the language of the Act to develop an alternative formulation of the question before the Court: "Could Congress rationally have found that 'violent crime in school zones,' through its effect on the 'quality of education,' significantly (or substantially) affects 'interstate' or 'foreign commerce'?"

Having articulated this deferential standard, Justice Breyer answered the question in the affirmative. He attached an appendix over twelve pages in length full of congressional materials and other resources that could have aided in reaching such a determination. Justice Breyer concluded: "Based on reports such as these, Congress obviously could have thought that guns and learning are mutually exclusive. ... Congress could therefore have found a substantial educational problem – teachers unable to teach, students unable to learn – and concluded that guns near schools contribute substantially to the size and scope of that problem."[51] He also observed that so holding, "would not expand the scope of (the Commerce

---

[44] *Id.* at 603.
[45] *Id.* at 608.
[46] *Id.* at 613.
[47] *Id.* at 614.
[48] *Id.* at 615.
[49] *Id.* at 616.
[50] *Id.*
[51] *Id.* at 619.

Clause). Rather, it simply would apply pre-existing law to changing economic circumstances."[52]

After *Lopez*, Congress in fact attempted to remedy the Commerce Clause infirmity in its statute by passing the revised Gun Free School Zones Act of 1996.[53] That statute prohibits any person from knowingly possessing a firearm "that has moved in or that otherwise affects interstate or foreign commerce."[54]

Before the Supreme Court ruled in *Lopez*, Congress also enacted the Gun-Free Schools Act of 1994. The statute has since been re-enacted as a part of the No Child Left Behind Act of 2001.[55] Under the statute, states receiving federal funds must require local educational agencies to expel for at least one year any student who brings a "firearm" to school. The statute was passed pursuant to Congress' power under the Spending Clause rather than the Commerce Clause. The statute comes close to requiring schools to enact strict "zero tolerance policies" for students who bring a firearm to school or possess a firearm on school grounds or at any school-sponsored event or activity conducted anywhere. The student must be expelled for at least one year.

But the statute also gives the school superintendent or chief administrative officer discretion to modify the expulsion on a case-by-case basis.[56] The statute also requires local education agencies to refer to the criminal justice system any student who brings a firearm to school. The statutory presumption that students who bring firearms to school must be expelled for at least one year (absent administrative modification) targets student behavior and is designed to deter students from bringing dangerous firearms to school. Such a policy, however, raises difficult political and prudential questions. In recent years, the Department of Education has struggled to answer them.

ESSA'S AMBIGUOUS TREATMENT OF EXCLUSIONARY DISCIPLINE

Passed in 2015, the Every Student Succeeds Act (ESSA) encourages schools to move away from using exclusionary discipline techniques. Throughout the bill, Congress urges school districts to suspend or expel students only as a last resort. Yet, ESSA does not repeal or even constrain the Gun-Free Schools Act of 1994 (GFSA).[57] GFSA requires school districts to expel any student who possesses a firearm on school grounds for one calendar year. It is the most prominent example of a zero tolerance policy in K-12 education. Like most zero tolerance policies, it also automatically triggers exclusionary discipline for its violators. Indeed, GFSA requires – as

---

[52] *Id.* at 624.
[53] 18 U.S.C. §922(q) (2)(A).
[54] See, e.g., *United States v. Danks*, 221 F.3d 1037, 1038 (8th Cir. 1999).
[55] 20 U.S.C. §7151.
[56] 20 U.S.C. §7151(b).
[57] 20 U.S.C.A. §7961.

a condition for receiving federal funds – each local educational agency to implement a policy mandating referral of any student in violation of GFSA to "the criminal justice or juvenile delinquency system."[58] This provision has provided ample fuel for the school-to-prison pipeline over the last quarter century.

Philosophically, zero tolerance policies operate under the premise that both major and minor violations deserve equally harsh treatment in order to serve as a warning to the rest of the community.[59] A pure zero tolerance policy thus draws no distinction between the troubled high school junior who intentionally carries a firearm in his backpack and the sixth-grade honor student who accidentally brings a lunchbox that contains a knife. Both have violated the policy. Russell J. Skiba notes that many districts with a pure zero tolerance policy have tended to impose ever-greater punishments over time. By punishing relatively minor or accidental infractions severely, districts must then elevate the penalty even higher for genuinely dangerous violators.[60]

While zero tolerance policies have proven popular nationwide, many concerns linger. In "The Gun-Free Schools Act of 1994: Zero Tolerance Takes Aim at Procedural Due Process," Kathleen M. Cerrone critiques school discipline on both legal and practical grounds.[61] Noting that a right to receive a free public education has been firmly established as a property interest, Cerrone argues that stringent zero tolerance policies contravene *Goss* v.*Lopez*. Paraphrasing *Goss*, she writes: "Suspension or expulsion deprives a student so completely of his or her property interest to attend school ... that such punishment can only be imposed if accompanied by the procedural safeguards guaranteed by minimum due process."[62] While nothing in GFSA prohibits schools from extending a pre-expulsion hearing to an alleged violator, nothing requires them to do so either. In fact, Cerrone cites a Nevada statute passed to comply with GFSA that explicitly removes procedural due process protections for alleged possessors of firearms.[63] Considering the widespread use of zero tolerance in schools, the ambiguity surrounding due process requirements invites constitutional challenges.

Cerrone also questions the premise that zero tolerance laws effectively deter students who would otherwise act violently. She contends that those students who bring a weapon to school through an honest mistake will feel disillusioned and alienated after enduring a harsh punishment. Conversely, Cerrone argues that those students who knowingly bring a weapon to school likely will not be deterred by a suspension or expulsion. Due to the realities of many students' home lives, such a punishment often has the effect of insuring unsupervised, unstructured free time.

[58] Id.
[59] Russell J. Skiba, "Zero Tolerance Zero Evidence: An Analysis of School Disciplinary Practice," Indiana Univ., Bloomington. Education Policy Center (2000), at 7.
[60] Ibid. at 13.
[61] 20 Pace L. Rev., Fall 1999, at 131.
[62] Id. at 178.
[63] Id.

When added to (in many cases) significant mental or emotional disturbances and the ready availability of firearms at home, this combination has proved disastrous on multiple occasions.[64] Cerrone concludes,

> Local school districts are no longer dealing with students who can be shamed into good behavior by a day or two of suspension. The current era is one of sophisticated ingenuity, and sometimes mental disease, at a young age ... (Districts) must diagnose the particular student they are dealing with.[65]

Added to this problem of implementation is a surprising lack of data from which objective conclusions can be drawn about zero tolerance. Skiba notes the irony of this gap in the context of an increasing national emphasis on standardized testing and statistical metrics of educational effectiveness.[66] Moreover, his research suggests that almost no investigation of the effectiveness of zero tolerance policies in improving school safety has occurred. What is clear, Skiba concludes, is that "the most consistently documented outcome of suspension and expulsion appears to be further suspension and expulsion, and perhaps school dropout."[67]

In sum, criticisms of zero tolerance policies in schools implicate both procedural and substantive concerns. Procedurally, zero tolerance policies often constrain – or eliminate – the due process rights of students. Substantively, zero tolerance policies tend to punish radically different violations with identical severity. They thus lump all offenders into a "one size fits all" category, allowing for no evaluation of situational or contextual factors. This can result in both an elevation of penalties for all offenders and a failure to effectively separate the truly threatening students from the more innocuous cases. Compounding all these issues is the lack of data on the effectiveness of zero tolerance policies. For a quarter century, GFSA has raised many questions while providing few satisfactory answers.

To date, the Department of Education's most ambitious analysis of zero tolerance policies is its Dear Colleague Letter of January 8, 2014, and the accompanying *Guiding Principles: A Resource Guide for Improving School Climate and Discipline*.[68] The Dear Colleague Letter addressed Civil Rights Data Collection (CRDC) findings that indicated a racial disparity in exclusionary discipline; essentially, the figures demonstrated that students of color are far more likely to be subjected to expulsion or suspension than their white classmates.[69] The Letter instructs schools that policies which either treat students of different races differently

---

[64] Id. at 183–184.
[65] Id. at 184.
[66] Russell J. Skiba, "Zero Tolerance Zero Evidence: An Analysis of School Disciplinary Practice," Indiana Univ., Bloomington. Education Policy Center (2000), at 10.
[67] Ibid. at 15.
[68] As we will see, this Guidance has since been rescinded by the Trump administration. However, it continues to offer an excellent template for those who would prefer a more holistic approach to student conduct that relies less on zero tolerance and exclusionary discipline policies.
[69] U.S. Department of Education, "Dear Colleague Letter on the Nondiscriminatory Administration of School Discipline," January 8, 2014, at 3.

or have disparate impacts on different racial groups constitute a civil rights violation. However, the Department of Education makes clear that misconduct rising to the level of discriminatory harassment – particularly sexual misconduct under Title IX – does not fall within the scope of the guidance.[70] The Letter as a whole leaves little doubt that by 2014 the Department took the improper use of exclusionary discipline techniques seriously and stood ready to intervene in response. The policies outlined in the Letter reveal a special attention to the disproportionate impact exclusionary discipline has on minority students.

While the Dear Colleague Letter reminds schools of the Department of Education's willingness to open civil rights investigations to insure compliance, the accompanying Resource Guide has a different focus.[71] It encourages schools to structure their disciplinary policies in accordance with the Department's three Guiding Principles for Improving School Climate and Discipline. It states that schools should: (1) create positive climates and focus on prevention; (2) develop clear, appropriate, and consistent expectations to address disruptive student behaviors; and (3) insure fairness, equity, and continuous improvement. The Resource Guide includes numerous Action Steps that suggest intermediate goals and tasks for schools to accomplish. These, the Guide adds, will help schools achieve the Guiding Principles. Overall, the document concerns itself with scaling back the cold, unforgiving tone so often set by zero tolerance policies. Rather than a system in which even routine disciplinary matters fall within the purview of school resource officers, it envisions building school communities in which all stakeholders play a role; teachers, administrators, support staff, mental health professionals, parents, guardians, and even fellow students each have their own responsibility to help achieve the Guiding Principles. This multi-tiered disciplinary approach offers a welcome respite from exclusionary discipline.

Despite its general rejection of exclusionary discipline and zero tolerance, however, the Resource Guide allows for one key exception. Under a heading entitled "Reserve for Serious Infractions," the Guide explicitly reminds schools of their obligations under GFSA.[72] The Department of Education calls for exclusionary discipline in situations "involving a serious and immediate threat to students, school personnel, or public safety."[73] Viewed through this lens, the continued vitality of GFSA can be squared with ESSA's broad rejection of zero tolerance and exclusionary discipline. In fact, the section hastens to add that GFSA does not require states or schools to craft zero tolerance policies for anything other than firearm

---

[70] Ibid. at 5.
[71] U.S. Department of Education, *Guiding Principles: A Resource Guide for Improving School Climate and Discipline*, Washington, D.C., 2014.
[72] Ibid. at 15.
[73] Ibid.

possession.[74] It also encourages schools that remove students in accordance with GFSA to nonetheless offer alternative educational services whenever possible.[75]

In light of the opposing forces of ESSA and GFSA, the Department of Education's stance on the use of zero tolerance and exclusionary discipline attempted to incorporate both laws. The Department's publications during the Obama administration all indicate both deep discomfort with such policies and a reluctance to abandon them entirely. By 2014, the Department of Education reached the following position: Zero tolerance and exclusionary discipline should be avoided in all cases except those which pose a serious and immediate threat of harm to the school community. Based on the Guidance, examples which constitute a serious and immediate threat under this standard are (1) violations of GFSA and (2) violations of Title IX prohibitions against sexual misconduct. While criticizing the overuse of zero tolerance and exclusionary discipline, the Department of Education maintained that certain violations of school rules are so harmful as to require these measures to protect the school community.

EVALUATING THE RECOMMENDATIONS OF THE FEDERAL COMMISSION ON SCHOOL SAFETY

In the wake of the horrifying mass shooting at Marjory Stoneman Douglas High School on February 14, 2018, President Trump established the Federal Commission on School Safety. Chaired by Secretary of Education Betsy DeVos, the Commission submitted its Final Report on December 18, 2018. The Report is thus the most recent systematic study of violence in schools.

Viewed through a social constructivist lens, the Report is a decidedly mixed bag. Particularly in its early sections, it emphasizes the critical need for healthy relationships, caring school communities, and an interconnected citizenry as the main defenses against school violence. The Commission deserves credit for making these astute observations and offering such worthy sentiments. As the Report progresses, however, its focus shifts dramatically. Apart from the occasional cursory reference to building strong relationships, the Commission myopically highlights security policies and practices. Many appear better suited for airports than classrooms. As it will likely set the tone in school security policies for years to come, the Report deserves a close analysis and a detailed explanation of its strengths and weaknesses.

Remarkably, the Report opens with a statement of principles that closely mirror the tenets of social constructivist pedagogy. In its Letter of Transmittal, the Commission states: "Our country's moral fabric needs more threads of love, empathy, and connection."[76] In other words, the Commission – which consists of four

[74] Ibid.
[75] Ibid.
[76] Federal Commission on School Safety, Final Report (2018), 1.

members of President Trump's Cabinet – explicitly endorses a goal achievable only by teaching students to construct knowledge together through meaningful relationships. This unlikely convergence between public officials and educational theorists speaks volumes about the potential of a school system premised on the tenets of social constructivism.

In the Report's very first chapter, the Commission calls for renewed efforts to develop the character of young students and create what it calls a "Culture of Connectedness." Specifically, the Commission concludes that to create safer schools, "[s]uccessful efforts must improve the culture in which students live and learn. This includes developing students of strong character who are connected in meaningful ways to their peers, educators, and communities."[77] The Commission additionally notes the efficacy of using Positive Behavioral Interventions and Supports (PBIS) to aid children in this effort.[78] In its recommendations, the Commission reiterates the centrality of "[r]elationship building ... emphasizing cooperative learning and teaching interpersonal skills."[79] At this early stage, the Report reads like an excerpt from a social constructivist teacher's manual.

The Commission continues to expound on the theme of meaningful connections and relationships. In particular, it notes the key role positive support networks can play in diverting youth from interaction with the criminal justice system.[80] The Report also champions the need for increased mental health services in schools – particularly for at-risk youth. Aware that most perpetrators of school violence had attracted the attention and concern of educators for extended periods of time prior to incidents[81] the Report calls for mental health screening to occur regularly in schools. It suggests schools conduct mental health exams alongside hearing and vision tests – with no more stigma attached to one than the other.[82] Insightfully, the Report calls for developing "Mental Health First Aid" resources to enable adults working with students to more readily appreciate signs that some degree of treatment may be required.[83]

The Commission briefly surveys the landscape of violent entertainment available to young Americans. While noting that multiple school shooters exhibited interest in violent videogames, it avoids drawing any conclusions on the subject.[84] By treading so lightly in this area, the Commission misses an opportunity to further address the themes of isolation and connectedness. In addition to the violent images prevalent in videogames, the games are also increasingly played alone. Where early systems lacked internet capabilities and thus lent themselves to groups of friends gathering

---

[77] Ibid. at 17.
[78] Ibid. at 18.
[79] Ibid. at 19.
[80] Ibid. at 38.
[81] Ibid. at 49.
[82] Ibid. at 40.
[83] Ibid. at 33.
[84] Ibid. at 63–67.

to play together, contemporary platforms are internet-based and thus have the effect of discouraging interpersonal contact. Accordingly, the road to unhealthy isolation through videogames is considerably easier to travel today than in years past. A closer examination of the interplay between gratuitously violent images in games and the attendant isolation of the player would have been fruitful.

Regrettably, the promising signs present in the early pages of the Report vanish in its later chapters. The Commission largely avoids the pressing issue of access to firearms, engaging in a cursory discussion only to express skepticism regarding increased gun control measures.[85] It says nothing of what effect a culture saturated with access to and use of firearms might have on adolescent minds. On a similar note, the Commission calls without reservation for an increased police presence in schools.[86] Although it concedes that local sensibilities should govern the question of arming teachers, it leaves such a decision within the discretion of school officials.[87] Whatever the intent of the Commission, it is difficult to imagine a measure more directly opposed to the formation of meaningful relationships between teachers and students than this policy. One wonders what Justice Powell would have thought of the state of the relationship between teachers and students if he could have seen a document entertaining the possibility of guns in the classroom.

Aspects of the Commission's recommendations regarding building security smack of attempts to apply counterterrorism measures to the school setting. The Report directs readers to a publication of the Department of Homeland Security (DHS) outlining principles for school safety.[88] In a similar vein, the Commission praises local police departments for measures such as a so-called "Threat Mitigation Unit."[89] While crafted with the best of intentions, these measures inevitably lead to a militarization of the school setting which in turn exacerbates the school-to-prison pipeline. It is hard to envision how the crucial task of educating citizens for democratic participation can take place effectively in such an environment. On a similar note, the Commission calls for DHS and the Department of Education to co-sponsor a "Peer-to-Peer Competition Challenge" in which "high school students develop school security campaigns."[90] The initiative manages to combine the grim acceptance of violence with the behaviorist emphasis on competition. Even school safety is reduced to a contest. Neither the subject matter nor the mechanism bear any resemblance to the vision of the Founders.

The Commission concludes its Report by unpacking the best practices surrounding the execution of active shooter drills. Given the spate of violent incidents in schools, one cannot criticize the Commission for including this discussion. Its

---

[85] Ibid. at 85–89.
[86] Ibid. at 106.
[87] Ibid.
[88] Ibid. at 121.
[89] Ibid.
[90] Ibid. at 56.

recommendations on this front, however, paint a picture of a deeply wounded society; it is impossible to read a list of expectations outlining the degree of assistance kindergarteners could render their teachers in the event of an active shooter situation without a feeling of despair.[91] The Commission endorses active shooter drills at all levels, though it cautions the drills should be "designed in a manner not to unduly traumatize any of the participants."[92]

The Final Report of the Federal Commission on School Safety offers recommendations tailored for an environment in which mass shooter events at schools are real possibilities. Given this context, the Report's emphasis on security measures, intense training, and possibly arming school personnel is understandable – though still disappointing. To its credit, the Report at the outset agrees that the very emphasis on relationships and connection facilitated by social constructivist pedagogy is, in the long run, the best antidote to school violence. The Report does not, regrettably, appear to grasp how some of the proposals offered would make this task more difficult.

THE TRUMP ADMINISTRATION RETHINKS THE "RETHINKING SCHOOL DISCIPLINE" GUIDANCE

As part of its wide-ranging report, the Commission also takes the opportunity to call for the rescission of the Department of Education's "Rethinking School Discipline" Guidance issued in 2014 and discussed earlier in the Chapter. It spends considerable space critiquing the 2014 Guidance.

The Trump administration advances three main criticisms of the Guidance. First, it claims that it creates a "chilling effect" on the use of classroom discipline through the threat of federal intervention.[93] In other words, students whose behavior would otherwise merit removal remain in class to disrupt the learning environment. Second, it argues that the Guidance's embrace of the "disparate impact legal theory" in evaluating exclusionary discipline is directly contradicted by Supreme Court precedent interpreting Title VI of the Civil Rights Act of 1964.[94] Third, it charges that the threat of investigations announced in the Guidance, "has likely had a strong, negative impact on school discipline and safety."[95]

The Report recites several studies purporting to document widespread teacher dissatisfaction with changes implemented in reaction to the Guidance.[96] It cites educators tracing an uptick in disruptive classroom behaviors and decline in academic performance to the mandates announced in the Guidance. In addition, it

---

[91] Ibid. at 142.
[92] Ibid. at 146.
[93] Ibid. at 67.
[94] Ibid.
[95] Ibid.
[96] Ibid. at 69–70.

directly questions the premise underlying the Guidance – claiming that any "racial gap" in exclusionary discipline "was completely accounted for by a measure of the prior problem behavior of the student."[97] Of course, this assumes that any prior disciplinary encounters were not driven by racially informed motives – an assumption that, the data suggests, is not one that can be made with confidence.

The Trump administration then proceeds to call for a restoration of "basic principles of federalism" by maintaining local control over education – including exclusionary discipline.[98] It signals unequivocally a withdrawal of federal oversight in this arena, stating: "Schools should also receive deference as to whether their policies promote a 'valid educational purpose' due to the 'special characteristics of the school environment,' and these policies should not be overturned merely because others disagree about their 'wisdom.'"[99] It finally concludes the discussion by calling for a full rescission of the Guidance with immediate effect.[100] Three days after the Report's release, a "Dear Colleague Letter" issued by the Department of Education and Department of Justice did precisely that.[101]

The horrific acts of violence that have occurred at schools, of course, call for a wide range of preventive responses and raise many difficult questions. Is zero tolerance sufficient to deter school violence? In fact, there is no evidence that zero tolerance policies make schools safer or improve student behavior.[102] School safety is a subtle, nuanced, and multi-faceted issue. What comprehensive steps should a school district take to promote a safe school environment? Do policies like these facilitate a school-to-prison pipeline with a disproportionate impact on minority students?[103] African American students are 3.5 times more likely than their white peers to be suspended. They represent only 18 percent of the public school population, but 37 percent of expulsions. Of the students who were referred by school to law enforcement in the 2009–2010 school year, 70 percent were Latino or African American.[104]

Across the country, zero tolerance policies and increased police presence are more common in schools with large populations of students of color.[105] Is it problematic that in many school districts across the country, "zero tolerance" policies have been expanded to apply to less severe student behavior that does not impact school

---

[97] Ibid. at 70.
[98] Ibid. at 71.
[99] Ibid.
[100] Ibid. at 72.
[101] www2.ed.gov/about/offices/list/ocr/letters/colleague-201812.pdf .
[102] ACLU, School to Prison Pipeline (2011).
[103] See, e.g., Avarita L. Hansen, Have Zero Tolerance School Discipline Policies Turned into a Nightmare?, 9 U.C. Davis J. Juv. L. & Pol'y 289 (2005).
[104] Code of Conduct: Safety, Discipline, and School Climate, 32(16) Educ. Wk. 4–12 (Jan. 10, 2013).
[105] Advancement Project, Alliance for Educational Justice, Dignity in Schools Campaign, & NAACP Legal Defense and Education Fund, Police in Schools Are Not the Answer to the Newtown Shooting (January 2013).

safety? The policies have also been accompanied by an increased police presence in schools.[106]

The number of school resource officers increased by 38 percent between 1997 and 2007. Despite the expanded investment in police presence in schools, there is no clear connection between police in schools and school safety; in fact, research shows that police in school may increase distrust and disorder in schools. These school-based law enforcement officers are increasingly asked to respond to incidents that are not a threat to safety. This has resulted in students being handcuffed or arrested for minor offenses, such as missing a class, writing "okay" on a school desk, or walking past a fight. This increased police presence and response poses a significant threat to educational achievement: a first-time arrest doubles the chance that a student will drop out of high school, and a first-time court appearance quadruples the student's chances of dropping out.[107]

THE MECHANICS OF THE SCHOOL-TO-PRISON PIPELINE

With its emphasis on deference to school officials, Supreme Court precedent has helped create a climate amenable to the widespread use of exclusionary discipline. At its most extreme, this has facilitated the expansion of the school-to-prison pipeline. Among its many pernicious characteristics, this system features racial biases, a reliance on punitive discipline methods, a criminalization of relatively benign juvenile behaviors, and an outsourcing of pedagogy to police.

In their pathbreaking study, *The School-To-Prison Pipeline: Structuring Legal Reform*, attorneys Catherine Y. Kim, Daniel J. Losen, and Damon T. Hewitt define the school-to-prison pipeline as:

> [T]he confluence of education policies in underresourced public schools and a predominantly punitive juvenile justice system that fails to provide education and mental health services for our most at-risk students and drastically increases the risk that these children will end up with a criminal record rather than a high school diploma.[108]

As Kim, Losen, and Hewitt demonstrate, this confluence of factors manifests itself most sharply in property-poor, majority-minority school districts. The school-to-prison pipeline thus combines the ills discussed in Chapter 4 and Chapter 6 with extreme elements of the behaviorist philosophies outlined in Chapter 3. As we will see, it is completely inimical to the tenets of social constructivist pedagogy.

---

[106] Code of Conduct: Safety, Discipline, and School Climate.
[107] Advancement Project, Alliance for Educational Justice, Dignity in Schools Campaign, & NAACP Legal Defense and Education Fund, Police in Schools Are Not the Answer to the Newtown Shooting (January 2013).
[108] (New York: New York University Press, 2010), 4.

A pronounced racial bias characterizes the school-to-prison pipeline. Research suggests that black students with disabilities are four times more likely than white students with disabilities to be placed in correctional facilities.[109] Relatedly, stationing police personnel in schools on a full-time basis opens the door to the use of racial profiling. This is especially true when unscrupulous actors abuse their authority. A trio of recent incidents in California illustrate this danger:

> In the Union City School District, school officials worked with police officials to target sixty minority students to be searched, interrogated, and photographed as part of a 'gang intervention' effort. In Fairfield, a school resource officer (SRO) and police officers required groups of Latino students to be lined up and photographed for a gang database. In Bishop, a police officer permanently stationed at the school physically threatened and abused students, causing one to lose consciousness.[110]

Even in cases where police officers proceed in the utmost good faith and avoid racial bias entirely, the increasing criminalization of behaviors historically treated as merely immature or counterproductive insures more students encounter the justice system. As Kim, et al. note, several states have passed statutes holding out the threat of criminal sanctions for "crimes" such as disruption of schools and talking back to teachers.[111] Indeed, the authors report that "disrupting schools" was the most common offense adjudicated in juvenile court in South Carolina during the 2007–2008 school year.[112]

School districts are also, in many cases, increasingly outsourcing their pedagogical responsibilities to police departments. All too often, the first instinct is not to educate but incarcerate. Rather than use a young child's verbal threat as a teachable moment that can be turned toward a constructive outcome, school officials frequently turn the matter over to law enforcement.[113] In doing so, they abdicate their responsibility as educators.

At present, many schools treat their students like suspects at best and inmates at worst. Too many educators have adopted heavy-handed investigative tactics and deployed them on their students, causing irreparable harm to the learning environment. Kim, et al. describe an alternative school in which, "in order to enter the building every day, students were required to take off their shoes, to open their mouths and show their tongues, and even to 'snap' their bras to demonstrate that they were not hiding contraband."[114] Such invasive and degrading searches transform a student's school from a place of joy and learning to an institution of fear and suspicion. One South Dakota district allegedly forced its students to write statements admitting disciplinary infractions on forms entitled "Affidavit" or "Affidavit in

[109] Ibid. at 51.
[110] Ibid. at 120.
[111] Ibid. at 124–125.
[112] Ibid. at 112.
[113] Ibid. at 126–127.
[114] Ibid. at 108.

Support of Criminal Prosecution" – which were then duly notarized and conveyed to law enforcement officials.[115] Students invariably find it difficult to trust their teachers in such an environment.

From a social constructivist perspective, the effects of the school-to-prison pipeline are disastrous. Its methods treat students – often young children – not as budding citizens capable of making new insights and unique contributions but rather as current or future lawbreakers. It ignores a student's talents and sees only a district's liabilities. It does not overstate the scope of the problem to say that the pipeline's combination of racial bias, abdication of educative responsibilities, and criminalization of adolescent behaviors ruins lives. Especially tragic is its impact on those communities that, if anything, are in need of special support rather than extra enforcement.

Over the long term, the continued expansion of the school-to-prison pipeline will render impossible this nation's efforts to implement the Founders' vision. It will remove an entire segment of the population from the mainstream of American life and will, in effect, make their participation in and contribution to national conversations impossible. It will combine familiar badges and incidents of discrimination with a new approach that views relatively minor infractions as appropriate grounds for imposing punitive discipline and its associated stigma. A democracy cannot afford to make this mistake. Law can play a key role in fixing this defect. Kim and her colleagues suggest: "The very fact that school officials are relying on the juvenile and criminal justice systems in new and unprecedented ways supports the argument that courts should revisit the dilution of constitutional standards in schools."[116] The present situation certainly calls into question the equity of relying on *Goss* and *T.L.O.* indefinitely.

The lasting repair, however, must come from education. Restorative justice techniques offer a compelling alternative to the harmful practices fueling the school-to-prison pipeline.

THE EMERGING ROLE OF RESTORATIVE JUSTICE

Restorative justice is a viable alternative to punitive approaches and has proven to be the most effective method of discipline. A restorative justice approach is one that is collaborative, relies on social justice curriculum, and progresses toward building community. Restorative justice heals rather than continues a cycle of disobedience and punishment. States and districts are recognizing that disciplining through restorative justice is far more effective than any other method. Illinois, for example, has recognized the "long-standing and well-documented negative effects of exclusionary discipline" and has thus worked to adopt best practices and develop policies

---

[115] Ibid. at 118.
[116] Ibid. at 119.

that reduce the time that children lose due to such policies and eradicate inequities in how discipline is administered.

In its Model Code of Conduct, the Transforming School Discipline Collaborative for the state of Illinois notes that developing a district or school's discipline philosophy "presents a meaningful opportunity for students, parents, guardians, families, district and school staff, school board members, and community members to engage in a collaborative process that results in a shared vision to which all stakeholders can be committed. All of these stakeholders must be involved in the development, implementation, and evaluation of [the school's] discipline policies." It also sets forth components of a discipline philosophy: a discipline creed, rights and responsibilities, and a discipline framework.

An example of a discipline creed found in the Illinois Model Code of Conduct follows:

> Discipline is any policy, procedure, or consequence used by anyone at the district or school to redirect student behavior, so that all the students involved are successfully engaged in a healthy and safe school climate and culture. Discipline should be used as an opportunity for support, learning, growth, self-awareness, and community building, instead of punishment.
>
> Our goals are to understand and address the causes of behavior, resolve conflicts, encourage students to take responsibility for changing their behavior, repair the harm done, restore the relationships in the school community, and reintegrate students into the school community.
>
> We use evidence-based, school-wide discipline policies developed, implemented, monitored, evaluated, and revised with meaningful, shared, and equal input by the school community, which includes students, parents, guardians, families, district and school staff, school board members, and community members to create a positive and inclusive school climate for everyone.
>
> Our district and schools are committed to applying school discipline policies and practices in a fair and equitable manner so as not to disproportionately impact students of color, students with disabilities, LGBT students, students with limited English proficiency, students with unstable family and home lives, homeless students, military-involved students, students who have been the target of bullying behavior, or other at-risk students.
>
> With regard to rights and responsibilities, the code of conduct should identify rights and responsibilities of parents, students, and teachers. Coming up with these rights and responsibilities should be a collaborative process, and, while all stakeholders will share some, others may be more specific to each stakeholder group.
>
> With regard to the discipline framework, schools will provide positive early and differentiated interventions for students using a multi-tiered system of support (supports that are schoolwide, provided to groups, or provided to individual students). Students who have fallen behind, students who are being disciplined, students who are at risk of leaving or being pushed out of school, or students who are disproportionately negatively affected by policies in a school community are

supported by specific academic, behavioral, mental health, and social-emotional practices at different tiers, based on data.

As such, "restorative measures" is defined in Illinois law as: a continuum of school-based alternatives to exclusionary discipline, such as suspensions and expulsions, that: (i) are adapted to the particular needs of the school and community, (ii) contribute to maintaining school safety, (iii) protect the integrity of a positive and productive learning climate, (iv) teach students the personal and interpersonal skills they will need to be successful in school and society, (v) serve to build and restore relationships among students, families, schools, and communities, and (vi) reduce the likelihood of future disruption by balancing accountability with an understanding of students' behavioral health needs in order to keep students in school.

The Illinois Model Code of Conduct sets forth various support services and interventions that may include:

Referral of those who experienced harm and caused harm to appropriate support services in the school and community, such as: counselors, psychologists, social workers, child welfare attendance personnel, or other school support service personnel for case management, counseling, and anything else that may address underlying behavior;

Notification of parents, guardians, and students in writing from all those involved;

Processes for resolution, such as mediation, restorative justice circles led by an experienced circle leader, conversations, and family groups;

Conferences, behavior contracts, instruction in anger and/or stress management, and social and emotional skill-building;

Academic interventions, such as tutoring and use of formative assessment;

Community service, including opportunities to reflect on service to the community with adult mentors; and

Study teams, guidance teams, resource panel teams, or other intervention-related teams that assess the behavior, and develop and implement individualized plans to address the behavior in partnership with the student and parents or guardians.

The district and the schools should provide structured opportunities for students, parents, guardians, families, staff, school board members, and community members to give input, get information, help make decisions, and participate in the educational process. All of these individuals must be informed in a timely and clear manner as to how and when they can participate, and trainings should be provided on how the individuals can effectively hold each other and schools accountable. Districts should also implement a grievance and complaint procedure, insuring that the due process rights of all stakeholders are respected.

Because the goal is to "create a safe and supportive environment where all students can develop the academic, social, and emotional skills needed to become engaged citizens," challenges in student conduct should be addressed in the most constructive way possible, and out-of-school suspensions and expulsions should be used only as a last resort and for legitimate educational purposes.

An educational environment inspired by neuroscientific research would also implement trauma-informed practices. In "The Pedagogy of Trauma-Informed Lawyering," Professors Sarah Katz and Deeya Haldar describe a traumatic event as one that "renders an individual's internal and external resources inadequate, making effective coping impossible."[117] They explain:

> A traumatic experience occurs when an individual subjectively experiences a threat to life, bodily integrity or sanity. ... External threats that result in trauma can include, experiencing, witnessing, anticipating, or being confronted with an event or events that involve actual or threatened death or serious injury, or threats to the physical integrity of one's self or others.[118]

Traumatic episodes are a common human experience.[119] Studies illustrate connections between trauma and experienced racism and between trauma and urban poverty.[120] Exposure to trauma has a direct impact on academic success.[121] As Professor Miranda Johnson illustrates:

> A childhood background of trauma enhances the likelihood of school failure. Many students from neighborhoods high in violence come to school traumatized by what they witness in their daily lives. Constantly in "fight or flight" mode, they may act inappropriately in response to even minor triggers. Traumatized students are more likely to have poor attendance as well as academic and behavioral problems.[122]

School leaders who seek to provide loving care for the whole person will implement trauma-informed practices. They will support students who have experienced, or are experiencing, trauma. Katz and Haldar explain:

> To be trauma-informed means to be educated about the impact of interpersonal violence and victimization on an individual's life and development. ... Trauma-informed practice recognizes the ways in which trauma impacts systems and individuals. Becoming trauma informed results in the recognition that behavioral symptoms, mental health diagnosis, and involvement in the criminal justice system are all manifestations of injury, rather than indicators of sickness or badness – the two current explanations for such behavior.[123]

---

[117] 22 CLINICAL L. REV. 359, 364 (2016).
[118] *Id.*
[119] *Id.* at 367.
[120] *Id.* at 364–365.
[121] Miranda Johnson, "Opinion, Education Investment Critical in Ending Chicago's Violence," HILL (Feb. 17, 2017), http://thehill.com/blogs/pundits-blog/education/320104-education-investment-critical-in-ending-chicagos-violence [https://perma.cc/SAP8-EVNR].
[122] *Id.*
[123] Katz & Haldar, at 369–370.

Trauma-informed practices include an additional layer of support services needed for students as well as structural changes needed to insure such services are available and feasible for use by the students.

While some suggest stricter security measures, including putting additional security officers in schools and allowing teachers and principals to carry weapons, others offer solutions that focus on altering the school climate.[124] Groups advocating changes to school climate as the most appropriate response to these tragedies point to model schools that are improving safety by fostering connectedness and communication among students, staff, and community. These schools embrace policies that allow teachers and students to solve school climate problems as equals.

Both informal discussions and more formal programs, such as restorative justice practices and use of social justice projects, can engage students in insuring that their schools are safe and supportive. Schools that have made these changes report that discipline incidents – particularly those that are a threat to safety – decrease, in part because students who feel connected to their school community are more likely to seek assistance and their peers are more likely to report rumors of threats or weapons in school.[125] Changing these aspects of school culture may come with additional benefits. Research shows that building a safe and supportive school climate often leads to improved academic achievement.[126]

Restorative justice's emphasis on connectedness, community, redemption, and respect all commend it to advocates of a pedagogy based on the tenets of social constructivism. Rather than encourage students to nurture grudges indefinitely or remove offenders from school permanently, restorative justice offers an effective antidote to the regime of exclusionary discipline. It teaches students the habits of mind critical for participation in a democratic polity. Disagreements and offensive behavior will face students throughout their entire lives; restorative justice trains them to cope with these obstacles and maintain and repair the strong relationships critical to living healthy, satisfying, productive lives.

Moreover, adopting restorative justice would make a genuine contribution toward creating the kind of school communities in which violence is unthinkable. The offended would be supported and the offenders would be offered a path toward enjoying full membership in the community once again. Relationships formed and strengthened through these techniques will in the long run do more to create safe schools and communities than all the guns and security drills in the world.

---

[124] See "Shootings Revive Debates on Security," 32(15) *Educ. Wk.* 1 (Jan. 9, 2013); "Code of Conduct: Safety, Discipline, and School Climate," 32(16) *Educ. Wk.* 4–12 (Jan. 10, 2013).
[125] Code of Conduct: Safety, Discipline, and School Climate; Advancement Project, Alliance for Educational Justice, Dignity in Schools Campaign, & NAACP Legal Defense and Education Fund, Police in Schools Are Not the Answer to the Newtown Shooting (January 2013).
[126] "Plucked from Back in the Pack, Unlikely Peers Step Up," 32(16) *Educ. Wk.* 19 (Jan. 10, 2013).

CONCLUSION

The nearly unfettered discretion bestowed upon school officials, coupled with political pressure to implement strict discipline policies, has created an environment in which zero tolerance and exclusionary discipline exert a harmful influence on the lives of many vulnerable students. Instances of shocking violence in schools have encouraged policymakers to double down on these deeply flawed and mistaken practices. These practices not only often exacerbate the badges and incidents of discrimination but also stand in direct opposition to the most basic tenets of social constructivist pedagogy.

By tracing Supreme Court precedent, congressional legislation, and executive policy, we have demonstrated that the present approach to student discipline in this country contradicts the vision of the Founders. The climate of fear, paranoia, and suspicion makes it nearly impossible for students to form the meaningful relationships so central to constructing knowledge and participating in a democracy. Restorative justice promises to heal these ruptures and create school climates more conducive to truly democratic education. In contrast to zero tolerance and exclusionary discipline, restorative justice more fully reflects how human beings live and learn together. Embracing its principles will lead to better schools and a healthier society.

10

Current Reform Initiatives and a Better Way Forward

The logic and language of behaviorism permeate so deeply that even the leading reform initiatives have incorporated its flawed principles. As we will see, these initiatives are of dubious academic benefit and clearly prove inimical to fostering a democratic citizenry.

This chapter will analyze the most recent, dominant educational reform initiatives, including: (1) greater "accountability," through reliance on standardized tests to evaluate students and teachers; and (2) greater "school choice" and privatization through expanding charter schools and voucher programs. Research from multiple disciplines, particularly Nobel Prize-winning work in the economic sciences, proves the inefficiency of these initiatives. Such initiatives actually deepen the disparities in educational resources given to students based on their color, gender, native language, socio-economic status, and disability. They do nothing to further the Founders' vision of an engaged, democratic citizenry and, in fact, contradict it. The chapter will conclude by discussing a superior alternative which offers far more promise than either of these unfortunate trends.

ACCOUNTABILITY

The first popular reform initiative is the call for greater accountability in education. There is little debate about the value of accountability as a broad concept. Yet, calls for accountability are often limited to arguments for evaluating teachers and schools based on the test scores of their students.[1] When reformers advocate for "accountability," they tend to mean reliance on standardized tests.[2] While advocates for accountability through a regime of testing undoubtedly are well intentioned, the research has revealed limitations on the value of standardized tests to assess student learning and teacher performance. A consensus has coalesced around eleven

---

[1] Phillip Harris, Bruce M. Smith, & Joan Harris, *The Myths of Standardized Testing: Why They Don't Tell You What You Think They Do* (New York: Rowman & Littlefield, 2011).

[2] Diane Ravitch, *Reign of Error: The Hoax of the Privatization Movement and the Danger to America's Public Schools* (New York: Knopf, 2013), 34.

principle reasons why reliance on standardized assessments of students and teachers is ineffective.

First, standardized tests do not assess social and emotional growth, including skills that reliably correspond to success such as motivation, perseverance, self-regulation, collaboration, and inter-subjectivity.[3] As James Heckman has concluded after conducting and analyzing numerous data sets, "using achievement tests alone to assess teacher effectiveness would miss important dimensions of teacher quality."[4] At best, standardized tests only assess student performance in narrowly defined academic tasks. And because of their nature, they assess student performance at only one moment in time. Long-term retention and ability to use this knowledge is not measured.

Second, students are tested on their "academic" performance in only a few of the many subjects covered in school.[5] Subjects such as math and literacy are emphasized while other subjects are not considered.

Third, even within each of the few subjects covered, the test questions do not cover the range of content within the subject itself.[6] A student's test scores thus do not measure the range and depth of student academic achievement in particular content areas.

Fourth, the test questions themselves are not objective. The authors of the test questions set the difficulty of the questions with reference to an anticipated range of student responses.[7] Successful questions are those that generate a significant percentage of incorrect answers.[8] The authors of the questions thus are incentivized to create questions that result in an easy stratification of student answers.[9]

Fifth, the choice of which questions to use in a particular test reflects a host of non-objective judgments. Particular subjects and narrow topics are privileged over numerous subjects and broad topics.[10] As Alfie Kohn has shown, high scores on typical standardized tests can often signify superficial thinking.[11]

Sixth, a student's score on standardized tests is not predictive of that student's success in life, or even future academic success within different educational institutions.[12]

---

[3] Ibid.
[4] James J. Heckman & Tim Kautz, "Fostering and Measuring Skills: Interventions that Improve Character and Cognition" (working paper, National Bureau of Economic Research, 2013), 86, www.nber.org/papers/w19656.pdf.
[5] Harris, Smith, & Harris, *The Myths of Standardized Testing*, 31.
[6] Ibid.
[7] Ibid.
[8] Ibid.
[9] Ibid.
[10] Ibid.
[11] Alfie Kohn, *The Case against Standardized Testing: Raising the Scores, Ruining the Schools* (Portsmouth, NH: Heinemann, 2000).
[12] Ibid.

Seventh, student learning is not improved by high stakes testing. Rather, in those states relying on high stakes testing, student learning stays the same or "actually goes down."[13]

Eighth, the use of standardized tests as a sole measure of evaluating student and teacher performance can have unintended, negative consequences. As David Berliner and Audrey Amrein have noted: "Because clear evidence of increased student learning is not found, and because there are numerous reports of unintended consequences associated with high-stakes testing policies (increased drop-out rates, teachers and schools cheating on exams, teachers' defection from the profession ...), there is need for ... transformation of current high-stakes testing policies."[14]

Ninth, as the significance assigned to test results increases, so too does the potential for abuse of those results. According to the "uncertainty principle," the likelihood of distortion and corruption of the political and social uses of test results increases when the consequences of those results increase.[15] When the "stakes" of standardized testing increased with No Child Left Behind, the distortion and corruption of the test results to serve cynical political ends predictably increased as well.

Tenth, the premise that a student's performance on a standardized test alone is a reliable indicator of the quality of a school or its teachers is flawed.[16] The test-based system of the No Child Left Behind Act has been extended by the Obama administration's Race to the Top program. Under the No Child Left Behind Act, the high-stakes tests are used to mark "nonperforming" schools with the stigma of failure and financial penalties. Under the Race to the Top program, states are incentivized to insure their testing systems are used to evaluate not just schools, but individual teachers as well.

Under the two regimes together, the federal government rewards states that punish schools and teachers who fail to perform on standardized tests. While the benevolent assumption undergirding both NCLB and Race to the Top is that every child can learn regardless of their socio-economic conditions or their family circumstances,[17] the sole measure of whether or not a child is learning is his or her performance on these high stakes tests. If the child's test scores do not improve, therefore, the child has not learned and the teachers must be the cause of this failure.[18]

---

[13] Audrey Amrein & David Berliner, "High-Stakes Testing, Uncertainty, and Student Learning," *Education Policy and Analysis* 10(2) (2002).
[14] Ibid. at 2.
[15] Ibid., see also Pelletier, et al., "Pressure from above and pressure from below as determinants of teachers' motivation and teaching behaviors," *Journal of Educational Psychology* 94 (2002):186–96
[16] See, e.g., John Ewing, "Mathematical Intimidation: Driven by the Data," Notices of the AMS 58(5) (May 2011): 667, www.ams.org/notices/201105/rtx110500667p.pdf.
[17] Ravitch, *Reign of Error*, 100.
[18] Ibid.

Yet, the opponents of the reliance on standardized tests to insure accountability have argued that the problems with "value-added assessments of a teacher's performance are legion."[19] Even if the tests themselves were perfect, they contend, the data they produce cannot be legitimately used to measure teaching quality. While individual teachers undoubtedly have an enormous impact on a child's growth and development, that impact cannot be accurately measured by high stakes tests across classrooms, schools, or grade levels. At best, "differences in the quality of schools can explain about one-third of the variation in student achievement."[20] Nonetheless, some advocates for testing insist that schools begin to discipline teachers whose students do not meet standards and reward teachers whose students do meet standards with merit-based pay.[21]

Eleventh, even within the school and the classroom, the variables cannot be sufficiently controlled to assess the "value" that any particular teacher in any particular year "adds." A student's performance on any given test can be shaped by factors in the school such as class size, class composition, instructional materials, availability of assistants, learning resources, wellness, peer culture, climate, prior teachers, prior in-school learning environments, and summer school programming. As one of the country's foremost education experts, Linda Darling-Hammond, has concluded: even when sincere efforts are made to control for student populations, test results "largely reflect whom a teacher teaches, not how well they teach."[22]

In a comprehensive study of teacher evaluation methods commissioned by proponents of using test scores to gauge teacher quality, the evidence indicates that test-based measures of student achievement cannot reliably be employed as the primary evaluation measure.[23] In fact, evaluation systems based primarily on student test-scores were proven to be the least reliable teacher evaluation model relative to models that stressed a diversity of classroom observations and student surveys.[24] Teacher evaluation systems based on standardized test scores were particularly poor at measuring a teacher's ability to help students acquire higher-order thinking skills.[25] Such systems have proven to be "inaccurate, unstable, and unreliable."[26]

---

[19] Ibid. at 108.
[20] Richard Rothstein, "How to Fix Our Schools," Economic Policy Institute, Oct. 14, 2010, www.epi.org/publication/ib286/.
[21] Ravitch, *Reign of Error*, 103–106.
[22] Linda Darling-Hammond, "Value-Added Evaluation Hurts Teaching," *Education Week*, March 20, 2012, www.edweek.org/ew/articles/2012/03/05/24darlinghammond_ep.h31.html.
[23] See "Ensuring Fair and Reliable Measures of Effective Teaching," Bill and Melinda Gates Foundation Measures of Effective Teaching Project, 2013, 10, www.metproject.org/downloads/MET_Ensuring_Fair_and_Reliable_Measures_Practitioner_Brief.pdf. ("Teaching is too complex for any single measure of performance to capture it.")
[24] Ibid. at 11–12.
[25] Ibid.
[26] Ravitch, *Reign of Error*, 113.

Accordingly, while proponents of utilizing high stakes tests argue that policy-makers need a valid way to determine whether all students are meeting the same high standards,[27] the reliance on standardized tests alone provides an imperfect and incomplete measure of student learning. The legitimate goal of accountability can be better served if those tests are augmented by documentation of student learning.

As the researchers from Project Zero at the Harvard Graduate School of Education have demonstrated, the practice of documentation provides an authentic measure of student learning and therefore an extremely effective method of accountability.[28] Through documentation, highly skilled educators are able to record the process and products of student learning, and then share their assessments with multiple stakeholders, including community members, taxpayers, and policy-makers.

Educators in extremely effective early childhood education programs already use documentation to make learning visible. They carefully observe, record, interpret, and share the ways in which children construct their knowledge through meaningful relationships. The skilled use of documentation by those educators provides a model of authentic assessment and genuine accountability. Advocates on all sides of the accountability debate therefore share a strong interest in supporting the development of a system of early childhood programs that make student learning visible through documentation. In addition, the best practices in documentation and "assessment" in early childhood education could and should find ready application in elementary, secondary, and even tertiary education. There is no compelling reason preventing the increased use of these methods for older students.

PRIVATIZATION

The second reform initiative that has generated substantial debate is the movement toward privatization or school choice, which includes vouchers and charter schools. Some advocates favoring the expansion of vouchers and charter schools argue that they offer a market-based solution to the problems associated with public education, and can offer families educational opportunities not otherwise available in the public schools. As we will see, advocates opposing the development of voucher programs and charter schools argue convincingly that the evidence does not support these claims.

VOUCHERS

Vouchers enable parents to take some or all of the money that would have been allocated to a public school to educate their children and use it for private school

---

[27] See, e.g., "Accountability Systems," Democrats for Education Reform Education Equality Project, March 2010, www.dfer.org/docs/DFER.EEP.Accountability.ESEA.March.2010.pdf.

[28] See M. Krechevsky, B. Mardell, M. Rivard, & D. Wilson, *Visible Learners* (San Francisco: Jossey-Bass, 2013); Project Zero & Reggio Children, *Making Learning Visible: Children as Individual and Group Learners* (Reggio Emilia, Italy: Reggio Children, 2001).

education.[29] Vouchers typically do not represent cash payments directly to parents. Rather, the state or the district in which the child otherwise would have been enrolled transfers funding from public to private school. The amount of the voucher often represents either some portion of state or local funding, or the amount of state aid that would have been paid for the child to attend public school in his or her school district. The actual cost to the school district can vary. In some programs, those costs exceed the amount of the voucher.

Although vouchers are frequently compared to tuition tax credit and tax deduction plans, they are different in several respects. Tax credit and deduction plans do not transfer funds from the state to a private institution. In effect, parents receive a discount from their tax obligations for tuition paid in a prior year rather than a grant or subsidy from a public agency that is remitted to a private school. Private schools tend to prefer vouchers because the schools receive the funds directly. Further, since vouchers are not derived from parents' income, they allow private schools to raise tuition more easily than do tax deductions or tax credits.

Vouchers also are often confused with charter schools and choice programs. More than half the states have passed laws allowing parents and teachers to establish charter schools at some cost to the public. Charter schools operate relatively independently of the public school system, and commonly receive public funds on a per-pupil basis.

At first glance, vouchers appear to resemble charter schools and thereby may add to state pressures to adopt them. However, there are several key distinctions. Most charters are granted by a public agency, such as a local school board. Charter schools are subject to criteria, expectations, operating conditions, and monitoring that are not required of private schools. Further, most charters are staffed by public employees, cannot charge tuition, and are subject to many of the same admissions requirements as public schools.

Despite these distinctions, there are some areas where the lines between charters and vouchers become blurred. Several states, including Arizona, Minnesota, and Wisconsin, allow private schools to become charter schools. Additionally, a distinction should be made between public charter schools that are created by local school boards and those created by other entities, such as the state or a public university. Although public in character, these charter schools, like private school vouchers, redirect local school district finances without traditional legal, fiscal, or performance accountability to the voters in the community.

Finally, vouchers should not be confused with public school choice programs. Choice programs can include public charter schools, magnet schools, and other public schools within the district and in other school districts. In these choice

---

[29] The National School Boards Association has prepared excellent materials regarding the political economy of vouchers. See, e.g., National School Boards Association Advocacy Tools on Vouchers, www.nsba.org.

programs, students remain within the public school system, and public resources are not redirected outside of the public school system.

In 1996, Cleveland, Ohio, instituted a voucher program that limited eligibility to low-income students. In its *Zelman* decision, the Supreme Court voted 5–4 to uphold the constitutionality of the Cleveland voucher program.[30] Although most of the voucher recipients used their subsidies to pay religious school tuition, the Supreme Court concluded that Cleveland's voucher program involved strictly individual, private choices and therefore did not offend the Establishment Clause of the First Amendment.

Milwaukee has operated a voucher program since 1990, and over the years, the Wisconsin legislature has expanded the original program. The Supreme Court in *Zelman* refers to Milwaukee's voucher program, suggesting that it has been successful. The program was amended in 1995, expanding eligibility to any child residing in Milwaukee whose family's income is below 125 percent of the poverty level. In 2011, the program was expanded to any child whose family's income is below 300 percent of the poverty line. For high school students whose family's income is below 300 percent but above 220 percent of the poverty line, however, participating private schools may charge tuition.

The program initially was open to all eligible public school children in grades K-12, with the maximum number of vouchers set at 7 percent of public school enrollment or a maximum of 7,250 students. The scope of the program was then allowed to double to 15 percent (or about 15,000 students in 1996–1997). In 2011, the cap on enrollment in the program was removed and the geographic boundaries were expanded to include students whose families reside in Racine as well as those with families in Milwaukee. Students are selected by random lottery.

Enrollment of voucher students in any one school initially was limited to 50 percent, then to 65 percent. Currently, there is no limit on the portion of the student body that can include voucher students. The amount of the voucher, which is nearly $6,500 per pupil (full-time equivalent), is equal to the amount of per-pupil state aid that would have been paid to the Milwaukee school system, but not greater than the cost of educating a child at the private school.

Over the first four years, the program grew from 341 to 802 students, or about half the authorized level. During that time, the number of participating schools expanded from 6 to 12. By comparison, Milwaukee's 130 private schools enrolled more than 24,000 students in 1995, or about 30 percent of the city's middle- and upper-income children and 7 percent of the children from the city's poorest neighborhoods. In the 2011–2012 school year, following the income level and geographic expansion of program eligibility, 22,762 students used vouchers at 106 participating schools located in Milwaukee and the surrounding area. Seventy-one percent of these students attended religious parish schools.

---

[30] *Zelman v. Simmons-Harris*, 536 U.S. 639 (2002).

The Milwaukee voucher program is one of the longest running and closest studied in the nation. By all legitimate measures, the program has not been as successful as was hoped. Voucher students have not outperformed public school students from the same area.[31] While utilizing resources from the public schools, the Milwaukee voucher program has produced few empirically sound advantages for its students relative to the corresponding public schools.[32]

The Milwaukee experience with vouchers is not atypical.[33] In 2004, there were more than two dozen privately funded voucher programs in the country. Two of the more established programs were in San Antonio and Indianapolis.

San Antonio set up a public school choice program emphasizing immersion into Latino language, culture, and history. In addition, the business community created a program to allow 2,000 poor children to attend private schools through a private scholarship program. Parents paid about one-half of the tuition cost. In this program, 99 percent of the students were enrolled in parochial schools, mainly Catholic, and 95 percent of the parents rated religious training as very important or important.

In Indianapolis, a privately financed trust was established in 1991 that supported the enrollment of about 1,000 children from low-income families in 67 private schools. As in San Antonio, parents paid about one-half of the tuition cost. The private schools were overwhelmingly parochial and enrolled 75 percent of the children involved in the program. Forty percent of non-Catholic parents participating in the voucher program sent their children to Catholic schools.

School voucher programs in Indiana have expanded and are receiving state support. There are now several "scholarship granting organizations," similar to this original privately financed trust that operate across the state to provide vouchers to students. In the summer of 2009, the Indiana legislature approved a generous tax deduction for donations to scholarship granting organizations. Additionally, in 2011, Indiana began operating a statewide publicly funded voucher program. In the 2012–2013 school year, this program served 9,324 families.

Proponents of these voucher programs contend that they will: (1) enhance parental choice; (2) spur competition between public and private education, thereby improving the academic achievement of all students as measured primarily by standardized test scores; (3) increase parental control over tax dollars; (4) open opportunities for minority and low-income families; (5) offer help for low-income parents whose children are currently in private school; (6) save money for public education; (7) save taxpayers' money; and (8) rescue public education.

---

[31] Ravitch, *Reign of Error*, 208–209, citing Matthew DeFour, "DPI: Students in Milwaukee Voucher Program Didn't Perform Better in State Tests," Wisconsin State Journal, March 29, 2011, http://host.madison.com/news/local/education/local_schools/dpi-students-in-milwaukee-voucher-program-didn-t-perform-better/article_4f083f0e-59a7-11e0-8d74-001cc4c03286.html.

[32] Ibid. at 209.

[33] See Alexandra Usher & Nancy Kober, *Keeping Informed about School Vouchers: A Review of Major Developments and Research* (Center on Education Policy, July 27, 2011), www.cep-dc.org/displayDocument.cfm?documentID=369.

Independent research demonstrates that these benefits have not materialized.[34] The voucher students in the Cleveland plan upheld by the Supreme Court in *Zelman*, for example, have performed worse on state achievement measures than those students left in the Cleveland public schools.[35] Even the voucher program in the District of Columbia created by Congress has produced "no conclusive evidence" of any impact on student achievement.[36]

According to the National School Boards Association (NSBA), vouchers weaken, rather than improve, public education because they re-direct much-needed public financial resources to private schools.[37] The NSBA has argued that, as such, vouchers do not improve public education but rather undermine the public schools' capacity to compete and improve.

Moreover, vouchers have not fulfilled their promise of providing genuine school choice. Geography and family finances limit most low-income students to a very narrow range of private schools. Even then, the private school, not the parent, determines which children are admitted and retained. Therefore, vouchers do not broaden the choices available to children from low-income families or those who do not meet the profile of private schools. Rather, vouchers provide more choices to private institutions to determine which children to accept or reject. In fact, according to the NSBA, vouchers reduce equity in educational opportunity. Even with vouchers, some low-income families still are unable to have access to realistic choices regarding their school enrollment.

Vouchers force taxpayers to support two education systems. With about 5.5 million children currently enrolled in private schools, a universal voucher of $3,000 per child would immediately reallocate over $16 billion from public to private schools. Such a reduction in public school funds would not help to improve the education of children enrolled in public schools. In fact, such shortfalls already have forced state legislatures and school boards to raise taxes to make up for at least some of the lost revenue. Given a finite amount of public money, the pressure to fund this growing entitlement comes at the expense of general funds for public schools.

Recognizing that the Louisiana voucher program diverted public funds dedicated to the minimum foundation level for public education, and redirected them to private and religious school tuition, the Supreme Court of Louisiana recently declared the program unconstitutional.[38] As the Louisiana Supreme Court understood, voucher programs necessarily entail the re-distribution of scarce public education funds to private institutions.

---

[34] Ibid.
[35] Ravitch, *Reign of Error*, 210.
[36] Ibid.
[37] Michael A. Resnick, *Why Vouchers Won't Work* (National School Boards Association, 1998).
[38] *Louisiana Federation of Teachers v. State of Louisiana*, No. 2013-CA-0120 (May 7, 2013).

In addition, according to U.S. Department of Education statistics, four out of every five students in private schools come from families whose annual incomes exceed $50,000. In the public schools, only about one out of five students come from families at that income level. High-income families, therefore, are the primary beneficiaries of vouchers.

Furthermore, arguments favoring and opposing private choice in the form of vouchers have been divisive. By encouraging more students to enroll in a diffuse collection of private schools, voucher systems dilute the public interest in promoting an American culture and identity. As the breadth of the voucher debate suggests, the issue of vouchers raises questions about the fundamental value of public education and the political will to share in the education of the community's children.

CHARTER SCHOOLS

Charter schools are "publicly funded elementary or secondary schools that have been freed from some of the rules, regulations, and statutes that apply to other public schools, in exchange for some type of accountability for producing certain results, which are set forth in each school's charter."[39] The National Educational Association has recognized that "charter schools and other nontraditional public school options have the potential to facilitate education reforms and develop new and creative teaching methods that can be replicated in traditional public schools for the benefit of all children. Whether charter schools will fulfill this potential depends on how charter schools are designed and implemented, including the oversight and assistance provided by charter authorizers."[40]

Proponents of expanding charter schools seek to rely on standardized test scores to claim that charter schools outperform their public school counterparts.[41] Charter schools attempting to justify their charters have a particular incentive to produce the kind of results that are measured by standardized tests. They also tend to attract the kind of students whose families self-select charter schools that promise those kinds of test results, and they accept and retain fewer students who are at risk of school failure as measured by standardized test scores.[42] The flaws in those standardized tests identified in this chapter therefore would tend to skew those scores in favor of charter school students.

Nonetheless, standardized test scores do not provide support for the expansion of charter schools. In 2004, the National Assessment Governing Board (NAGB) released an analysis of charter school performance based on the 2003 National Assessment of Educational Progress (NAEP), also known as "The Nation's Report

[39] See "Charter Schools," National Educational Association, www.nea.org/charter.
[40] Ibid.
[41] See, e.g., G. Tirozzi, "It's Déjà Vu All Over Again for Charter Schools," *Education Week*, August 27, 2014, 22.
[42] Ibid. at 23.

Card." The report found that charter school students, on average, score lower than students in traditional public schools. While there was no measurable difference between charter school students and students in traditional public schools in the same racial or ethnic subgroup, charter school students who were eligible for free or reduced-price lunch scored lower than their peers in traditional public schools, and charter school students in urban areas scored lower than their peers in math in the fourth grade.

NAGB looked at the impact of school characteristics and found that:

(1) Charter schools that were part of the local school district had significantly higher scores than charter schools that served as their own district.
(2) Students taught by certified teachers had roughly comparable scores whether they attended charter schools or traditional public schools, but the scores of students taught by uncertified teachers in charter schools were significantly lower than those of charter school students with certified teachers.
(3) Students taught by teachers with at least five years' experience outperformed students with less experienced teachers, regardless of the type of school attended, but charter school students with inexperienced teachers did significantly worse than students in traditional public schools with less experienced teachers. (The impact of this finding is compounded by the fact that charter schools are twice as likely as traditional public schools to employ inexperienced teachers.)

Recent evidence confirms that most charter schools do not perform as well as their public school counterparts. After conducting a meta-analysis of all of the available data, the National Alliance for Public Charter Schools and the Center for Research on Education Outcomes both concluded that the majority of charter schools perform the same or worse than their public school feeders. In fact, 37 percent of charter schools performed "significantly worse" than public schools in math and literacy.[43]

Opponents of the expansion of charter schools also have raised concerns regarding student attrition, high rates of teacher turnover, student access, and inclusiveness. In particular, they argue that some charter schools are able to skim the highest-performing students from public schools by discouraging other students from applying or by "counseling out" students with educational disabilities. In *Schools without Diversity: Education Management Organizations, Charter Schools, and the Demographic Stratification of the American School System* (2010), the authors conducted a comprehensive study of charter schools and concluded that they have produced stark segregation by race, income, English language acquisition, and disability.[44]

---

[43] See, e.g., Ibid.; Scott A. Imberman, "Achievement and Behavior in Charter Schools: Drawing a More Complex Picture," *The Review of Economics and Statistics* 93(2) (2011), www.mitpressjournals.org/doi/abs/10.1162/REST_a_00077?journalCode=rest#.VAaDuRZJnG4.

[44] See "Strengthening Charter School Policies," National Education Association Policy Brief (2011), www.nea.org/assets/docs/PB33charterschoolpolicies2011.pdf; Ravitch, *Reign of Error*, 175.

Despite the data challenging charter school performance, charter schools continue to garner public support. The number of students served by charter schools has continued to grow rapidly. In the 2011–2012 school year, more than 2 million students – nearly 5 percent of total enrollment in public schools – attended charter schools in 41 states and the District of Columbia. More than 100 school districts have at least 10 percent of their students in charter schools.[45]

THE LIMITS OF CURRENT REFORM INITIATIVES

As we have seen, a closer look at accountability and privatization initiatives casts serious doubt upon the effectiveness of these approaches. However, even if their proponents could prove these programs yielded quantifiable academic benefits, a broader, threshold question would still remain. Can accountability and privatization produce a truly democratic educational system?

Noted educational theorist Henry A. Giroux answers this question in the negative. In his recent book, *Education and the Crisis of Public Values: Challenging the Assault on Teachers, Students, & Public Education*, Giroux places current reform initiatives in education within a framework of what he views as a wider attack on democracy.[46] His observations on the theory and practice of accountability and privatization demonstrate the shortcomings inherent in these reform initiatives.

Giroux describes the broader social landscape to contextualize current trends in educational reform. He argues, "[a] survival-of-the-fittest ethic has replaced any reasonable notion of solidarity, social responsibility, and compassion for the other."[47] This ethic, Giroux claims, has migrated from the business world to the classroom – following the trail blazed by behaviorist practices a century ago. Giroux critiques this development severely and questions the propriety of using the language and practices of business in the context of education. To say the least, pedagogy does not lend itself to the clear-cut, bottom-line analysis of a balance sheet. He develops his criticism further by noting that the ethic of unbridled competition and acquisition in the financial markets led to an economic meltdown in 2008. To introduce such an ethos into schools and make it the guiding principle of education, Giroux shows, could only end in disaster.

Giroux thus claims that current reform initiatives harm not only students but democracy itself. He writes:

> The rhetoric of accountability, privatization, and standardization ... does more than deskill teachers, weaken teacher unions, dumb down the curriculum, punish students, and create a culture of ignorance. It also offers up a model for education

---

[45] "A Growing Movement: America's Largest Charter School Communities," National Alliance for Public Charter Schools (November 2012), www.edweek.org/media/napcsmarketshare-13charters.pdf.
[46] (New York: Peter Lang Publishing, 2012).
[47] Ibid. at x–xi.

that undermines it as a public good while disinvesting in a formative culture necessary to creating critical citizens.[48]

The Founders understood that democratic citizens are formed, not born. The task of self-government is undoubtedly a demanding one. As Giroux demonstrates, citizens who have been formed in an environment in which public spaces are either permeated with unceasing competition or hollowed out through privatization will not see their fellow Americans as collaborators in a democratic system. Instead, they will inevitably view them as threats to their individual wellbeing – as competitors in a zero-sum game. In this paradigm, fellow citizens are enemies rather than allies. Under accountability, schools are pitted one against the other for access to an ever-shrinking pool of resources. Under privatization, large numbers of citizens isolate themselves from the broader population. Giroux and like-minded theorists view these trends as a direct threat to the American project initiated by the Founders. "Removed from democratic ideals, education is aligned with both a culture that sets individuals in competition with each other and an order of privatization increasingly positioned at odds with public institutions that promote the social foundations of human solidarity."[49]

Giroux concludes his commentary with a bleak assessment of the current American classroom, writing:

> Dominated by pedagogies that are utterly instrumental and geared toward memorization, conformity, and high-stakes test taking, public schools have become intellectual dead zones and punishment centers as far removed from teaching civic values and expanding the imagination of students as one can imagine.[50]

Essentially, Giroux characterizes the present landscape as a dystopia in which behaviorist principles have been taken to their logical conclusion. While his critique at times descends into a jeremiad against American society at large, his central point is quite sound: namely, accountability and privatization initiatives cannot inculcate democratic values in students and, accordingly, are inimical to the democratic project itself.

In light of the clear shortcomings of accountability and privatization, the discussion must move from diagnosis to treatment. If accountability and privatization cannot produce democratic citizens, which educational theories and practices are best suited to this task? As this book has emphasized, human beings learn by constructing knowledge together through meaningful relationships. The missteps found in the history of American education law arise as a result of a failure to grasp this fundamental principle. This failure has inhibited the progress of countless citizens and of our democracy as a whole. It has also maintained and aggravated the lingering badges and incidents of discrimination. Having examined this history

---

[48] Ibid. at 11.
[49] Ibid. at 65.
[50] Ibid. at 117.

in detail together, the time has come to explore a better path forward. In the pages that remain, we will see that early interventions and social constructivism offer the best chance for human beings to learn and for our democracy to grow.

A BETTER PATH FORWARD: EARLY INTERVENTIONS AND SOCIAL CONSTRUCTIVISM

Even if the accountability and privatization initiatives were successful in improving educational opportunities for all children, these strategies would not be as cost-effective as an investment in early childhood education. The evidence adduced by James Heckman and others demonstrates that interventions early in the lives of children are much more efficient than later educational interventions. Heckman specifically analyzed the relative costs and benefits of efforts to remediate a deficient early learning environment, including GED programs, job training, educational rehabilitation, adult literacy and tuition subsidies.[51]

These efforts to correct deficiencies in early learning environments may be effective, but they are not as cost-effective as early childhood education programs.[52] As James Heckman concludes: "for studies in which later intervention showed some benefits, the performance of disadvantaged children was still behind the performance of children who experienced earlier interventions in the preschool years."[53] Moreover, "[e]arly interventions promote economic efficiency and reduce lifetime inequality." Remedial interventions, by contrast, can reduce inequality somewhat, but "are difficult to justify on the grounds of economic efficiency."[54]

The most recent evidence demonstrates:

> Only early interventions ... improve IQ in a lasting way, consistent with the evidence that early childhood is a critical period of cognitive development. ... The most successful interventions target preschoolers and primary school children. They improve later-life outcomes by developing character skills.
>
> The most effective adolescent remediation programs are those that develop character by integrating work and education.[55]

But the development of essential character skills in pre-K is much more cost effective than their remediation later in life. The positive effects from effective early childhood programs "arise primarily from lasting changes in character skills, not

---

[51] Heckman, "School, Skills and Synapses," 4, 21.
[52] Ibid. at 20–21.
[53] Ibid. at 21.
[54] Heckman, "School, Skills and Synapses," 22. See also C. Raver, P. Garner, & R. Smith-Donald, "The Roles of Emotion Regulation and Emotion Knowledge for Children's Academic Readiness: Are the Links Causal?" in *School Readiness and the Transition to Kindergarten in the Era of Accountability*, ed. Robert Pianta, Martha Cox, & Kyle Snow (Baltimore, MD: Paul H. Brookes Publishing, 2007).
[55] Heckman & Kautz, "Fostering and Measuring Skills," 35, 66.

from changes in IQ."⁵⁶ The acquisition of general knowledge depends on "persistence, curiosity and focus."⁵⁷ There is "substantial evidence that high-quality early childhood programs have lasting and beneficial effects on character skills."⁵⁸ Early childhood education programs that develop essential relationship-building skills thus show significant positive long-term educational, social, and economic benefits. The bottom line is that:

> Most successful remediation programs are not as effective as the most successful early childhood programs. Building on an early base of skills that promote later-life learning and engagement in school and society is a better strategy. Prevention is more effective than remediation.⁵⁹

Based upon his careful analysis of the most significant education reform initiatives, David Kirp, one of the world's foremost education experts, has arrived at the same conclusion: "Every successful educational initiative of which I'm aware aims at strengthening personal bonds by building strong systems of support in the schools. The best preschools create intimate worlds where students become explorers and attentive adults are close at hand."⁶⁰

As Kirp insightfully demonstrates:

> It's impossible to improve education by doing an end run around inherently complicated and messy human relationships. All youngsters need to believe that they have a stake in the future, a goal worth striving for, if they're going to make it in school. They need a champion, someone who believes in them, and that's where teachers enter the picture. The most effective approaches foster bonds of caring between teachers and their students.⁶¹

Accordingly, an investment in the "best" early childhood programs – ones designed to build those indispensable bonds – will provide a model of success that will advance the shared goals of all advocates of genuine education reform.

Research from economics and neuroscience demonstrates that advocates on all sides of contemporary education reform movements have a shared interest in fostering a legal and political structure that supports education programs that have proven to be particularly effective – those in which prudent investments are made in professional educators who are trained to enable students at all levels to construct their own knowledge by developing meaningful relationships in diverse and connected learning communities. Such an investment would be built on a solid legal

---

⁵⁶ Ibid. at 44.
⁵⁷ Ibid. at 45.
⁵⁸ Ibid. at 89.
⁵⁹ Ibid.
⁶⁰ David Kirp, "Teaching is Not a Business," N. Y. Times, August 16, 2014, www.nytimes.com/2014/08/17/opinion/sunday/teaching-is-not-a-business.html. See also David L. Kirp, *Improbable Scholars: The Rebirth of a Great American School System and a Strategy for America's Schools* (New York: Oxford University Press, 2013).
⁶¹ Kirp, "Teaching is Not a Business."

foundation in civil rights jurisprudence, would reduce educational inequities, and would produce robust educational, social, and economic benefits for all children and for the nation.

The debate over the effectiveness of charter schools is intense and sometimes divisive. But advocates on all sides of that debate have a mutual interest in supporting a substantial investment of resources in effective early childhood education programs. Those programs can provide a laboratory for the kind of innovative, research-based teaching practices that were the original promise of charter schools.[62] As James E. Ryan has shown in his pathbreaking article entitled "A Constitutional Right to Preschool," a vibrant system of government-supported early childhood programs also will serve as a model, demonstrating that the investment of public funds to support a range of genuine educational choices for families can produce significant benefits for children and for the country.[63]

SOCIAL CONSTRUCTIVISM: A MODEL FOR REFORM EFFORTS

Social constructivist education programs have produced, and will continue to produce, robust educational, social, and economic benefits. By developing habits of mind and heart that enable children to construct knowledge through meaningful relationships, these programs help to: (1) realize the Founders' vision of a regime that depends for its survival on the capacity of individuals to advance and disseminate knowledge through their associations; (2) dismantle the badges and incidents of bias and discrimination; and (3) build skills such as inter-subjectivity, cognitive integration, attachment, executive function, self-regulation, discipline, synthesis, creativity, respect, and ethics. Those particular skills bring economic success and wellbeing and reduce harmful, externalizing behaviors that would otherwise increase the personal and social costs of crime, health care, imprisonment, grade retention, and remedial education programs.

Many of the insights developed by the classical, modern, and American educational philosophers are now the foundation for contemporary ideas about education in the American regime. In the current debates about the proper direction of education in America, the following principles are generally well accepted:

(1) Plato's view that education is a public, political matter that plays a vital role in shaping the character of children and the nature of a regime;
(2) Aristotle's understanding that a democratic regime requires for its health a unique democratic form of education that trains all children both to govern and to be governed;

---

[62] See Richard D. Kahlenberg & Halley Potter, *A Smarter Charter: Finding What Works for Charter Schools and Public Education* (New York: Teachers College Press, 2014).
[63] 94 Calif. L. Rev. 49 (2006).

(3) Locke's view that society must educate its children in the self-restraint necessary for self-government;
(4) Montesquieu's view that children can be free to govern themselves only if given through education a love of their community;
(5) Rousseau's perception that education must be attuned to the natural, developmental needs of each child so that each citizen can come to understand their connection with the community;
(6) The Founders' belief that the general diffusion of knowledge to all citizens through a public educational system is vital to creating a unified American regime;
(7) Mann's insight that such an education should be accomplished by the creation of uniform, comprehensive, state-centralized "common" schools, funded by property owners for the good of society; and
(8) Dewey's doctrine that American education must be designed to allow children the freedom to "construct" their own experience and to find the common human bonds that link all persons, regardless of race, class or religion.

John Dewey's uniquely American educational philosophy has had a profound impact upon the law and practice of education in America. Writing in the early 1900s, Dewey creates a comprehensive educational philosophy built upon democratic principles of equality and individuality. In *Democracy and Education*, Dewey argues that because "a democratic society repudiates the principle of external authority, it must find a substitute in voluntary disposition and interest; these can be created only by education." Education serves democratic institutions, where it facilitates the "breaking down of those barriers of class, race, and national territory which kept men from perceiving the full import of their activity."[64]

Dewey then traces the development of educational philosophy from the social constructs of Plato to the individualist model of the Enlightenment ideals exemplified by Locke and Rousseau. He advances a specific "democratic ideal" of education that makes educational resources available in America regardless of class or status and uses those resources to encourage American children to reach beyond their borders and discover things that unite mankind: "The emphasis must be put upon whatever bind people together in cooperative human pursuits and results, apart from geographical limitations."[65] Dewey understands democratic education as a "freeing of individual capacity in a progressive growth directed to social aims."[66]

In *Experience and Education*, Dewey declares that the educator must understand that learning is "a continuous process of reconstruction of experience."[67] Dewey is

---

[64] See John Dewey, *Democracy and Education*, reprinted in Cahn, *Classic and Contemporary Readings*, 288–293.
[65] Ibid.
[66] Ibid.
[67] See John Dewey, *Experience and Education*, reprinted in Cahn, *Classic and Contemporary Readings*, 362.

often credited with the fundamental belief that students learn by "doing." Children actively construct their own knowledge in relationships through their shared experiences.

Dewey also believed that the "scientific method" was "the only authentic means at our command for getting at the significance of our everyday experiences of the world in which we live."[68] Only by having the freedom to explore their environment and to test their interactions with materials and with others can children truly develop the capacity for constructing knowledge.

With the help of the scientific method adapted to various degrees of student maturity, students can freely construct for themselves patterns discernible in everyday experience. That method, and the "constructivist" learning process that results, include "the formation of ideas, acting upon ideas, observation of the conditions which result, and the organization of facts and ideas for future use."[69]

Dewey shows that knowledge is not delivered or revealed by an authority figure. To the contrary, children construct knowledge as they explore, experiment, mess about, and question their environment. Educational programs therefore must be designed to encourage children to construct meaning in their lives by interacting with their environment in cooperation with teachers and peers. Dewey's remarkable discoveries owe much to the tenets of social constructivism.

Social constructivism is an educational approach that recognizes that true knowledge is not passively or individually consumed; instead, knowledge is co-constructed socially through meaningful relationships with family, caregivers, teachers, peers, the environment, and the community.

This educational approach was founded on the discoveries of Russian lawyer and psychologist Lev Vygotsky. Vygotsky was born in Orsha, Belorussia (Belarus) in 1896 and graduated from Moscow University with a degree in law.[70] He authored more than 180 pathbreaking articles and books on child psychology and human development.[71]

Vygotsky demonstrated, and eventually convinced Jean Piaget, that learning is a social construct. Indeed, after he studied Vygotsky's work, Piaget developed his constructs to recognize the primal role of social relationships in the development of mental processes and language.[72] Vygotsky's conclusions illustrated the idea that all of *"human learning presupposes a specific social nature and a process by which children grow into the intellectual life of those around them."*[73] The social, interpersonal process of the construction of knowledge is altered by the child into an

---

[68] Ibid.
[69] Ibid.
[70] Kaufman et al., Learning Together, at 116.
[71] See, e.g., Elena Bodrova & Deborah J. Leong, *Tools of the Mind* (Upper Saddle River, NJ: Prentiss Hall, 1996); Lev Vygotsky, *Thought and Language* (rev. ed., Boston: MIT Press, 1986); L. S. Vygotsky, *Mind in Society: The Development of Psychological Processes* (Boston: Harvard University Press, 1978).
[72] Vygotsky, Mind in Society, at 67.
[73] Ibid. at 88.

internal one.⁷⁴ Every function of a child's development happens twice: "first *between* people ... and then inside the child."⁷⁵ In fact, all the higher mental functions, including attention, memory, and the formation of concepts, "originate as actual relations between human individuals."⁷⁶

Vygotsky's research revealed that "human beings become ourselves through others."⁷⁷ This fundamental rule that knowledge is constructed through meaningful social relationships "applies not only to the personality as a whole, but also to the history of every individual function."⁷⁸ The child's social context is an integral part of the construction of knowledge and the very process of cognition.⁷⁹ That context includes the child's direct interactions with individuals and materials that are proximate to the child. Yet, the social context also includes the child's family, school, culture, and society.⁸⁰ All of these social networks are not merely received by a child, they shape the way in which the child thinks.⁸¹

Significantly, Vygotsky revealed how a child's mental processes are actually shaped by social interactions.⁸² Mental processes grow in an exchange among human beings.⁸³ Children "acquire a mental process by *sharing*, or using it when interacting with others."⁸⁴ The child must first share an experience with another human being before internalizing the mental process and being able to perform that process independently.⁸⁵ Without a shared social experience, knowledge cannot be genuinely constructed.⁸⁶

The social constructivist approach is exemplified in the remarkable schools of Reggio Emilia, Italy. The Reggio Emilia experience is named after the city in which it originated and for the community of people that was dedicated to changing the culture of early childhood.⁸⁷ Its schools have become the gold standard and are deemed to be the best in the world.⁸⁸

After World War II had seriously damaged their city, the community of Reggio Emilia came together and decided that the rebuilding process must be focused upon children and their early education.⁸⁹ In a city torn by trauma and violence, its

---

74 Ibid. at 57.
75 Ibid.
76 Ibid.
77 Ibid.
78 L. S. Vygotsky, "Development of the Higher Mental Functions," 1 Psychological Research in the U.S.S.R. 43 (A.N. Leontyev et al. eds., 1966).
79 Kaufman et al., Learning Together, at 117.
80 Ibid.
81 Ibid.
82 Ibid.
83 Ibid.
84 Ibid. at 117.
85 Ibid.
86 Ibid.
87 Kaufman et al., *The Pre-K Home Companion*, at 31.
88 Ibid.
89 Ibid.

leaders were determined to place children at the center of policymaking.[90] They dedicated themselves to establishing a new kind of education in which children are vital, contributing members of the democratic community and in which the community is an active participant in the development and wellbeing of children and their families.[91] The educators in Reggio Emilia were guided by the fundamental image of the child as a capable, caring, creative, curious, and connected member of the community who has "legitimate rights."[92]

The following educational pillars are central to the Reggio Emilia experience: (1) the environment is a "teacher" that encourages the co-construction of knowledge through relationships; (2) the curriculum emerges from and inspires children's curiosities, relies on teachers' collaborative research, and values multiple forms of representation; (3) the learning of each child and the community is made visible through documentation; (4) shared projects arise naturally from the interests of groups of children and are as brief or lengthy as seems constructive; (5) all materials in the environment are respected – whether naturally designed, human-designed, or repurposed; and (6) collaboration is emphasized – among children, among teachers, and among children and teachers, including perspective taking, role playing, dialogue, negotiation, problem solving, listening, and respect for different perspectives.[93]

In Reggio schools, educators celebrate the spectrum of diversity brought to the learning environment by students.[94] As the city of Reggio Emilia has become increasingly diverse, educators in Reggio Emilia understand the integration of immigrant families into the centers and schools as an opportunity for tremendous growth and learning.[95]

Moreover, "[c]hildren with special needs (or 'special rights' as they are called in Reggio Emilia) are not limited by adult perceptions of their cognitive functioning and are included in all activities."[96] Children with special rights are not defined by perceived limitations; rather, they are fully included in a classroom in Reggio Emilia and are respected for their capability to use all their senses to learn through play, touching, dancing, moving, listening, seeing, and creating.[97]

The Reggio Emilia experience also reflects the work of highly skilled educators who provide authentic assessment through documentation of a variety of learning experiences, which is then used as a tool for additional learning and advocacy for children.[98]

---

[90] Ibid.
[91] Ibid.
[92] Ibid. at 29.
[93] Ibid. at 22, 25.
[94] Ibid. at 26.
[95] Ibid.
[96] Ibid.
[97] Ibid.
[98] Ibid. Documentation is the practice of observing, recording, interpreting, and sharing through a variety of media the processes and products of individual and community learning.

Documentation is vital to individual and group learning: it is an intentional act of reflecting on the process of individual and group growth, and it collects and holds up artifacts of shared group learning experiences to assist the group in reflecting on its own progress.[99] The documentation informs all subsequent teaching in the classroom and outside the classroom.[100] It makes visible to multiple stakeholders the learning that takes place in an early childhood education program.[101]

Moreover, documentation provides direct evidence of learning that can be shared with the community surrounding the school.[102] In this way, documentation provides an authentic assessment of the learning process.[103] The promise of documentation is that it will augment forms of assessment and accountability based primarily on standardized tests.[104]

The fundamental belief that students construct knowledge through meaningful relationships also creates a foundation from which those students are inspired to become engaged citizens.[105] In a Reggio-inspired education program, the community beyond the doors of the school is a vital partner in the learning.[106] The community provides a forum for expression in common spaces. The city surrounding the school may become involved in a community-wide activity.[107]

Not only do students learn outside of their school walls, but community members learn to appreciate the abilities of young children to construct knowledge.[108] Through documentation, Reggio-inspired educators make the learning that takes place within the school visible to the community surrounding the school.[109] This form of authentic assessment provides evidence of the profound effectiveness of the children's experience to community stakeholders, including policymakers, taxpayers, and funding sources.[110]

Accordingly, students emerge from a social constructivist learning experience with the habits of mind and heart that they need to lead, to create, to respect the environment, to problem-solve, to collaborate, to express themselves, to negotiate, to build alliances, to focus, to listen, to absorb, to relate to each other, and to find joy in learning.[111] Educators in these environments also nurture, inspire, and empower

---

[99] Kaufman et al., *Learning Together*, at 14.
[100] Ibid.
[101] Ibid.
[102] Ibid.
[103] Ibid. at 14–15.
[104] Ibid. at 15.
[105] Kaufman et al., *The Pre-K Home Companion*, at 27.
[106] Ibid. at 30.
[107] Ibid.
[108] Ibid. at 31.
[109] Ibid.
[110] Ibid.
[111] Ibid.

their students to pursue their natural instinct to build the kind of relationships from which knowledge and social justice are created.[112]

In a social constructivist learning community, the environment is a source of tremendous value and meaning. It becomes a critical "third" teacher. Natural materials of all kinds are praised and repurposed rather than misappropriated or thrown away. Schools can encourage this way of appreciating natural and repurposed materials by creating "maker spaces," either in common areas or in library space no longer needed for hard copy materials.

Students both in and out of the classroom should be prompted to pursue collaborative projects in which learning grows from "compassionate care"[113] and "dialogue with others."[114] The best collaborative exercises require students to perform self-examination, dialogue, and generous encounters between persons. The pedagogy of perspective taking also requires that students understand and work to overcome implicit biases in themselves and others. It fosters the development of cultural competencies.

In addition, the most effective collaboration includes projects in which faculty are partners with students in their learning. In the social constructivist law school, for example, tenured faculty, untenured faculty, adjunct faculty, and staff would all become partners in the learning community. All members of the school community would be given dignity in their work.

In collaborative and experiential learning settings, students also break down the artificial divisions between domains of learning. They understand questions not as either a math problem or a literacy problem, but as a human and social problem that requires a transdisciplinary, multifaceted solution.

In the social constructivist school environment, students experience the pedagogy of "perspective taking." They learn to understand, recognize, appreciate, respect, and respond helpfully to the thoughts, feelings, and intentions of others.

A school that uses social constructivist approaches, such as perspective taking, experiential learning, valuing the environment as a teacher, and collaborative projects, would become a learning community that transforms students from passive consumers of information to collaborative innovators who construct knowledge and social justice by building meaningful relationships.

Members of a social constructivist learning community also understand that all students can contribute to the learning environment, particularly those who display neurodiversity. The consumptive and behaviorist model of education leads to an understanding of human development that treats learning differences as deficits. Students who process information in a common way set the standard for rewarded behavior. All students who learn in ways that depart from the norm are identified as disabled and are given treatment to try to standardize their learning. But, as we have

---

[112] Ibid. at 29.
[113] Ibid. para. 210.
[114] Ibid. para. 81.

seen, research into brain development belies that model; different approaches to learning are not deficits. Rather, they reflect neurodiversity: the variations in learning strategies that are the result of the natural evolution of human brain development.

CONCLUSION

Social constructivism has as its unifying principle an accurate view of the manner in which human beings live and learn: by constructing knowledge together through meaningful relationships. This realization opens up a world of possibilities.

An educational system premised upon social constructivism would welcome and celebrate each and every child. It would embrace diversity, inclusion, and collaboration and reject the tenets of behaviorism. To the extent race, gender, and learning style mattered, it would be as a learning opportunity rather than as a source of division. Occasions for discipline would become a platform for mending and improving relationships rather than retribution and punitive action.

American students would learn how to build, repair, and maintain meaningful relationships with their fellow citizens more effectively. As these students grew into leaders, they would take these skills and competencies and use them to build a society that reflects these lessons. In time, an education based on social constructivist principles would do much to cure our society's present ills of isolation, incivility, and fear with solidarity, respect, and joy.

Index

Abbott ex rel Abbott v. Burke (Abbott IV) (N.J. 1997), 119–121
academic mismatch argument, 88–91
accommodation of learning differences, neurodiversity and, 171–174
accountability reforms
  limits of, 212–214
  overview of, 201–205
Adarand Constructors Inc. v. Peña (1995), 85, 86
Adequate Yearly Progress benchmarks, 122–124
adversarial pedagogy, gender discrimination and, 146–151
affirmative action policies. *See also* race-conscious admissions policies
  Bakke decision, 70–71, 84–85
  ballot initiatives against, 97–98
  educational benefits of, 103–105
  Michigan cases involving, 85–91
  political process doctrine and, 98–103
  race-conscious admissions policies and, 70–71, 72–73, 78–81
  strict scrutiny standard and, 91–97
  Supreme Court desegregation rulings and, 74–75
  Supreme Court restrictions on, 98–103
African Americans
  affirmative action programs and, 84–85
  in Head Start program, 110–111
  parallel educational institutions developed by, 55–61
  post-Civil War rights of, 17–19
  school desegregation cases and, 57–59
  slavery's impact on education for, 15–17
  state human and civil rights violations against, 133–135
  student body composition and learning outcomes in segregated schools and, 75–76
  in student population, 108–109

Alexander v. Holmes County Bd. of Educ, 65–66
Alito, Samuel (Justice), 98–103
"all deliberate speed" standard, 62–63, 65–66, 77
American Association of University Women (AAUW), 155–158
American School Board Journal, 40
Americans with Disabilities Act (ADA) (1990), 160, 161
Amrein, Audrey, 203
Aristotle, 216–217
  on education, 4
  Founders' educational thought and, 3
assimilation, Native American education and, 6n.15
associations, human development and role of, 50
attachment theory, human development and, 42–43
Aune, Beth, 171–172

Bakke decision. *See University of California Regents v. Bakke*
ballot initiatives, prohibition of race-conscious admissions policies through, 97–98
behaviorism, 27–28
  criticism of, 42–46
  gender discrimination and, 155–158
  human development research vs., 47–53
  limits of, 201, 212–214
  No Child Left Behind Act and, 122–124
  origins, principles and influence of, 32–42
  race-conscious admissions policies and, 80–81
  school-to-prison pipeline and, 193–195
Behavior Solutions for the Inclusive Classroom (Aune, Burt & Gennaro), 171–172
Berg, Barbara J., 157
Berliner, David, 203
Bertocchi, Graziela, 16–17

"Bill for the More General Diffusion of Knowledge," 8–9
binaries in human nature, behaviorism and, 36
Blackmun, Harry (Justice), 128–129, 162–163
Board of Education of Oklahoma City Public Schools v. Dowell, 66–69
Board of Education of the Westside Community Schools v. Mergens, 29
Board of Education v. Rowley, 162–166, 174–175
Bracey, Glenn E. II, 24–25
Bradley, Joseph P. (Justice), 19–21
Brennan William J. (Justice), 126–129
  affirmative action cases and, 81–85
  on IDEA, 162–163, 166–168
  on students' Fourth Amendment rights, 180–181
Breyer, Stephen (Justice), 69–75, 99–100, 181–184
Brown v. Board of Education, 14n.18
  Civil Rights Act of 1964 and, 61–62
  criticism of, 60–61
  Founders' theory and, 55
  legal background and precedent for, 55–61
  limits on legacy of, 69–75, 77, 107
  resegregation after, 62–69
Burger, Warren (Chief Justice), 80–81, 128–129
Burlington v. Dept. of Ed, Massachusetts, 166–168
Burt, Beth, 171–172
busing programs, Supreme Court rulings on, 66–69

California Constitution, right to education and, 129–132
Callahan, Raymond, 38–39, 41–42
Campaign for Fiscal Equity, Inc. v. State of New York, 129–132
Cannon v. University of Chicago, 140–141
Carr v. Koch, 132
Catholicism, Native American education and, 6
Cedar Rapids Community Sch. Dist. v. Garret F, 163
Cerrone, Kathlene M., 185–186
charter schools, 210–212
Chetty, Raj, 119–121
Chicago Urban League, 133–135
church-sponsored schools, in colonial America, 7
citizenship
  in classical philosophy, 4
  diversity and strengthening of, 103–105
  secular education and, 3
City of Richmond v. J. A. Croson Co., 85, 86
civil rights
  Congressional legislation for, 61–62
  educational philosophy and, 17–19
  gun rights and, 181–184

state laws for, 133–135
student discipline and, 176
Civil Rights Act of 1866, 17–19
Civil Rights Act of 1875, 18–19
Civil Rights Act of 1964, 61–62
Civil Rights Cases, 19–22, 23–24
Civil Rights Data Collection (CRDC) research on exclusionary discipline, 186–188
Civil Rights Movement, 55
  Title IX and, 137–138
Civil Rights Restoration Act of 1987, 139–140
classical philosophy
  Founders' educational thought and, 3
  political regime and, 4
Coleman Report, 121–122
collaborative learning, 219–223
colonial America, private education in, 6–7
color-blind diversity strategies, Supreme Court rulings using, 71–75
The Color of Law: A Forgotten History of How our Government Segregated America (Rothstein), 23–24
Columbus Bd. of Educ. v. Penick, 66
Commerce Clause
  civil rights and, 29–30
  gun rights and, 181–184
Committee for Educational Rights v. Edgar, 129–132
common schools, Founders' model of, 13–14
community-based education
  in colonial America, 6–7
  individual relationships and, 7–9
compelling interest principle
  affirmative action cases and, 81–84, 88–97
  desegregation rulings and, 69–75
compulsory attendance
  institution of, 14
  parental rights *vs.*, 31–32
conditioned response, learning and, 34–35
Congress
  educational policy and role of, 29–30
  equal education legislation and, 61–62
  promotion of knowledge by, 48
  special education legislation passed by, 160–162
  term limits in, 47
constitutional structure, Founders' embrace of, 11, 25–26
Constitution of the United States. *See also* specific Amendments, e.g. Fourteenth Amendment; specific Clauses, e.g., Commerce Clause
  democratic government structure and, 25–26
  educational rights and, 111–117
  intellectual property protections in, 48
  limits on local control in, 30–31

Constitution of the United States (cont.)
  parents and guardians constitutional rights, 31–32
  post-Civil War amendments to, 17–19
  right to education and, 132
  term limits in, 47
counterterrorism measures, student safety and, 190–191
Craig v. Boren, 145–146
critical mass principle, 88–91, 92–93
critical race theory, 24–25
"Culture of Connectedness," 189
curriculum development, gender discrimination and, 155–158

Darling-Hammond, Linda, 35, 37–38, 204
Davis v. Monroe County Board of Education, 142–144, 153–155
Dayton Board of Education v. Brinkman, 66
"Dear Colleague Letter" (Department of Education), 186–188
"Dear Colleague Letter" (Office of Civil Rights), 151–155
The Death and Life of the Great American School System: How Testing and Choice are Undermining Education (Ravitch), 122–124
de facto gender discrimination, 155–158
de facto segregation, 55, 60–61
  race-conscious admissions policies and, 78–81
  resegregation and, 62–69
  Supreme Court consideration of, 72–73
de jure segregation, 55, 60–61
  Brown decision and end of, 62–63
  racial quotas for ending, 65–66
  Supreme Court rulings on, 66–69, 70, 71–75
"deliberate indifference" standard, 141–142, 143, 153–155
Deming, David J., 46
de minimis standard
  special education litigation rulings and, 164–166
  students' Fourth Amendment rights and, 180–181
democracy
  associations and, 50
  community and individual relationships and, 7–9
  diversity and strengthening of, 103–105
  education and, 52–53
  Founders' views on education and, 10
  social constructivist educational reforms based on, 216–223
Democracy and Education (Dewey), 217–218
Democracy in America (de Tocqueville), 50
Department of Education
  Civil Rights Guidelines, 144–145
  Dear Colleague Letter on zero tolerance and, 186–188
  "Rethinking School Discipline" Guidance from, 191–193
Department of Homeland Security, 190–191
Department of Justice, 145
DeRolph v. Ohio, 129–132
desegregation. *See also* segregation
  history of, 55–61
  resegregation following, 62–69
  student body composition and learning outcomes and impact of, 75–76
desire, reason and, 52–53
de Tocqueville, Alexis, 50
DeVos, Betsy, 188–191
Dewey, John, 36–38, 217–218
Dimico, Archangelo, 16–17
disabilities, students with
  early cases and legislation involving, 160–162
  early childhood special education for, 168–169
  ethics of inclusion and, 159
  least restrictive environment principle and, 166–168
  procedural and substantive guarantees for, 162–166
diversity
  affirmative action in pursuit of, 82, 83–84, 85–91
  charter schools' impact on, 211–212
  educational benefits of, 103–105
  Reggio Emilia educational model and, 219–223
  in student population, 108–109
  Supreme Court restrictions on pursuit of, 98–103
documentation, accountability assessment and, 205
  Reggio Emilia educational model and, 219–223
Does Local Tax Financing of Public Schools Perpetuate Inequality? (Chetty & Friedman), 120–121
Due Process Clause
  educational policy and, 30–31, 47–48
  exclusionary discipline and, 176–179
  parental rights and, 31–32

early childhood education. *See also* Head Start program
  documentation techniques in, 205
  Head Start program, 110–111
  social constructivism and early intervention models, 214–216
  special education inclusion in, 168–169
  Vygotsky's research on, 218–219

Early Head Start program, 110–111
Eason, Anne I., 172–173
economic conditions
　educational policy and, 27–28
　inequality in education and, 114–117, 121–122
　race-conscious admissions policies and, 79–80
　school vouchers and, 207–210
Edgewood Independent School District v. Kirby, 129–132
Education Act of 1972, Title IX, 137–138
educational inequality
　Equal Protection Clause and, 64–65
　gender discrimination and, 137–138
　inadequate and inequitable funding and, 119–121
　No Child Left Behind and, 122–124
　overview of, 16–17
　post-Reconstruction legacy in, 22–24
　race-conscious admissions policies and, 81–84, 88–91
　segregation and, 55–61
　Supreme Court tolerance for, 111–117
　Title IX provisions involving, 138–145
educational philosophy and policy
　accountability initiatives and, 201–205
　behaviorist model in, 27–28, 32–42
　charter schools and, 210–212
　citizenship and, 3
　classical philosophy and, 4
　community and individual relationships and, 7–9
　Congressional power over, 29–30
　Enlightenment perspectives and, 4–6
　federal vs. state control over, 28
　future challenges for, 201
　Jefferson's views on, 8–9
　limits of reform initiatives and, 212–214
　local control of education and, 28–29
　of Native Americans, 6
　origins of civil rights and, 17–19
　in post-Reconstruction era, 27–28
　privatization initiatives and, 205
　Reconstruction and setbacks to, 17–19
　slavery and, 15–17
　social constructivist reform model for, 216–223
　voucher programs and, 205–210
Education and the Cult of Efficiency: A Study of the Social Forces That Have Shaped the Administration of the Public Schools (Callahan), 38–39
Education Trust, 119–121
efficiency
　behaviorist educational policy and, 32–34, 39
　school administrators decisions based on, 40–42
Einstein, Albert, 27–28, 51–52

Elementary and Secondary Education Act of 1965, 61–62
　Title I Grants, 109–110
emancipation, fears of educated black population and, 15–16
Emerson, Harrington, 39
Emile (On Education) (Rousseau), 4–6
empathy, human development and role of, 51
Endrew F. v. Douglas County School District, 164–166, 174–175
Enlightenment philosophy
　education and, 4–6
　social constructivist educational reforms and, 217–218
equal employment opportunity, race-conscious admissions policies and, 80–81
Equal Protection Clause, 30–31
　funding inequalities in education and, 111–113, 117–119
　race-conscious admissions policies and, 81–84, 97–103
　right to education and, 126–129
　school desegregation and, 57–61
　state educational policies and, 126–132
　Supreme Court decisions involving, 64–65
　Supreme Court desegregation rulings and, 74–75
　Title IX jurisprudence and, 144–151
Equity and Excellence Commission, 119–121
"equivalent substitute" principle, school funding inequality and, 117–119
essential character skills development, 214–216
Every Student Succeeds Act (ESSA), 124–126, 184–188
"The Evolution of the Racial Gap in Education and the Legacy of Slavery" (Bertocchi & Dimico), 16–17
exceedingly persuasive justification standard, gender discrimination and, 151
exclusionary discipline
　due process and, 176–179
　Every Student Succeeds Act provisions on, 184–188
　school-to-prison pipeline and, 193–195
　students' Fourth Amendment rights and, 180–181
Experience and Education (Dewey), 217–218

factory model, 27–28
Federal Commission on School Safety, 188–191
federal government
　Congressional power over education and, 29–30
　education policy and, 28
　equal access to education and, 61–62

federal government (cont.)
  Every Student Succeeds Act and, 124–126
  funding for education from, 109–110
  Head Start funding and, 110–111
  intervention in student discipline by, 191–193
  special education funding and, 170–171
  special education legislation and, 160–162
  Title IX enforcement and, 144–145
Federalist Papers, 11–13
Fifteenth Amendment, 18–19
Fifth Amendment, 30–31
First Amendment
  educational policy and, 28
  free speech and free press in, 47
Fisher v. University of Texas (Fisher I and II), 91–97, 105–106
five habits of mind, Gardner's theory of, 45–46
Florence County School Dist. v. Carter, 166–168
Foner, Eric, 18–19, 22–24
Foster, John Bellamy, 51
Founders
  on community and individual relationships, 7–9
  constitutional structure developed by, 11
  democratic government and role of, 25–26
  educational philosophy of, 3
  on human nature and development, 11–13, 47–53
  public education model of, 13–14
  slavery and role of, 15–17
  social constructivist educational reforms based on vision of, 216–223
Fourteenth Amendment. *See also* Due Process Clause
  citizenship rights and, 10, 17–19
  educational policy and, 28
  enforcement of, 19–21
  Equal Protection Clause, 30–31
  exclusionary discipline and, 176–179
  race-conscious admissions policies and, 81–84
  right to education and, 126–129
  school desegregation and, 57–61
  state educational policies and, 126–132
Fourth Amendment, school environment and, 179–184
Franklin, Benjamin, 7–9, 25–26
Franklin v. Gwinnett County Public Schools, 140–141
Free, Appropriate Public Education (FAPE) standard, 162–166
freedom of choice principle, school desegregation and, 65–66
Freeman, Joshua B., 137–138
Freeman and Jenkins, 149–151
Freeman v. Pitts, 66–69
Friedman, John, 120–121

funding for education
  federal, state and local sources for, 109–110
  inadequate and unequal structures for, 119–121
  inequalities in, 111–113, 117–119
  No Child Left Behind Act disparities and, 122–124
  quality of education and, 121–122
  school vouchers impact on, 209–210
  special education, 121, 170–171
  Title IX litigation related to, 139–140

Gardner, Howard, 45–46
Gebser v. Lago Vista Independent School District, 141–142, 153–155
gender discrimination
  equal protection jurisprudence for, 145–151
  historical context of Title IX and, 137–138
  intermediate scrutiny in cases of, 64–65
  overview of, 137
  recent enforcement issues for, 151–155
  social constructivism and, 155–158
  Title IX damages for victims of, 144
Gennaro, Peter, 171–172
Gilded Age, educational policy in, 27–28, 53–54
Ginsburg, Ruth Bader (Justice), 100, 142, 146–151, 158
Giroux, Henry A., 212–214
Giving Kids a Fair Chance (A Strategy that Works) (Heckman), 44–45
Goddard, David Hamilton, 80–81
Goss v. Lopez, 176–179, 185–186, 195
government, slavery and role of, 15–17
Gratz v. Bollinger, 85–91
Green v. County Sch. Bd. of New Kent County, 65–66
Griggs v. Duke Power Co., 80–81
Grove City College v. Bell, 139–140
The Growing Importance of Social Skills in the Labor Market (Deming), 46
Grutter v. Bollinger (2003), 70–71, 100–103, 105–106
guardians. *See* parents and guardians
Guiding Principles: A Resource Guide for Improving School Climate and Discipline (Department of Education), 186–188
Gun-Free Schools Act (1994), 181–184, 185–188
Gun Free School Zones Act (1996), 184
"The Gun-Free Schools Act of 1994: Zero Tolerance Takes Aim at Procedural Due Process" (Cerrone), 185–186
gun safety
  Federal Commission on School Safety recommendations, 188–191
  students' rights and, 181–184
  zero tolerance policies and, 184–188

Haldar, Deeya, 198–199
Hamilton, Alexander, 11–13
Harlan, John Marshall (Justice), 21
Harvard College Admissions Program, race-conscious admissions policies and, 83–85
Hawkins, David, 44
Head Start program, funding for, 110–111
Heckman, James, 44–45, 120–121, 214–216
Hernandez v. Texas, 59
Hewitt, Damon T., 193–195
Heyneman, Stephen, 38–39
higher education
  special admissions programs in, 81–84
  Supreme Court race-conscious admissions policies and, 70–71, 72–73, 78–81
Honig, California Superintendent of Public Instruction v. Doe, 166–168, 174–175
Hopwood v. Texas, 93–94
hornbooks, 7
Houston, Charles "Charlie," 56, 58, 77
human nature and development
  behaviorism *vs.* research in, 42–46
  Founders' understanding of, 11–13, 47–53
  limits of behaviorist pedagogy and, 47–53
human rights, state laws for, 133–135
Humphrey, Hubert, 61–62
Hunter case, 98–103

IEP and Inclusion Tips for Parents and Teachers (Eason & Whitbread), 172–173
Illinois Model Code of Conduct, 195–199
important governmental objective, gender discrimination and, 151
inclusion
  neurodiversity principle and, 171–174
  special education and role of, 159
income level
  educational disparities and, 16–17
  educational inequality and, 114–117, 121–122
  school vouchers and, 207–210
  segregation and, 75–76
Individualized Education Program (IEP), 159
  Congressional establishment of, 29
  least restrictive environment principle and, 166–168
  procedural and substantive guarantees in, 162–166
individualized family services plan, 168–169
Individuals with Disabilities Education Act (IDEA), 159
  early childhood special education in, 168–169
  funding mandates in, 170–171
  least restrictive environment principle and, 166–168

passage of, 169
procedural and substantive guarantees in, 162–166
state grants from, 109–110
industrialization, educational policy and influence of, 27–28, 39
intellectual property
  Constitutional protections for, 48
  Locke's discussion of, 48–49
intermediate scrutiny
  equal protection cases and, 64–65
  gender discrimination jurisprudence and, 145–151
  right to education and, 126–129
intradistrict school integration, limitations of, 66–69
Irving Independent School District v. Tatro, 163

Jefferson, Thomas, 8–9, 25–26, 27–28, 49–50
Johnson, Lyndon, 78–79
judicial branch, democracy and role of, 13
judicial restraint doctrine
  affirmative action case and, 91–97
  Supreme Court desegregation rulings and, 74–75

Kahneman, Daniel, 44
Katz, Sarah, 198–199
Kennedy, Anthony (Justice)
  affirmative action cases and, 91–97, 98–103
  Commerce Clause jurisprudence and, 181–184
  segregation rulings and, 69–70, 71–75
  sexual harassment rulings and, 143
Kersjes, Mike, 173–174
Kim, Catherine Y., 193–195
Kirp, David, 215–216
knowledge
  Constitutional protections for, 48
  cooperation and, 47
  Jefferson's analysis of ideas and, 49–50
Kohn, Alfie, 202–203

labor law, race-conscious admissions policies and, 80–81
Latino students
  demographics on, 108–109
  in Head Start program, 110–111
  student body composition and learning outcomes in segregated schools and, 75–76
Law and Modern Society: Toward a Criticism of Social Theory (Unger), 52–53
learning
  behaviorist approach to, 34–35
  gender discrimination's impact on, 155–158

learning (cont.)
  impact of integration and resegregation on, 75–76
  neurodiversity and, 171–174
  Vygotsky's research on, 218–219
least restrictive environment principle, 166–168
Library Company of Philadelphia, 8
local government
  Constitutional limits of, 30–31
  early childhood special education and, 168–169
  educational infrastructure of, 28–29
  funding for education and, 109–110
  Head Start program operation by, 110–111
  restorative justice programs and, 195–199
  Title IX litigation and, 138–145
Locke, John, 3, 4–6, 48–49, 217–218
Losen, Daniel, 193–195
Louisiana Federation of Teachers v. State of Louisiana, 209–210

Madison, James, 11–13, 25–26, 48
Magill, S. W., 16
magnet schools, desegregation and, 69
Majority-Minority districts, educational rights and, 133–135
management theory, educational policy and, 32–34
Mann, Horace, 14, 216–217
Marjory Stoneman Douglas High School mass shooting, 188–191
Marshall, Thurgood (Justice), 58, 77, 114–117, 162–163
mass production, 27–28
McLaurin v. Oklahoma State Regents for Higher Education, 57–59
Meyer v. Nebraska, 31–32, 113–117
Milliken v. Bradley, 66–69, 77
Mills v. Board of Education of District of Columbia, 160–162
Mind: A Journey to the Heart of Being Human (Siegel), 43–44
minimal impact principle, affirmative action and, 95–97
minority-owned businesses, affirmative action and, 84–85
missionaries, Native American education and, 16
Mississippi University for Women v. Hogan, 145–146
Missouri ex rel Gaines v. Canada, 57–59
Missouri v. Jenkins (Jenkins II), 66–69
Montesquieu (Charles-Louis Secondat), 3, 4–6

NAACP
  school desegregation lawsuits and, 58–59
  Seattle desegregation lawsuit by, 72–73
National Assessment Governing Board (NAGB), 210–211
National Assessment of Educational Progress (NAEP), 210–211
National Organization for Women (NOW), 137–138
National School Boards Association (NSBA), school vouchers assessment by, 209–210
Native Americans, approach to education of, 26
natural rights, Civil Rights Cases and, 21–22
neurodiversity, 105–106
neuroscience
  diversity and, 87–88, 105–106
  human development and, 42–46
  special education policies and, 171–174
  trauma-informed practices and, 198–199
NeuroTribes: The Legacy of Autism and the Future of Neurodiversity (Silberman), 171–174
New England Primer, 7
New Jersey v. T.L.O., 179–184, 195
No Child Left Behind Act, 122–124, 184, 203

Obama, Barack, 151–155
O'Connor, Sandra Day (Justice), 85–91, 141–144
Office of Civil Rights (OCR) (Department of Education), Title IX enforcement and, 151–155
"Old Deluder Satan Act," 6–7
"one-race" schools, school desegregation cases and role of, 65–66
operant conditioning, education and role of, 36–38

Papasan v. Allain, 117–119, 135–136
P.A.R.C. v. Commonwealth of Pennsylvania, 160–162
parents and guardians
  constitutional rights of, 31–32
  school voucher programs and rights of, 207–210
  special education litigation and, 162–166
Parents Involved in Community Schools v. Seattle School Dist. No. 1 (PICS)., 69–75, 77, 98
Patterson, James T., 58–59
Paul, Catherine A., 62
Pavlov, Ivan, 34–35
pedagogy, in post-Reconstruction era, 27–28
"The Pedagogy of Trauma-Informed Lawyering," 198
"Peer-to-Peer Competition Challenge," 190
Pell Grants, 109–110

per-pupil expenditures, inadequate and inequitable funding and, 119–121
Perry, Bruce (Dr.), 42–43
Philadelphia Academy, Franklin's establishment of, 8
Piaget, Jean, 218–219
Pierce v. Society of Sisters, 31–32, 113–117
"pit schools," slaves' education in, 15–16
Plato, 216–217
    educational philosophy and, 4
    Founders' educational thought and, 3
Plessy v. Ferguson, 57–59, 77
Plutarch's Lives, 8
Plyler v. Doe, 117–119, 126–129, 135–136
police presence in schools, 191–193
    school-to-prison pipeline and, 193–195
political philosophy, Founders' educational thought and, 3
political process doctrine, race-conscious admissions policies and, 98–103
political regime
    ballot initiatives against race-conscious admissions policies, 97–98
    educational philosophy, 4
    Madison's analysis of, 11–13
Poor Richard's Almanack (Franklin), 7–9
Positive Behavioral Interventions and Supports, 189
positive reinforcement, education and role of, 36–38
poverty
    educational inequality and, 114–117, 121–122
    segregation and, 75–76
Powell, Louis (Justice)
    race-conscious admissions rulings and, 81–91
    on right to education, 114–117, 128–129
    on student discipline, 178–179
    on students' Fourth Amendment rights, 180–181
The Principles of Scientific Management (Taylor), 32–34
private choice
    civil rights and, 19–22
    state and actions and, 25
private education
    in colonial America, 6–7
    school vouchers and access to, 207–210
privatization of education, 205
    limits of, 212–214
Progressive Era, educational policy in, 27–28, 39, 53–54
Project Zero, 205

property taxes
    educational funding and, 109–110
    inadequate and inequitable school funding and, 119–121
Proposal 2 (Michigan), 97–103
Proposals Relating to the Education of Youth in Pennsylvania (Franklin), 8
Proposition 209 (California), 97–98
Protagoras dialogue (Plato), 4
protected classes principle, equal protection cases and, 64–65
Psychology as the Behaviorist Views It (Watson), 34–35
public education
    Founders' model of, 13–14
    Jefferson's views on, 8–9
Pyle, Christopher, 149–151

quality of education, funding linked to, 121–122

race-conscious admissions policies. *See also* affirmative action policies
    ballot initiatives against, 97–98
    court restrictions on, 98–103
    educational benefits of, 103–105
    Michigan cases involving, 85–91
    standardized testing, 81
    strict scrutiny standard and, 91–97
    Supreme Court decisions on, 70–71, 72–73
Race to the Top program, 109–110, 203
racial inequality
    behaviorism and, 36
    education and, 16–17
    equal protection cases involving, 64–65
    exclusionary discipline and, 186–188
    history of school segregation, 55–61
    legacy of Reconstruction and, 22–24
    micro-aggression against minorities and, 88–91
    race-conscious admissions policies and, 81–84
    school-to-prison pipeline and, 193–195
    school vouchers and, 207–210
    standardized testing results and, 203
racial quotas
    affirmative action and, 88–91
    school desegregation and use of, 65–66
rational basis review
    equal protection cases and, 64–65
    funding inequalities in education and, 111–113
    right to education and, 126–129
rationalization, education and, 51
Ravitch, Diane, 122–124
reason, desire and, 52–53

Reconstruction
  educational philosophy and setbacks of, 17–19
  legacy and consequences of, 22–25
Reggio Emilia educational model, 219–223
Rehabilitation Act of 1973 (RHA), *Mills v. Board of Education of District of Columbia*
Rehnquist, William (Justice)
  on affirmative action, 90
  on gender discrimination, 149–151
  on gun rights, 181–184
relationships, learning and role of, 44–45
religion, free exercise of, educational policy and, 31–32
remediation, early intervention vs., 214–216
Republic (Plato), 4
respondeat superior liability, Title IX litigation and, 141–142
restorative justice, student discipline and, 195–199
"Rethinking School Discipline" Guidance (Department of Education), 191–193
revenue sources for American education, 109–110
  unequal distribution of, 111–113
right to education
  federal constitutional arguments for, 132
  legal arguments for, 132
  state constitutional arguments for, 133
  state-level policies and, 129–132
  statutory arguments based on civil or human rights law, 133–135
  Supreme Court's denial of, 111–117, 126–129
  unconstitutional denial of access and, 133
Roberts, John (Chief Justice), 69–75, 98–103, 164–166
Rothstein, Richard, 23–24
Rousseau, Jean-Jacques, 3, 4–6, 217–218
Rush, Benjamin, 13–14, 77

San Antonio Independent School District v. Rodriguez, 36
  critical analysis of, 113–117
  educational inequality and, 111–113, 135–136
  funding linked to educational quality in, 121–122
  right to education and, 126–132
  special education and, 163
  state educational policies and, 126–132
Savannah Educational Association, 16
Scalia, Antonin (Justice), 98–103
school administration, efficiency principles adopted by, 40–42
school boards
  education policy and, 28–29
  efficiency principles and composition of, 40–41

school choice
  privatization initiatives and, 205
  voucher programs and, 205–210
school construction, efficiency principles and, 40
school districts
  boundaries and attendance zones in, desegregation cases and role of, 65–66, 71–75
  inadequate and inequitable funding and, 119–121
  Majority-Minority districts, educational rights and, 133–135
  student population demographics and, 108–109
school environment
  diversity in, educational benefits of, 103–105
  Federal Commission on School Safety recommendations, 188–191
  Fourth Amendment rights in, 179–184
  gun rights and, 181–184
  impact of integration and resegregation on learning and, 75–76
  learning and impact of, 44
  Reggio Emilia educational model and, 219–223
  trauma-informed practices and, 198–199
school principals, efficiency principles and, 40
Schools Without Diversity: Education Management Organizations, Charter Schools, and the Demographic Stratification of the American School System (2010), 211–212
school-to-prison pipeline, 193–195
Schuette v. BAMN, 98–103, 105–106
scientific management, educational policy and, 27–28, 39
scientific method, educational reforms and, 217–218
Second Treatise of Civil Government (Locke), 48–49
secular education, Founders' belief in, 3
security measures, student violence and, 190–191
segregation. *See also* desegregation
  Congressional legislation ending, 61–62
  history in schools of, 55–61
  legacy of Reconstruction and, 23–24
  limits on legacy of *Brown* in, 69–75
  resegregation following *Brown*, 62–69
  student body composition and learning outcomes, impact of resegregation on, 75–76
Self-Taught, African American Education in Slavery and Freedom (Williams), 15
separate but equal doctrine
  de jure segregation and, 77
  gender discrimination and, 149
  as violation of Equal Protection Clause, 55–61
Serrano v. Priest I & II, 129–132
sex discrimination. *See* gender discrimination
sexual harassment

Department of Education Civil Rights
  Guidelines on, 144–145
Office of Civil Rights definition of, 153–155
Title IX litigation related to, 141–144
sexual violence, Title IX responses to, 151–155
Shaffer v. Weast, 167–168
Siegel, Daniel, 43–44
Silberman, Steve, 171–174
single-sex education, gender discrimination and, 146–151
Skiba, Russell J., 185, 186
Skinner, B. F., 34–35, 36–38
slavery
  badges and incidents of, 15–17
  economic effects of, 16–17
  race-conscious admissions policies and legacy of, 81–84
  Thirteenth Amendment and abolition of, 17–19
social constructivism, 49–50
  early intervention and, 214–216
  educational reform based on, 216–223
  Federal Commission on School Safety recommendations, 188–191
  gender equity and, 155–158
  school-to-prison pipeline and, 195
  Supreme Court desegregation rulings and, 74–75
social justice, Civil Rights Cases and, 21–22
social skills, worker productivity and, 46
Some Thoughts Concerning Education (Locke), 4–6
Sotomayor, Sonia (Justice), 100–103
Souter, David (Justice), 181–184
Southeastern Comm. College v. Davis, 161–162
special education
  early cases and legislation involving, 160–162
  in early childhood, duty to provide, 168–169
  funding for, 121, 170–171
  future challenges in, 174–175
  inclusion model and, 159
  least restrictive environment principle and, 166–168
  neurodiversity principle and, 171–174
  procedural and substantive guarantees for, 162–166
Spending Clause, 28, 29–30
  special education funding and, 170–171
The Spirit of the Laws (Montesquieu), 4–6
sports activities, Title IX litigation on discrimination in, 140–141
standardization
  accountability initiatives as alternative to, 201–205
  educational policy and, 32–34, 38–39

standardized testing, race-conscious admissions policies and, 81
state government
  civil rights and, 19–22, 107
  critical race theory on, 24–25
  early childhood special education and, 168–169
  educational inequality and school funding mechanisms and, 111–113
  education policy and, 28, 122–124
  Every Student Succeeds Act and, 124–126
  funding for education from, 109–110
  parents and guardians constitutional rights and, 31–32
  restorative justice programs and, 195–199
  right to education and policies of, 129–132
  school voucher programs and, 205–210
  special education funding and, 170–171
  statutory arguments based on violation civil or human rights law in, 133–135
  Title IX litigation and, 138–145
  unconstitutional denial of access to education and, 133
"stay-put" provisions in IDEA, 166–168
stereotype threats, diversity as solution to, 88–91, 103–105
Stevens, John Paul (Justice), 29, 180–184
Stewart, Potter (Justice), 114–117
"stop and frisk" searches, student rights and, 179–184
strict scrutiny standard
  equal protection cases and, 64–65
  funding inequalities in education and, 111–113
  gender discrimination and, 151
  race-conscious admissions policies and, 83–84
student achievement
  accountability initiatives for measurement of, 201–205
  charter schools impact on, 210–211
  school vouchers and, 207–210
  testing and, 122–126
student discipline
  civil rights and, 176
  Department of Education Resource Guide on, 186–188
  Department of Education "Rethinking School Discipline" Guidance and, 191–193
  due process and exclusionary discipline, 176–179
  Every Student Succeeds Act provisions on, 184–188
  Federal Commission on School Safety recommendations, 188–191
  federal intervention in, 191–193
  future challenges involving, 200

student discipline (cont.)
  restorative justice and, 195–199
  school-to-prison pipeline and, 193–195
student population demographics, 108–109
Students for Fair Admissions v. Harvard University, 95–97
Supreme Court (U.S.)
  affirmative action rulings of, 70–71, 81–91, 105–106
  behaviorist theory and decisions by, 36
  Brown v. Board of Education ruling by, 59–61
  Civil Rights Cases before, 19–22
  Congressional powers over education and, 29–30
  education and jurisprudence of, 27–28
  equal protection cases before, 64–65
  First Amendment decisions in, 47–48
  Fisher I and II affirmative action cases and, 91–97
  funding inequalities in education rulings of, 111–113
  gender discrimination jurisprudence and, 145–151
  gun rights rulings and, 181–184
  higher education race-conscious admissions policies and, 70–71, 72–73, 78–81
  least restrictive environment principle in special education rulings of, 166–168
  legacy of Reconstruction and, 22–24
  limits on *Brown* desegregation legacy by, 69–75
  Michigan affirmative action cases and, 85–91
  parental rights rulings by, 31–32
  post-*Brown* decisions on segregation, 62–69
  restrictions on race-conscious admissions policies by, 98–103
  school-to-prison pipeline and rulings by, 193–195
  school voucher program cases and, 207–210
  student body composition and learning outcomes, effect of rulings on, 75–76
  student body composition and learning outcomes linked to diluted segregation rulings, 75–76
  students with disabilities rulings and, 161–162
  Title IX cases and, 138–145
  tolerance for educational inequality on, 111–113
"A Survey Method for Characterizing Daily Experience: The Day Reconstruction Method" (Kahneman), 44
Swann v. Charlotte-Mecklenburg Board of Education, 65–66
Sweatt v. Painter, 57–59, 149

taxation
  educational funding and, 109–110
  inadequate and inequitable school funding and, 119–121
  voucher programs and, 205–210
Taylor, Frederick Winslow, 32–34, 53–54
teachers and teaching
  accountability initiatives and, 204
  behaviorist theory and, 35, 36–38
  training and standardization for, 40–42
teaching machine, Skinner's development of, 34–35
Tenth Amendment, 28
testing and test scores
  accountability initiatives as alternative to, 201–205
  charter schools and, 210–212
  education policy linked to, 122–126
  school vouchers and, 207–210
"Texas Minimum Foundation School Program," 111–113
(school)*The School-To-Prison Pipeline: Structuring Legal Reform* (Kim, Losen & Hewitt), 193–195
Thirteenth Amendment, 17–21
Thomas, Clarence (Justice), 91–97, 181–184
Threat Mitigation Unit, student safety and, 190–191
Title IX of Education Act of 1972
  backlash against, 153–155
  Department of Education Civil Rights Guidelines and, 144–145
  equal protection jurisprudence and, 145–151
  historical context of, 137–138
  ongoing legacy of, 155–158
  parameters of, 138–145
  recent developments in enforcement of, 151–155
trauma-informed practices, student discipline and, 198–199
Trump, Donald, 153–155, 191–193

underperforming schools, education policy and, 122–124
undocumented immigrants, right to education for, 117–119, 126–129
Unger, Roberto Mangabeira, 52–53
United States v. Virginia, 145–151, 158
University of California Regents v. Bakke
  affirmative action and, 70–71, 84–85
  Supreme Court ruling on, 81–84
University of Michigan, race-conscious admissions at, 85–91
Urban, Wayne, 7–9
U. S. Department of Education, budget appropriations by, 109–110
U.S. v. Lopez, 181–184

violence in schools
   Federal Commission on School Safety recommendations, 188–191
   trauma-informed practices and, 198–199
violent entertainment, student violence and, 189–190
Virginia Constitutional Convention, 11–13
Virginia Military Institute (VMI), 146–151
Virginia Women's Leadership Institute (VWLI), 146–151
voucher programs, 205–210
Vygotsky, Lev, 218–219

Wagoner, Jennings, 7–9
Warren, Earl (Chief Justice), 59–61, 77
Washington v. Davis, 99
Watson, John, 34–35

Whitbread, Kathleen, 172–173
White, Byron (Justice), 114–117, 162–163, 176–179
   on students' Fourth Amendment rights, 180–181
Williams, Heather Andrea, 15–16
Williams, Juan, 56–57
Wisconsin v. Yoder, 31–32
women
   affirmative action programs for, 84–85
   Title IX and discrimination against, 137–138
Women's Liberation Movement, 137–138

Zelman V. Simmons-Harris, 207–210
zero tolerance policies
   federal intervention and, 191–193
   future challenges involving, 200
   limitations of, 184–188
   school-to-prison pipeline and, 193–195

Lightning Source UK Ltd.
Milton Keynes UK
UKHW020838150522
402927UK00019B/457